1989

PERSPECTIVES ON
Irish Nationalism

PERSPECTIVES ON
Irish Nationalism

EDITED BY

THOMAS E. HACHEY &
LAWRENCE J. McCAFFREY

THE UNIVERSITY PRESS OF KENTUCKY

Scholarly publisher for the Commonwealth,
serving Bellarmine College, Berea College, Centre
College of Kentucky, Eastern Kentucky University,
The Filson Club, Georgetown College, Kentucky
Historical Society, Kentucky State University,
Morehead State University, Murray State University,
Northern Kentucky University, Transylvania University,
University of Kentucky, University of Louisville,
and Western Kentuky University.

Editorial and Sales Offices: Lexington, Kentucky 40506-0336

Library of Congress Cataloging-in-Publication Data
Perspectives on Irish nationalism / edited by Thomas E. Hachey &
    Lawrence J. McCaffrey.
        p.   cm.
    Bibliography: p.
    Includes index.
    Contents: Components of Irish nationalism / Lawrence J. McCaffrey
— Nation, nationalism, and the Irish language / R.V. Comerford —
The folklore of Irish nationalism / Mary Helen Thuente —
Nationalism / Thomas Flanagan — The land question in nationalist
politics / James S. Donnelly, Jr. — The Irish political tradition /
Emmet Larkin — Irish nationalism and the British connection /
Thomas E. Hachey.
    ISBN 0-8131-1665-1 (alk. paper).   ISBN 0-8131-0188-3
(pbk. : alk. paper)
    1. Irish question.   2. Nationalism—Ireland.   3. Ireland—Politics
and government—19th century.   4. Ireland—Politics and
government—20th century.   I. Hachey, Thomas E.   II. McCaffrey,
Lawrence John, 1925-   .   III. Title: Irish nationalism.
DA950.P47   1988
941.508—dc19   88-20818

This book is printed on acid-free paper meeting
the requirements of the American National Standard
for Permanence of Paper for Printed Library Materials. ∞

CONTENTS

To our fellow members in the
American Conference for Irish Studies

PREFACE

IRISH NATIONALISM exhibits a composite of the Irish historical experience. The rhetoric of the Irish demand for sovereignty and its liberal democratic ethos represent the English impact on Ireland, conveyed through Old English Catholic and Anglo-Irish Protestant patriotisms, and the values of British radicalism and Whiggery that Daniel O'Connell injected into the Irish freedom movement. Modern Irish nationalism found its structure and popular force in the agitation for Catholic emancipation when a religious identity became a national self-consciousness. In post-Famine Ireland, the struggle to transfer the land of Ireland to its people gave Irish nationalism the passion and cohesiveness provided by the Catholic issue earlier in the century. Emigration added American egalitarianism to Irish nationalism, strengthening its democratic and republican dimensions. Journalism and literary genius, influenced by European romanticism, and Gaelic scholarship contributed a cultural ideology to Irish nationalism. In no country have literature and folklore played more significant roles in shaping, reflecting, and explaining the desire for national independence in both political and cultural forms.

In October 1986, supported by a Loyola-Mellon grant, the Midwest regional meeting of the American Conference for Irish Studies invited a number of distinguished scholars to the campus of Loyola University of Chicago to discuss various aspects of Irish nationalism. *Perspectives on Irish Nationalism* is the result of their efforts.

Thomas E. Hachey
Lawrence J. McCaffrey

Lawrence J. McCaffrey

COMPONENTS OF
IRISH NATIONALISM

EXCELLENT LITERATURE and stirring patriotic ballads have extended the appeal of Irish nationalism beyond those with heritages rooted in Ireland. In paying homage to the long struggle against colonialism, Irish nationalist literature and music have neglected to show the positive British impact on Irish political values.

When the Norman English arrived in late twelfth-century Ireland, they encountered a Gaelic nation united in language and tradition with a clan social structure, a system of Brehon laws, and a Catholicism that was more monastic than diocesan and remote from Rome in both distance and loyalty. But politically Ireland was in chaos. The árd-rí was high king in name only. Feuds and jealousies started and perpetuated conflict between kingdoms and clans. It was a civil war that brought Richard fitz Gilbert de Clare, Earl of Pembroke, known as Strongbow, to Ireland to assist Dermot MacMurrough in the recovery of his lost Leinster throne.

The Normans initiated the anglicization of Irish political, social, cultural, and economic life and advanced the romanization of Irish Catholicism. From the fourteenth to the late sixteenth century, however, the English hold on Ireland outside Leinster (the Pale) was tenuous. Still, the Norman political administration and Parliament that claimed authority over the complete island represented at least a facade of political nationhood.

Descendants of the original English colonizers rejected Protestantism as a religious-cultural dimension of sixteenth-century Tudor conquest. Twice in the next century they joined with Gaels to reverse the property and power results of Elizabethan and Cromwellian victories and Tudor, Stuart, and Cromwellian plantations. However, the goals of the allies were dissimilar. Gaels hoped to restore their cultural order; the Old English intended to reassert command of the Irish political nation. William III's conquest over this shaky, cross-purpose coalition assimilated in common defeat and suffering Old English and Gael into one oppressed Irish Catholic nation.[1]

The New English punished and terrorized Catholics with Penal Laws aimed at their religion, property, and civil liberties. If the religious clauses had been enforced, they would have gone a long way toward destroying Catholicism in Ireland. But that was not their purpose. Anti-Catholic legislation was intended to demoralize its victims so that they would become psychologically incapable of resisting minority rule. While the rural masses remained Catholic, most of the Gaelic and Old English aristocracy and gentry turned Protestant to protect their property, influence, and status.[2]

In the course of the eighteenth century there was a remarkable similarity in the emergence of Anglo-American and Anglo-Irish patriotisms. The Penal Laws' effectiveness in suppressing Catholic Ireland, and the British defeat of the French and their Indian allies in the New World, made the Anglo-Irish and Anglo-Americans feel so secure that they resented British colonialism. They argued that British mercantilism restricted economic growth in their countries and that British parliamentary supervision over their legislatures amounted to tyranny. They both relied on the precedent of the Glorious Revolution and its John Locke apologia to insist that local concerns and interests necessitated local sovereignty.

After the Americans rebelled, declared their independence, and received French and Spanish military and naval aid, Anglo-Irish patriots raised a volunteer army, ostensibly to defend their country against Bourbon invasion. But they used it to intimidate Britain into free trade and parliamentary sovereignty. While royal veto power, on the advice of British ministers, restricted the authority of the Irish Parliament, in 1782 the Anglo-Irish moved close to an authentic nation-state. Memories of the Parliament in College Green inspired nineteenth-century Irish nationalism.

Sentimental recollections of the Anglo-Irish nation played down its Protestant exclusivity. Certain that Catholic access to property and civil equality would destroy Protestant ascendancy, Parliament perpetuated the religious, social, economic, and political disabilities of the Penal Laws. To please their Hapsburg ally in the war against the French Revolution, the British, however, pressured the economically dependent Anglo-Irish nation to lighten Catholic burdens. Responding, the Irish Parliament in the 1790s permitted Catholics first to lease and then to purchase property, to establish schools, and to practice law. It even endowed a Roman Catholic seminary at Maynooth, County Kildare, to keep Irish candidates for the priesthood out of French revolutionary nests on the Continent. Parliament also gave the vote to Catholic 40s freehold farmers. But they could only vote for Protestant candidates designated by their landlords.[3]

Not all Anglo-Irish patriots were satisfied with parliamentary sovereignty. Inspired by American democracy and British popular sovereignty radicalism, some insisted that Parliament should represent people rather than property. A few, such as Henry Grattan, the hero of 1782, wanted to include Catholics in the body politic, arguing that Ireland would never be truly free or Protestants secure until all Irishmen were integrated into one nation. Irish and British political reformers were associated with the French Revolution, which had considerable popularity in its early, constitutional phase. However, once it gravitated toward democratic republicanism, governments in both islands equated demand for parliamentary reform with Jacobinism and suppressed movements for change.

Repression, as well as French examples, radicalized many Irish reformers. Organized into the Society of United Irishmen, they concluded an alliance with the Defenders, a Jacobin-indoctrinated Catholic, secret, agrarian society. Although he had little regard for the timid Catholic upper and middle classes or their "superstitious" religion, Theobald Wolfe Tone, the society's most influential leader, considered the Catholic peasantry, "the people of no property," excellent revolutionary potential.[4]

A worried Irish Parliament in 1796 enacted a coercion package, including civil liberty restrictions, expanded police power, and habeas corpus suspension. The next year, the government sent Gen. Gerard Lake to smash the Ulster United Irishmen. When coercion and military force worked in the north, they were applied to the south. In March 1798, officials arrested most of the Dublin-area United Irishmen leaders.

Government precautions weakened the United Irishmen, but they failed to prevent insurrection. In May 1798, pike-armed Catholic peasants in Wexford slaughtered Protestant landlords. A month later, United Irishmen in Antrim and Down raised the standard of revolt. Government troops crushed the risings in Leinster and Ulster, but in August, Gen. Jean Joseph Humbert sailed into Killala Bay, County Mayo, with about a thousand French soldiers. Reinforced by a small force of peasants, he put on a good show for about a month. Then he ran out of supplies and realized that the masses throughout the country were not going to rise in a concerted effort. So Humbert surrendered to Charles Marquis Cornwallis, viceroy and commander of British forces in Ireland. The British repatriated Humbert and his troops, but brutally executed native Irish rebels. In October, they captured Wolfe Tone, wearing the uniform of a French adjutant general, off the Donegal coast. He chose suicide over execution.

Nationalist mythology has distorted Catholic-Protestant cooperation in 1798. The oppression that triggered the risings emanated directly from the Anglo-Irish Protestant government, not the British government. Catholics were numerous in the militia that General Lake took into Ulster. By 1798 it was apparent that the fiercely anti-Catholic Orange Order, founded in County Armagh three years earlier, represented Protestant opinion more than the United Irishmen. Orange yeomen terrorized Catholics in the south before and during 1798. In the north, United Irishmen were reluctant to recruit and arm Catholics. In Mayo, Catholics joined Humbert to fight for "the pope and Blessed Virgin," not "liberty, equality, and fraternity." And Catholics were prominent in Cornwallis's army.[5]

In 1798, British anxieties concerning Ireland as a security risk were confirmed. Since Tudor times, the British had worried that this neighboring island in the hands of their Continental enemies—Spain in the sixteenth century and France thereafter—would threaten the survival of Britain. That fear was something more than paranoia. The Spaniards had landed at Kinsale in 1601, and now Humbert had invaded Connacht. And there was a good chance that the French would come again in more formidable numbers.

William Pitt the Younger, the British prime minister, decided that Irish Anglican and Presbyterian middle-class radicalism, allied with Catholic discontent, encouraged French intervention. Doubting Anglo-Irish ability to control the situation, he proposed combining Ireland and Britain in a united kingdom. But he knew that such an arrangement could not last if the large Irish Catholic majority remained oppressed. Therefore, he promised Catholic clerical and lay leaders that their emancipation would accompany the union. Many of the Anglo-Irish shared Pitt's doubts about their ability to rule Ireland in an effective way and his belief that a united kingdom would protect the security of both countries. However, since their main concern was the continuation of Protestant ascendancy, they opposed Catholic equality. Since the British king, the House of Lords, and public opinion shared the anti-Catholicism of Irish Protestants and Nonconformists, Pitt had to surrender on the emancipation issue. Therefore, Ireland in January 1801 entered the United Kingdom with most of its people as second-class citizens.[6]

Despite betrayal of the nation they created, the Anglo-Irish authored the principles of Irish political nationalism. Daniel O'Connell (1775-1847) built on the Anglo-Irish Protestant Whig and radical heritages, linking them to Catholic aspirations. Born to County Kerry Catholic gentry,

O'Connell was first exposed to liberal ideas through reading as a law student at Lincoln's Inn, London. William Godwin's emphasis on moral force democracy as an instrument of change permanently influenced his politics. Adam Smith persuaded him of the merits of a free economy. Thomas Paine strengthened O'Connell's democratic convictions and challenged his Catholic faith. He would return to Catholicism from Deism, but he never reneged on democracy, freedom of conscience, religious tolerance, separation of church and state, the equality of all people, and laissez-faire. When O'Connell transferred from Lincoln's Inn to King's Inn, Dublin, he attended sessions of the Irish Parliament. Admiring Henry Grattan, he projected himself as the Liberator of Irish Catholics.[7]

Although O'Connell flirted with the United Irishmen, they were too extreme for his taste. In 1798 he returned to Kerry to avoid arrest. But he decried Wexford atrocities perpetrated in the name of liberty. O'Connell's condemnation of the United Irishmen and the 1798 rebels, and his persistent and consistent post-Union rejection of physical force resistance to British rule and landlordism, expressed pragmatism more than pacifism. Frequently he praised Americans who shaped a nation out of revolution. He collected money and gave much of his own, and he contributed a son to Simón Bolívar's victorious assault on Spanish imperialism in Latin America. But the events of 1798, added to Godwin's moral force argument, convinced O'Connell that revolution was not for Ireland. It would release the passions of ignorant peasants made desperate by tyranny and injustice. They would fight and lose after a bloody slaughter. Their enemies, as they did with the Act of Union, would use failed violence as a pretext to further enslave Ireland. Instead of physical force, O'Connell advised Irish Catholics to exploit the British constitutional tradition and process to free themselves and their country.

In 1798 O'Connell became a member of the Irish bar. In the Dublin Four Courts and on theMunster circuit he defended poor Catholics, blaming British rule for their crime and misery. Although the Union promised religious equality, in 1800 O'Connell was one of the few prominent membes of his faith to publicly oppose it. He said that he would rather be a second-class citizen, striving for civil rights in an Irish nation, than a first-class one in a British province. In 1805 he joined the Catholic Committee, soon becoming its most prominent personality. The committee's upper- and middle-class members sent annual petitions pleading for emancipation to Henry Grattan, M.P., who then presented them to the British House of Commons.

Merging Catholic and Irish interests, O'Connell united with Irish bishops in opposing an 1812 emancipation compromise. A number of

Whigs and a few Tories decided that the dictates of reason and the best interests of the United Kingdom necessitated Catholic equality. But they did not trust popery and demanded securities against the appointment of anti-British Catholic bishops. They suggested that either a committee of loyal Catholic laymen or the government have veto power over papal choices for United Kingdom sees. Most Irish and British Catholic lay leaders approved of a compromise that would give them access to opportunity and respectability. So did Rome, because it wanted friendly relations with the world's great power. But O'Connell strengthened the resolve of Irish bishops objecting to government or lay meddling in the affairs of a relatively healthy church. Their hostility to the compromise killed it, postponed emancipation, and divided the Catholic Committee.

O'Connell's long-range motives, unlike those of the bishops, in preventing the veto compromise were more national than Catholic. He realized that the defeat of Gaelic Ireland, and its assimilation with the Old English into Catholic Ireland, had made Catholicism as culture and identity, as well as faith, the only cohesive force among the Catholic majority. He intended to make it their nationality as well. In O'Connell's strategy, the agitation for Catholic emancipation would create national self-consciousness and a mass demand for repeal of the Union. He understood the potential of bishops and priests as leadership rivals to landlord agents of British colonialism. Most of the hierarchy and clergy came from the farmer or shopkeeper classes and remained loyal to their family roots. However, he feared that if the British government could manipulate the appointment of bishops, the Catholic church would speak for Britishness rather than Irishness. Nationalism would have a difficult time recruiting popular enthusiasm against the wishes of a hostile, even a neutral, Catholic church. Consequently, O'Connell decided it was better to postpone emancipation if it meant sacrificing Ireland's most important institution to British influence.

In 1823 O'Connell closed ranks with two leaders of the pro-veto faction, Richard Lalor Sheil and Sir Thomas Wyse, and together they founded the Catholic Association. It did not enjoy success until the next year when O'Connell invited peasants and urban and town workers to join as associate members at only a shilling a year. In other parts of the United Kingdom a shilling was a modest sum, but in Ireland it was a considerable sacrifice, indicating an investment of emotion. Participation in the emancipation effort had a liberating impact on the Irish Catholic mind, lifting spirits, injecting the dignity of freemen, and reducing a serflike inferiority complex. O'Connell directed the shillings of the poor to the emancipation cause and organized mass enthusiasm into a powerful instrument of public opinion.

The Catholic Association added repeal of the Union, security of tenant farmers at fair rents, compensation for improvements to farmers' holdings (tenant right), democratic suffrage with a secret ballot, and shorter parliaments to its platform, melding Irish nationalism with the principles of British radicalism. This merger politically civilized Irish Catholicism at a time when its Continental counterpart was a bulwark for aristocratic power, property, and privilege. Catholic bishops and priests assisted O'Connell as lieutenants in an agitation advocating popular sovereignty, property rights limited by moral duty, and the separation of church and state. This paradoxical blend of loyalties to liberal political and authoritarian religious values would long perplex the Irish national personality.[8]

From the beginnings of the agitation for Catholic emancipation in the 1820s to the end of his career as a promoter of repeal of the Union in the 1840s, O'Connell instructed his followers to obey the law and to avoid violence. He promised them that organized public opinion operating within the guidelines of the constitutional process would culminate in individual and national freedoms. However, moral force threatened physical force. O'Connell frequently warned British politicians that if they did not extend justice to Irish constitutional nationalism, the people, now united and expectant, would turn violent. And if Britain had to depend on the army to suppress the will of Catholic Ireland, it would be an admission that the Union was a fraud.

During the general election of 1826 priests led 40s freeholders to the polls to vote for proemancipation Protestant candidates. Two years later they did the same thing in a County Clare by-election where O'Connell ran against Vesey Fitzgerald, a government minister. Association victories in the general election and in Clare convinced the prime minister, the Duke of Wellington, and his home secretary, Sir Robert Peel, that Protestant ascendancy in Ireland would have to bow to expediency. To preserve order and the security of the Union, in 1829 the government passed a relief bill opening most political offices in the United Kingdom and seats in both houses of Parliament to Catholics. But Wellington and Peel were not gracious in their concession. The relief bill outlawed the Catholic Association, forced O'Connell to recontest Clare, eliminated the 40s freehold vote, and imposed insulting loyalty oaths on Catholics entering Parliament.

For the average Irish Catholic digging his potato patch or cutting turf in the bog, emancipation was more symbolic than real. It did not relieve his poverty or open opportunities. Few Catholics had the income or leisure for politics, a hobby and pastime for the landed aristocracy and gentry. Emancipation's importance was its glimmer of hope that public opinion could force change, and its role in the formation of nationality.[9] Although modern

Irish nationalism emerged from Catholic cohesiveness, O'Connell insisted that Irishness was inclusive. He rejected Catholic ascendancy as a substitute for Protestant ascendancy. He pleaded with Protestants to join Catholics in a united front against the British presence in Ireland.

Post–O'Connell constitutional and physical force Irish nationalisms retained his liberal democratic values and his appeal for Catholic-Protestant harmony. Young Irelanders in the 1840s called for cooperation between Anglo-Irish and Celt, Protestant and Catholic, in an effort to end the political and cultural scourge of Anglo-Saxonism.[10] In the next decade, Charles Gavan Duffy, Frederick Lucas, John Gray, George Henry Moore, and William Sharman Crawford launched the Independent Irish party to unite Catholic, Protestant, and Nonconformist farmers around the tenant right issue.[11] Although the Irish Republican Brotherhood in the 1860s condemned O'Connell's constitutional nationalism, it held fast to his faith in liberal democracy and to his insistence that the Irish people were one.[12]

In 1870 Isaac Butt established the Home Rule movement with a demand for a federal political structure in the United Kingdom. He hoped that the moderation of this request, and his assurances of the conservative instincts of Irish Catholics and their willingness to follow the lead of the landed aristocracy, would attract considerable Protestant support. His version of Home Rule projected Ireland as a conservative fortress against the secularism and egalitarianism sweeping through urban, industrial Britain. Butt also believed that a self-governing Ireland would enthusiastically share the burdens as well as the glories of the British Empire.[13]

Because Butt's Home Rule movement excluded agrarian and Catholic issues from its program and could not convince a significant number of Protestants to participate, it did not attract a dedicated constituency. Charles Stewart Parnell, like Butt an Anglo-Irish Protestant, forged to the front of Home Rule and made it popular by combining the demand for an Irish Parliament with a war on landlordism. Still, he did not abandon the inclusive ideology of Irish nationalism. He said that Ireland needed the talents of all classes and creeds.[14]

John Redmond and John Dillon, the last two leaders of the Irish party, angered some Irish and British bishops by refusing to turn the party into a Catholic lobby.[15] After the Easter Week 1916 "Blood Sacrifice," Sinn Féin captured the imagination of Irish nationalism and routed Home Rule in the December 1918 general election. But the 1916 declaration of an Irish republic, the pronouncements of Dáil Éireann during the 1919-21 Anglo-Irish War, and the stated policies of the Free State and Republic that followed the 1921 treaty all attested to the all-embracing oneness of the Irish nation.[16]

Despite its good intentions, Irish nationalism failed in its appeal to non-Catholics. The victory of Catholic emancipation convinced Anglican and Presbyterian communities that it was the beginning of a priest-led peasant democracy attack on their property and influence. They became increasingly attached to the Union as protection in a hostile environment. Home Rule's war on landlordism and its alliance with British liberalism strengthened the Irish Protestant garrison mentality.

The links between religion and nationality in Ireland that began with the Tudor conquest were tightened by the anti-Catholic essence of British nativism. Its paranoia and hate increased with the momentum of Irish nationalism. Conservative politicians manipulated British and Irish Protestant and Nonconformist opposition to popery to frustrate Irish nationalism and British liberalism. Following the 1886 alliance between Gladstone and Parnell, and the introduction of the first Home Rule bill, Conservatives changed their party label to Unionist, insisting that Irish self-government was a threat to the constitution, property rights, Protestantism, the United Kingdom, and the empire. From 1910 to 1914, during the House of Lords and third Home Rule bill crises, Unionist politicians played the "Orange card" to the precipice of civil war.[17]

Emigration and the displays of anti-Catholic nativism it encouraged in urban Britain and America also affected the associations between Irish and Catholic. It also gave Irish nationalism an English-speaking world dimension, making it more difficult for the British to contain. While Irish emigrants settled in many places, most went to the United States. Before 1820, the North American emigration was essentially Ulster Presbyterian. After that date, periodic famines, increasing rural violence, and population pressure on a primitive agrarian economy transformed North America into a Catholic escape hatch. The 1845-49 famine institutionalized emigration as a safety valve, with Irish parents raising most of their children for export. Irish nationalism described emigration as a consequence of British misrule. And it used Irish-American success stories as evidence that the Irish in a free environment were ambitious and enterprising.

Since Irish Catholicism accepted the principles of liberal democracy, and because they arrived in the United States skilled in Anglo-style politics, the Irish adjusted to the American political consensus and led later Catholic immigrants into a similar accommodation. Political power and leadership of an increasingly significant American Catholicism provided the Irish with social mobility leading to respectability. But the process was slow and regionally uneven.

Early Irish nationalism in the United States reflected the alienation experienced by the pioneers of America's urban ghetto who were having social, economic, and psychological difficulties with the transition from rural Ireland. Their poverty, crime, vices, and neuroses resulted in a major social problem. But to Anglo-Americans, Irish Catholicism was even more offensive than Irish social behavior. Stemming from English nativism, American prejudice against the Irish also considered superstitious, authoritarian popery a menace to Anglo-Protestant culture and institutions. Irish America replied to this bias that grouped religion and nationality with a militant Catholicism that was even more closely linked to ethnic identity than it had been in Ireland.[18]

When success finally came to Irish America, it did not always reduce inferiority complexes. Frequently, Anglos and other Protestants, even French Catholics in Louisiana, did not accept middle or upper working-class Irish Americans as equals. This encouraged a quest for respectability in their nationalism. Linking social subordination in the United States with Ireland's bondage, many of the economically mobile Irish decided that by liberating their mother country they would improve their American situation.[19]

Irish-American nationalism had two strategies: the first was to attempt to influence American foreign policy in anti-British directions; the second was to employ the United States as an arsenal for freedom movements in Ireland. Despite their acknowledged political abilities, Irish Americans were ineffective in shaping American foreign policy for several reasons. For most of them, nationalism was third on their priority list behind Catholicism and bread-and-butter Democratic politics. Another reason was the deep affection of the Anglo-American establishment for things British.[20]

Irish America's Irish strategy worked better than its American strategy. Without the diaspora, the Irish nationalism would have had survival problems. Repeal clubs in the United States sent dollars to O'Connell in the 1840s. After 1848, Irish Americans preferred physical force nationalism. They gave the name Fenianism to revolutionary republicanism in the 1860s. When Irish Republican Brotherhood insurrections failed in 1867, and the Fenian Brotherhood began to fade, the Clan na Gael picked up the green flag in the United States. Clansmen in New York designed the New Departure in the late 1870s to mobilize the Irish peasantry for a war on landlordism as a prelude to rebellion against British rule.[21]

Through the Land League, Parnell checkmated the Clan and captured the Irish-American majority for Home Rule. After the land war concluded with tenant right, a step toward peasant proprietorship, Parnell diverted Irish-American dollars to restructuring the Irish Parliamentary party and the Irish National League, its constituency organization. When the fanaticism of Ulster unionism, encouraged by the British Conservatives' determination to overcome the Irish-Liberal alliance, and by British Liberal timidity, undermined Home Rule in 1914, the Clan na Gael again was able to lead Irish America toward physical force nationalism. The Clan was part of the conspiracy that produced Easter Week, and during the Anglo-Irish War Irish Americans sent supplies to the Irish Republican Army. They also contributed to the force of world opinion that persuaded the British government to concede dominion status to a twenty-six-county Irish Free State.[22]

Irish-American nationalism was imprinted on the personality as well as the progress of Irish nationalism. Emigration meant Irish associations with American republicanism and egalitarianism; these strengthened democratic values in Ireland. Anglo-Irish landlords and Catholic bishops and priests observed that after the famine Irish Catholics were increasingly assertive and less deferential to status or authority. They attributed this change to the American influence, particularly as it was manifested in Fenianism.[23]

Emigration involved the agrarian as well as the Catholic dimensions of Irish nationalism. The mass exodus to America emphasized the problems of rural poverty, focusing attention on landlordism as the source. Tenant security had been an issue in the O'Connell and Young Ireland versions of Irish nationalism, but the famine and emigration made it the number one consideration.

In the 1840s James Fintan Lalor insisted that the land of Ireland belonged to its people. His words became the slogan for a variety of agrarian agitations, but it was interpreted in various ways. Until the 1870s, most land reformers would have settled for tenant right: secure tenures at fair rents with the right of a farmer to sell his contributions to the holding on leaving.

The Catholic clerical and inclusive ideology components of Irish nationalism limited its approach to the agrarian problem. Bishops and priests, sympathetic to the plight of the peasantry they came from, did not hesitate to support tenant right, but they could not distance themselves too far from the conservative, private property views of Roman Catholicism. As long as lay leaders clung to the fantasy that there was a potential Protestant constituency for Irish nationalism, they could not militantly confront landlordism.

Tenant right was the principal objective of the Independent Irish party of the 1850s. However, improvements in the postfamine economy, a revival of sectarian animosities, membership defections for government office, landlord political resurgence, and the opposition of many Catholic bishops to Independent opposition destroyed the party. But tenant right continued to be significant in Irish politics. Along with Protestant disestablishment, it was a goal of the National Association in the 1860s.

William Ewart Gladstone, the Liberal prime minister, reacting to Fenianism and the National Association with its connections to British radicalism, disestablished the Church of Ireland in 1867, and three years later passed a land act.[24] Although the act failed to secure tenures at fair rents with free sale, it established precedents for government limitations on property rights. And the Bright clause of the land act pointed the way to the ultimate solution of the land question, land purchase.

Although Isaac Butt was an advocate of tenant right, his decision to exclude it from the Home Rule program lost mass enthusiasm for federalism. Parnell did not make the same mistake. He realized the war on landlordism aspect of the New Departure was the way to recruit for Home Rule. On the invitation of its founder, Michael Davitt, Parnell became president of the National Land League. Davitt and his Irish-American mentor, Patrick Ford of *The Irish World,* wanted to nationalize land. Instead, Parnell accepted Gladstone's 1881 land act conferring tenant right. Most Irish peasants were happy with this decision.[25]

Postfamine Irish landlords were insecure, defensive, almost friendless. They had become the scapegoats of the Irish question. Even British politicians, who once considered landlords the glue of the Union and defended their property interests, now branded them the core cause of Irish discontent. Gladstone's first land act angered landlords; his second made them despair. Realizing that they were the targets of Irish nationalism, and that the British thought them greedy and cruel, they lost faith in the future. They cooperated with Arthur Balfour's progressive unionism.[26] Under the 1903 Wyndham Act, the government loaned Irish farmers money at a low interest and long payment period to buy their holdings, and gave landlords a generous bonus to sell.[26] Supplemented in 1907 by a Liberal government, this measure converted Ireland into a land of peasant proprietors.

The land war introduced a shopkeeper leadership class into Irish nationalism. It had strong kinship, customer, and money-lending ties with the peasantry. Most shopkeepers had farmer roots; many still tilled the soil on a part-time basis. Their connections with town life, their visits to cities such as Dublin, Cork, and Galway, and their diverse economic associations gave shopkeepers an aura of knowledge and sophistication, rivaling that of priests. When bad harvests and North American grain competition in a United Kingdom free trade market combined to produce a devastating agricultural depression in the late 1870s, shopkeepers shared the risks of farmers. When bishops and priests condemned violence and property attacks associated with the Land League, shopkeepers filled the local leadership vacuum. Realizing that the laity was marching on with new leaders, the clergy hurried to catch up, but they had to share command.[27] As Ireland moved into the twentieth century, a troika of priests, shopkeepers, and prosperous farmers controlled rural politics.

All or part of the Catholic, American, and agrarian features of the nationalist profile offended, or at least troubled, sections of Irish opinion. Young Irelanders blamed O'Connell for linking Catholic and Irish. But when they proposed Gaelic as an alternative to Catholic nationalism, Protestants could not see the difference. Young Ireland's message did impress a Catholic middle class searching for a respectable cultural identity. The mythology of an ancient, noble Irish race, with a significant literary and historical tradition, more sensitive and spiritual than coarse Anglo-Saxons, also had an impact on the inferiority complex of Irish America.[28]

Anglo-Irish Protestants reacted to the advancing Irish nationalism that was associated with Catholicism, indoctrinated in American egalitarianism and republicanism, and fueled by agrarian radicalism with ultraunionism. Two of their scholar-intellectuals, Standish O'Grady and Samuel Ferguson, thought this defensiveness mistaken. Like Young Irelanders before them, they urged their coreligionists to join with Catholics in mutual appreciation of the Gaelic tradition. But unlike Young Irelanders, they offered Irish cultural identity as an alternative rather than a supplement to political nationalism. They believed that admiration for the aristocratic character of the Gaelic heritage would wean Catholics away from democratic nationalism, reviving deference for the Anglo-Irish aristocracy and gentry. They also expected that if the Irish identity search was satisfied culturally, political nationalism would fade away, and Ireland would find a unique but integral place in the United Kingdom.

Ferguson and O'Grady failed to lure Anglo-Irish Protestantism out of its mental ghetto or to distract Catholics from Home Rule and land. But they did energize cultural nationalism. Reactions to Anglo-Saxism racism, immensely popular in British academic, intellectual, and popular culture circles, and disillusionment with politics after Parnell's fall in 1891 and the split in Home Rule ranks, also contributed to the revival of cultural nationalism.[29]

Not all of the Anglo-Irish interested in the Gaelic tradition shared the Ferguson-O'Grady distaste for Irish nationalism. Although not overtly political, Douglas Hyde, cofounder and first president of the Gaelic League, and William Butler Yeats and others in the literary renaissance were enemies of the British connection. They accused it of discouraging a creative, distinct, and vital indigenous culture. They had no problem with Home Rule.

Started in 1893 by Hyde and Eoin MacNeill, an Ulster Catholic, the

Gaelic League set out to de-anglicize Ireland by reviving the Irish language. It accepted the Young Ireland thesis that a political nation could not
be free if it remained in cultural slavery. The league was even more
committed to Irish than Young Ireland. Leagues believed that the language
was as much an expression of cultural values and a particular mind-set as it
was a means of written and verbal communication. To be truly sovereign,
the Irish must think and speak in their own tongue.[30]

The Gaelic League reprinted examples of ancient Gaelic literature,
and published contemporary writing in Irish. Many of the urban middle
class joined the league, even some who never bothered to learn Irish, or
knew it only superficially. Members cycled off to remote Irish-speaking
districts or crossed over to the Aran and Blasket islands to polish their
language skills in conversations with native speakers. They also became
Irish folk music and dancing enthusiasts.

Gaelic scholarship and the language movement also inspired literature
in English. In glorifying unsophisticated peasants as people with great folk
wisdom and spiritual sensitivity while lamenting the baneful effects of
Anglo-Saxon urban industrial culture on Ireland, writers of the literary
renaissance were in the Young Ireland tradition. In attempting to rescue
the peasant soul from secular materialism, writers believed they were
preserving the leaven of a Gaelic culture that would flourish again and teach
the world that there were things better than Anglo-Saxon greed and
utilitarianism.

Despite its intellectual energy and achievements, the Gaelic revival
was negative in its challenge to inclusive Irish nationalism. Founded in
1884 by Michael Cusack, the Gaelic Athletic Association spread through
rural and small-town Ireland, promoting such "ancient" Irish games as
Gaelic football and hurling for men and camogie (a sort of field hockey) for
women. Intolerant of all things English, the GAA banned participation in
such sports as rugby, cricket, soccer, or field hockey. Gaelic Leaguers also
were hostile to "foreign" influences. They labeled those indifferent to their
Irish-Ireland objective as West Britons or Shoneens (little John Bulls). This
provincialism and xenophobia estranged the self-confident and cosmopolitan young James Joyce from the Gaelic movement.

Within the revival there was conflict over the role of literature. Gaelic
League and GAA leaders viewed writers as propagandist for Irish Ireland.
Hyde insisted that authentic Irish literature must be in Irish. Yeats and his
friends drew on the Gaelic tradition for material and inspiration, but
refused to jettison English with its flexibility as a literary language and its
wide, international reading public. They were experimenting with a literature in English that was instructed by Irish experience, insight, and

perspective. Literary renaissance writers rejected a role subordinate to the purposes of nationalism. They demanded freedom to interpret Ireland in an honest, creative way.

Conflicting views on the role of literature resulted in two Abbey Theatre riots. In 1907, during the first performance of John Millington Synge's *Playboy of the Western World*, Irish-Ireland members of the audience protested, arguing that the playwright had libeled the noble Irish peasant. Irish Americans in New York treated Synge's masterpiece in a similar fashion. The thin skin of Irish cultural nationalism again was irritated in 1926 during the performance of Sean O'Casey's Dublin working-class play, *The Plough and the Stars.* In both instances, the exclusive nationalism of the Gaelic revival defended the mob against the artist.[31]

Irish Ireland began as a Gaelic alternative to Catholic nationalism, but ended as its captive. At first, bishops and priests suspected the Protestant prominence in the Gaelic revival. They feared the prospect of an Irish Ireland separate from a Catholic Ireland. They came to realize, however, that Gaelic nationalism's protest against the influence of British secularism and materialism and its cultural isolationism synchronized with Catholic values. Catholic leaders exploited the Gaelic revival's anglophobia and diverted its hope for a culturally monolithic, religiously pluralistic Irish Ireland into an essentially Catholic Irish Ireland.[32] They were assisted in their endeavor by Anglo-Irish Protestant and Scotch-Irish Presbyterian rejections of nationalism, cultural as well as political.

The Blood Sacrifice message of Easter Week poets Patrick Pearse, Joseph Mary Plunkett, and Thomas MacDonagh was a heretical integration of Catholic and Irish Ireland. They insisted on an Ireland "Gaelic as well as free" and wove Catholic atonement and redemption themes into a revolutionary tapestry. Ireland, said the poets, needed a baptism of blood to purge the stain of Anglo-Saxonism. Although the British would smash the first advance of revolution, the blood of a small band of martyrs would cleanse the Irish soul of Home Rule's collaboration with Britain, thus redeeming the nation. A more idealistic generation would then take up and succeed at the task of cultural and political liberation.[33]

Since British vengeance and insensitivity converted Blood Sacrifice ideology into historical reality, folklore and popular history have overlooked the significance of constitutional nationalism. Despite the failure of British politicians to respond in time and adequately to Irish agitations, the Irish were patient in their search for justice. Militancy and martyrology in nationalist literature, journalism, and folklore have obscured the basic moderation of nineteenth-century nationalists. Most followed O'Connell and Parnell; few rallied to Young Ireland in 1848 or the Fenians in 1867.

General acceptance of Home Rule illustrated the temperate quality of majority nationalism.[34] During the Home Rule years, the Irish were rewarded by excellent parliamentary representation that did much to solve the social and economic aspects of the Irish question. If the British had responded as well to the moderation of the Irish party as they did to the fanaticism of Ulster unionism, much of the turbulence of twentieth-century Anglo-Irish relations could have been avoided.

After the Irish party won the parliamentary game in 1910-14 and then lost Home Rule to the extraparliamentary bigotry of Ulster unionism, the cyncism and opportunism of British conservatism, and the timidity of a Liberal government, the faith of Irish nationalists in constitutionalism diminished. Still, until 1916 the Irish party continued to enjoy most of the nationalists' support. During and just after Easter Week, the overwhelming majority of nationalists thought of Pearse, James Connolly, the socialist leader of the citizen army, and their comrades as traitors, German dupes, or hooligans. But when the British, brutalized by the slaughter on the western front, reacted to what they considered a stab in the back by slowly, torturously, and sadistically executing the rebel leaders to teach the Irish a lesson, they presented a face of barbarity rather than justice. Men who had been denounced and spat on became gallant heroes. Their photographs appeared in Irish homes, and people read Blood Sacrifice poetry.

The swing in Irish nationalist opinion became apparent in December 1918 when voters rejected the Irish party for Sinn Féin inheritors of the Easter Week legend. After the general election, Sinn Féin M.P.s refused to take Westminster seats. Instead, they organized Dáil Éireann, the Parliament of the redeclared Irish Republic.

Britain's refusal to acknowledge the republic led to the Anglo-Irish conflict, the model of twentieth-century wars of liberation. Lloyd George and his coalition government in 1920 attempted to satisfy both Irish nationalists and Ulster unionists by creating two Home Rule parliaments, one in Belfast, the other in Dublin. In the north, unionists who militantly rejected Home Rule for all of Ireland in 1912-14, now accepted it for themselves to create "a Protestant nation for a Protestant people." In the south, nationalists took advantage of the election for a Dublin parliament to reassert their demand for a republic. Finally, in 1921, Irish, British, and world opinion pressured the government into conceding dominion status to a twenty-six-county Irish Free State.[35]

Posttreaty Ireland exhibits all of the strands in the texture of Irish nationalism.[36] While honed in revolution, it has survived and functioned within the constitutional tradition. Both the Irish Free State and its successor, the Republic of Ireland (1948), have featured a British parliamentary system with ministerial responsibility. But their written constitutions, bills of rights, personal rather than ideological politics, and egalitarianism represent an American addition to Irish nationalism. Although less socialistic, Ireland, because of its Gaelic and Catholic heritages, is more communal than Britain.[37] The Catholic element also distinguishes liberal democracy in Ireland from that in Britain or America. Since over 95 percent of the population is Catholic and mostly devout, and since Catholicism has represented culture and nationality, boundaries between religion and politics are more ambiguous and fragile in Ireland than in more pluralistic societies. Catholic homogeneity encourages the Irish to insist that problems concerning the family, marriage, procreation, and education have moral as well as socioeconomic implications.[38]

Although church and state technically are separate in Ireland, Eamon de Valera's 1937 constitution gave Catholicism a special status as the majority religion, and the Dáil has enacted Catholic morality and values in such areas as censorship, divorce, contraception, and education. Since this legislation has expressed majority rule more than clericalism, Ireland, like Israel, is a confessional state rather than a theocracy.

The ideals of Irish Ireland that inspired revolutions and produced the modern Irish state have been incorporated into its purpose. Governments have tried to preserve native-speaking districts (the Gaeltacht) and to revive the use of the language in the rest of the country by decreeing that it be taught in the schools and that it be required for civil service employment. The people have reacted inconsistently to these policies. Although Irish Ireland remains a nationalist objective, and voters have supported its political advocates, most Irish have made little effort to become proficient in the language. English remains the vernacular of the Irish nation.[39]

Gaelic, combined with Catholic dimensions of nationalism, cultivated a puritan and provincial Ireland. Censorship of the best in Irish and foreign literature symbolized the narrow perspective of Irish life. Daniel Corkery, a writer of considerable talent and accomplishment, became the leading postindependence champion of Irish Ireland. He wrote in English, but like Hyde, he maintained that Irish literature ideally should be in Irish. Corkery condemned the work of the literary renaissance as a provincial English literature that ignored the three dynamic forces in Irish history: language, religion, and land.[40]

Corkery did not represent the main themes of postrevolutionary Irish literature. The majority of Irish writers followed Yeats's lead in trying to free cultural nationalism from the restrictions of clericalism and chauvinism. While there was continuity in Irish literature's refusal to bend the artistic knee to religious or nationalist authoritarianism, the new generation of mostly Catholic, lower middle- or working-class, reform-conscious Irish writers shed the reactionary romanticism of the Anglo-Irish Protestant literary renaissance. They did not want to preserve Ireland as a folk museum.

There are few noble peasants in postrevolutionary Irish prose, poetry, or drama. Writers reflect the realism of Joyce rather than the romanticism of Yeats. For example, in Liam O'Flaherty's novel *Famine* or in Patrick Kavanaugh's novel *Tarry Flynn* and long poem *The Great Hunger*, peasants struggle for existence on small, infertile farms. The complacent fatalism, spirituality, and hospitality extolled by the literary renaissance has been transformed by economic hardship and a puritanical Catholicism into boredom, frustration, and thrift to the point of meanness, the worst kind of materialism.

Unlike their predecessors, writers such as Sean O'Casey, Sean O'Faolain, and Frank O'Connor exhibited more concern with city life than rural life, describing the latter as stultified by limited economic opportunities, Catholic puritanism, and anti-intellectualism. Their work emphasized the dilemma of talented youth caught in a motionless society, choosing between death of mind and spirit in Ireland or the emigrant ship and exile.

O'Faolain and O'Connor were the most distinguished Irish writers from the 1930s until the 1960s. Both were masters of the short story. They also wrote novels, literary criticism, travelogues, historical essays, and biographies. O'Faolain and O'Connor came from Cork where Daniel Corkery tutored them in Irish-Ireland cultural nationalism. They were active in the Irish Republican Army during the Troubles, fighting on the republican side against the free state in the 1922-23 civil war. Although Corkery inspired their cultural nationalism and their literary ambitions, the young men rejected his narrow vision of Ireland. They did not want to freeze their country in a Catholic, peasant past. They resisted Catholic clericalism and the conservative establishment of priest, large farmer, and shopkeeper. O'Connor and especially O'Faolain, through the journal he founded and edited, *The Bell*, deserve credit for preserving the liberal democratic impulses of Irish nationalism.

Although they tried, Gaelic and Catholic adherents ultimately failed to isolate Ireland from American and British cultural influences. Emigrants who returned to Ireland wearing fancy clothes with money-filled pockets fascinated friends and relatives with tales of exciting adventures on other shores, planting seeds of discontent. Hollywood movies, British newspapers, American and British television, and records and tapes of popular music penetrated the Shamrock Curtain, offering the Irish glimpses, often fantasies, of experiences far different from their own. To halt emigration, or at least slow its pace, the government in the 1960s and 1970s encouraged industrialization with subsidies and tax breaks for foreign investors. Urban industrialism diluted the rural Catholic content of Irishness. Imaginative changes in foreign policy also widened Irish perspectives. Consistent with its history, Ireland in 1956 entered the United Nations as a champion of the Third World. Seventeen years later, as a new member of the Common Market, its emphasis became European.

Economic and social changes; diplomatic, economic, tourist, and popular cultural relations with other countries; and new directions in Catholicism spawned by Vatican II made Ireland more secular and less rustic. Although pleased with a more open and more cosmopolitan working environment, some writers began to worry about materialism corrupting the Irish spirit.[41]

Since 1968, Protestant bigotry in Northern Ireland, Catholic resistance, British surrender to Orange fanaticism, British soldiers shooting and torturing Irish nationalists, Irish rebels ambushing British soldiers and members of the Royal Ulster Constabulary, Irish Americans financing the Irish Republican Army, and writers such as Seamus Heaney, Benedict Kiely, Seamus Deane, Brian Friel, and John Montague expressing the frustrations and anxieties of their people have telescoped centuries of Irish history into twenty short years.

Violence in British Ulster, which spread to the Republic, has forced Catholics in the south to reexamine their nationalism. They still blame Britain for promoting sectarian conflict as a divide-and-rule technique, for partitioning Ireland, and for tolerating Protestant oppression in the Six Counties, but many have come to realize that the Gaelic and Catholic threads in nationalism contributed to a divided Ireland. Consequently, Irish is no longer a requirement for a secondary school certificate or for civil service appointments. Censorship has abated, and a referendum has removed the special status of Catholicism from the constitution. The government also has permitted contraception for married couples. However, puritan Ireland has not entirely vanished, and Catholic Ireland continues to resist the liberal element in nationalism. A privately initiated referendum, finally sponsored by the government, permanently outlawed abortion no matter what the reason. A more recent referendum resulted in a conclusive rejection of divorce.

In the Northern Ireland fallout, writers north and south, Catholic and non-Catholic, are engaged in a task familiar in Irish literature, the search for a comprehensive Irish identity. They are trying to give it a pluralistic meaning independent of sect, ethnic origins, and language. Considering the Irish historical experience and the components of Irish nationalism, their effort could be an exercise in futility.[42]

R.V. Comerford

NATION, NATIONALISM, AND THE IRISH LANGUAGE

THE HISTORIOGRAPHY of nations as practiced in the nineteenth and twentieth centuries has typically been conducted on the assumption that the nation—each nation—is predestinate. However much historians in more recent times have endeavored to challenge and abandon that assumption, it remains stubbornly lodged in the mind of the typical general reader. So, the emergence of each nation and its rise to independent statehood is seen as the inevitable and obligatory fulfillment of the designs of nature or of the Creator, helped on of course by the endeavors of heroic personages. National boundaries are taken to be self-evidently right and natural, and various national characterisitics are seen as essential preconditions for the happiness and prosperity of the citizens. National language fits very comfortably into this scheme of things. It is at once the product and the vehicle of the national genius. If it is not universal within the national territory, the nation is incomplete. Those citizens who do not speak the national language are disadvantaged, not simply in a practical way but in the far more serious sense that they are cut off from the wellsprings of the national being; they are shut out of the spiritual communion that embraces the contemporary nation and the generations that have gone before. There follows the obvious obligation to promote and exalt or, if necessary, to restore or revive the language.

The predestinate nation is a satisfactory working model for many practical purposes and in many places. In many other places, including Ireland, it does not stand up for practical purposes. For the purposes of intellectual analysis it does not stand up anywhere. In treating of the Irish language and its relationship with modern Irish nationalism, I am particularly anxious to disallow predestinarian assumptions, and to that end I shall treat separately of the relationship of the Irish language to the bases of actual (as distinct from theoretical) Irish nationality in the nineteenth century and the involvement of the language in the superstructure of Irish nationalism in the early twentieth century. Subsequently I shall look at what is to be learned from the fate and fortunes of the language in a self-governing Irish state.

The sociopolitical grouping that came to assume the character of the Irish nation in the nineteenth century was as impressive an entity as most of its European contemporaries. It could on occasion effect spectacular mobilizations, and in and out of season it commanded an impressive level of communal and individual loyalty. The principal criterion by which Irish people, in practice, decided whether they belonged to this collectivity or not was one of religion. The sense of belonging from which the collectivity drew its strength was that of being Irish and Catholic. For its most effective mobilizations it depended on the organizational structures of the Catholic church. Its essential bond with Catholicism is not contradicted by the fact that it attracted the support of a number of individual Protestants. Some of these, most notably Thomas Davis and John Mitchell, expounded a theory of Irish nationality to comprehend Irish people of all religious affiliations, but it was a prescription for the ideal rather than a description of the actual.

Irish Catholics were particularly susceptible to the attractions of collective action because they had a strong collective sense of deprivation. The degree to which individuals felt this might at times seem to be in inverse ratio to actual individual deprivation. Catholics were particularly preoccupied with the matter of land. The desire of individuals for land, or for more land, was subsumed in a collective conviction that the Catholics of Ireland as a group had been robbed of the land.

Land and religion were obvious obsessions of the Irish Catholics; the Irish language was not. That is not to say that linguistic considerations were of no significance to them. Europe's nationalities in the nineteenth century had a very distinct tendency to simplify the linguistic situation within their boundaries. The thrust toward linguistic uniformity is not based in the first instance on ideology but is grounded in practical considerations. Political mobilization, the rise of popular nationalism, linguistic uniformity, and increased ease of communication all go hand in hand. If the language that gains the monopoly is an indigenous one, it can at once acquire the mystique of being the national language and be regarded as the repository of such sacred things as "the spirit of the race." And it can serve—even more decisively than religion—as the criterion for membership of the nation. The Irish national collectivity of the nineteenth century, however, chose English rather than Irish as its uniforming tongue.

To say that English was "chosen" is, of course, to beg a number of questions. There is no question of particular individuals or coherent groups having decided the issue. Somebody like Daniel O'Connell apparently did not see the matter in terms of choice: an old world was passing away inexorably and its language would go with it. O'Connell's attitude, so frequently lambasted by the language enthusiasts of later generations as one of carelessness or of active hostility to Irish, was in reality the expression of a pragmatist's verdict on the outcome of developments over which he had no control.[1] At the same time it is worth noting that Irish was by no means ineligible as a language of political mobilization in early nineteenth-century Ireland. One authority has cited a series of examples of political speech making in Irish during O'Connell's political career.[2] With the burgeoning of population in the decades before the Great Famine the absolute number of Irish speakers was actually increasing, even though they constituted a decreasing proportion of the population.

There is a clearly discernible dualism in the outlook and world view informing the O'Connellite mobilizations. The supporting masses were entering a modernizing world of ordered, pragmatic politics, while at the same time expressing themselves—as examination of the relevant folklore makes particularly clear—in terms of an Irish version of the millennialism characteristic of the old European peasantry. The imagery and vocabulary of the millennium were particularly readily available to those who were still Irish speakers. Much is sometimes made of the cultural losses that accompanied the change from Irish. But even if Irish had become the language of modernization the old ways and the old attitudes would have undergone transformation in the new environment.

The decline of literacy in Irish almost to the point of disappearance militated against the language's chances. In this respect the position of Welsh, for instance, was immeasurably stronger. On the other hand, a number of the modernizing languages of the nineteenth century—unlike Irish with its rich literary heritage—had no written forms until taken up as national languages. Slovak is a case in point. The determining factor in the case of Ireland in the early nineteenth century was not the weakness of Irish but the strength of English.

English became the language of Irish nationalist mobilization in the early nineteenth century not simply because it was the language of place and privilege, which it had been for a very long time, but because for a generation or two beforehand it was being adopted on a large scale as the language of opportunity.[3] The opportunities in question, accompanied by many painful dislocations, were based on greatly enhanced economic links with England and the colonies in the second half of the eighteenth century. There were therefore obvious utilitarian reasons for a shift to the English language.

In the sixteenth and seventeenth centuries the English state may have been second to none in the ferocity of its campaigns against indigenous language and culture in Ireland and elsewhere, but its efforts in this respect in nineteenth-century Ireland were pusillanimous. The mainspring of cultural and linguistic change was popular response to economic realities. It was popular demand for education in English that created the flourishing—and chaotic—growth of pay schools in the early decades of the nineteenth century. In many of these institutions, teachers eager to secure the results expected by parents in return for their precious fees, resorted to the crudest of methods, including the use of the notorious tally stick. Parental determination was vital. Increasingly, Irish-speaking parents adopted the most effective tactic of all by simply not using the language with their children. A recent ingenious analysis of the census data—which, while not a fully satisfactory guide in language matters, are all we have to go on— suggests that of Irish children born from 1801 to 1811, 45 percent may have been brought up speaking Irish. For those born 1831-41, the estimated percentage dropped to 28, and for those born 1861-71, to 13.[4]

The national school system instituted in 1831 was a response to the public demand for education. It answered a need and it also imposed standards and controls. In advancing English at the expense of Irish, the national board in charge of the new system was serving the "popular will" as surely as any state board has ever done. It was also, in promoting linguistic and cultural uniformity, behaving as the agents of all nineteenth-century European states tended to do, but by the standards of foreign contemporaries, it was a rather blunt instrument of acculturation.

While there were easily comprehensible economic reasons for learning English, this utilitarianism does not explain everything. The necessity of having English for commerce scarcely demanded the banishment of Irish from every other area of life. The heightened preoccupation with respectability and conformity in manners that marked the period from about 1830 to the First World War everywhere in western Europe was embraced unreservedly in Ireland. Educated and/or comfortable Irish Catholics were especially anxious to show that their kind was as good as the rest. That was a major source of pressure on the unfashionable and supposedly uncouth Irish language. Such prejudice went hand in hand with the imperatives of modernization to ensure that there was a movement not simply to acquire English but simultaneously to reject and abandon Irish.

A further cause of hostility to Irish on the part of many Catholics was its association with Protestant missionary endeavors. Humphrey O'Sullivan (Amhlaoibh Ó Súilleabháin) of Callan, in an entry for June 1827 in his celebrated diary, summed up the situation as a politicized Catholic who was also a lover of Irish: "How long until this Irish language in which I am writing disappears? Fine big schoolhouses are being built by the day for the teaching of the new tongue, i.e., English. But alas! nobody shows interest in the lovely, soft Gaelic tongue except little swaddlers trying to win the Irish people over to their accursed new religion."[5] The swaddlers were itinerant Protestant missionaries.

Throughout the first half of the century, evangelicals operating under the auspices of various churches and societies endeavored to bring the Scriptures to the speakers of Welsh, Scots Gaelic, and Irish in their native languages. In Ireland from 1811 onward they had the use of the Irish Bible published in that year by the British and Foreign Bible Society.[6] In previous centuries Irish may have acted as a barrier against the spread of a Protestantism served by agents lacking competence in the language. But in the first half of the nineteenth century there was a feeling—not confined to optimistic evangelicals—that Irish-speaking Catholics, like the speakers of "backward" indigenous languages elsewhere, were in a pristine, volatile state and ripe for evangelization, whereas the English-speaking Catholics of Ireland were seen to be fixed securely within a set politico-religious framework. Evangelicals making use of an indigenous language did not necessarily have its long-term survival at heart. Nevertheless, in the cases of Welsh and Scots Gaelic, the initiatives of the evangelicals had beneficial linguistic effects, while with the Irish it was ultimately otherwise.

What deserves to be reiterated is the way in which language as such lay outside the list of subjects, such as religion, land, the constitution, and access to office and employment, that fueled the intense political animosities of nineteenth-century Ireland. On 30 October 1834 a great demonstration was held at the residence of the Marquis of Downshire, Hillsborough Castle, County Down, attended by Anglicans and by Presbyterian followers of Rev. Henry Cooke, all resolved to stand together in a Pan-Protestant alliance against politicized Irish Catholicism and its English allies.[7] The same Marquis of Downshire was president of the Ulster Gaelic Society founded in 1830. This Belfast-based society kept up the romantic-antiquarian interest in Irish language and associated matters that had flourished in the city since the late eighteenth century.[8]

Similary in Dublin, Irish language, literature, and antiquities constituted an acceptable area of cultural interest for aristocratic and upper middle-class coteries. They formed such bodies as the Gaelic Society of Dublin (1806), the Hiberno-Celtic Society (1818), the Irish Archaeological Society (1840), the Celtic Society (1845), and the Ossianic Society (1853). This proliferation betokens cliques and factional conflicts for which one basis of division was the interconfessional animosity that entered into every area of Dublin social life at the time. But there was no question of Irish language or antiquities being seen as the property of any one religious group or as constituting a political badge of any kind. The Irish Archaeological Society succeeded in having Queen Victoria's husband, Prince Albert, as its nominal patron. The greatest services to language, ancient sources, and folklore were rendered by John O'Donovan and Eugene O'Curry who did much of their basic work in the 1830s while in the employment of the Ordnance Survey.

While the actual Irish nation was resolutely turning its back on the language, a few individual Irishmen under the influence of Continental theories of nationalism were uneasy. Thomas Davis, who in the pages of the *Nation* (founded 1842) did more than anyone else to impose standard European concepts on Irish political reality, declared that a people without a distinctive language was only half a nation.[9] He called for the preservation and cultivation of Irish. Another Young Irelander, William Smith O'Brien, was similarly convinced. Between 1856 and his death in 1864, he devoted himself to various nonpolitical forms of nation building, including cultivation of the Irish language, which he began to study himself in his last years.

The proprietor of the *Nation* from 1855 onward was A.M. Sullivan. Though apparently not a speaker of Irish himself, his deep immersion in romantic nationalist sentiment made of him a language enthusiast. In 1858 he acquired a font of Irish type (the paper had not had one since 1848) and began publication of an Irish language column. The following year he provided accommodation for a group of young artisans and clerks holding a weekly Irish class under the auspices of the Society for the Promotion and Cultivation of the Irish Language founded in Dublin in 1858. The society also had a branch in Belfast. In both cities it was a vehicle for young Catholics seeking an occasion for socialization. But they were not choosy about what occasion or pretext they might have for fraternal association, and they drifted off to other outlets not demanding the tedious effort involved in learning a new language.[10]

One of the few leaders of Catholic society after the famine who tried to organize the social activity of the young was Dean Richard O'Brien, a priest of the Limerick diocese. The Catholic Young Men's Society, founded in 1849, was his creation and remained under his guidance for many years. The CYMS had many branches in Ireland and in Britain. In 1861 (and perhaps in other years also) O'Brien used the annual convention of the CYMS to exhort the various branches to establish Irish classes and to promote the use of the language.[11]

A better-known organization that catered to the social needs of young Irishmen in the 1860s was the IRB. It is commonly known as the Fenian movement because it had an American counterpart, the Fenian Brotherhood, so named by its leader, John O'Mahony, in evocation of the Fianna of ancient Ireland. O'Mahony was a graduate of Trinity College, Dublin, where he spent little time, and a gentleman farmer with interests in northeast Cork and south Tipperary who had fled to France in 1848. Living in straitened circumstances in New York from 1853 on, he managed to pursue his interest in Irish language and history, and in 1857 his translation of Keating's *Foras Feasa ar Éirinn* was published.[12] However, he did not make an interest in Irish a noticeable feature of his organization on either side of the Atlantic. Of course, many of the IRB's adherents in Connacht and Munster had Irish, and a handful of its Dublin activists had shown some brief interest in acquiring the language. One of the latter, John Devoy, wrote on the subject of the Fenians and the language many decades later, and in a greatly changed context, in terms that can be best understood as a highly defensive admission that the language was not a preoccupation of the early IRB.[13]

It ought to be clear from the above that interest in the preservation of Irish during the mid-Victorian period was not predominantly a Protestant matter in the way sometimes suggested. There were even attempts to link the language with Catholic nationalism, though in vain.

Dean O'Brien, Davis, Smith O'Brien, O'Mahony, and Sullivan were motivated by a linguistic nationalism that meant nothing to the masses. But, ideology apart, the five of them also saw the Irish language as a precious inheritance whose loss would be a tragedy and a cause of impoverishment. The same realization, that the disappearance of the language was a grievous loss, also affected many others who unlike them were untouched by romantic nationalism; how many, it is impossible to say. Most of them probably shrugged their shoulders, realizing that the matter was as much beyond their control as the weather and the seasons. Humphrey O'Sullivan was a case in point, as the quotation from him above suggests. Those who took a less fatalistic line included Archbishop John MacHale of Tuam who had learned his English at school. He advised his flock to learn English, too, but to retain the use of Irish as he had done.[14] MacHale took up the writing of Irish late in life and translated inter alia the *Iliad* and some of Moore's melodies. Vastly more competent as an Irish scholar was his cousin and protégé, Fr. Ulick Bourke (1829-87), whose "Easy Lessons in Irish" were carried serially in the *Nation* before being published in book form.[15] His work was used in the 1870s by an Irish revivalist movement in the United States that operated under the designation of the Philo-Celtic societies.[16]

The British prime minister, William E. Gladstone, on a number of occasions in the 1870s, praised the people of Wales for cultivating their national language and remarked on how badly, by comparison, the Irish had neglected theirs. This view of the indigenous cultural institutions of the Celtic fringe as possessing their own authenticity and as being worthy of preservation had never been completely lost, but for most of the century it had almost disappeared. The last quarter of the nineteenth century witnessed a softening in the attitudes of certain sections of fashionable opinion toward the Celtic languages and the manifestations of ethnicity and folk life generally.

In this atmosphere the Society for the Preservation of the Irish Language was founded in 1876. Its officer board and council had a preponderance of people associated with the Home Rule side in Irish politics, but a society founded for any purpose in the Ireland of the 1870s was likely to have had some such bias. There was no question of the society's purpose itself having anything to do with Home Rule politics. Council members included the professor of Greek at Edinburgh, the professor of Oriental languages at Trinity College, Dublin, the professor of Celtic languages at Oxford, and the president of Queen's College, Galway. The Tory government of the day granted the society's request for the inclusion of Celtic as a recognized examination subject under the new board for intermediate education established by an act of 1878.[17] In the same year the national education commissioners, acceding to a widely subscribed petition organized by the society, permitted the introduction of Irish to the national school curriculum as an optional subject outside of normal hours. The list of signatories to the petition showed a strong weighting toward Catholic and Home Rule Ireland, but there was no question of the language being a Catholic or a Home Rule issue, as was shown by the signatures of a Protestant bishop and three deans, fifty other Protestant or Presbyterian clergymen, and ten professors of Trinity College.

The concessions made to Irish in the schools in 1878 had little enough immediate impact, but the new attitudes that had made them possible led to a notable increase in the pace of revivalist activity. Conflicts within the Society for the Preservation of the Irish Language produced the Gaelic Union (1880), which two years later set up the influential *Gaelic Journal*. In 1893 came the Gaelic League.

Nothing can be more easily made to seem like the pure product of idealism than a language revival movement. True, one could scarcely occur without a measure of idealism, but the idealism can make an impact only if its realization, or the working for its realization, serves some social purpose. By 1900, Irish revivalism was an idea whose time had come in the sense that there were various groups and interests ready to propagate, operate, use, and benefit from such a cause.

There is evidence from the 1880s, and even earlier, of an interesting group from a Protestant background who were detached from their collective bearings and in search of something new. For many of them, their old world had been shaken by the land war (1879-82) and its sequel, by the Home Rule crisis of 1886, and by the inroads of religious doubt. Some—such as Standish James O'Grady, William Butler Yeats, John M. Synge, and Douglas Hyde—were sons or grandsons of evangelical clergymen.[18] Literature and journalism were their obvious métier.

A strong element in the literary fashion of the age encouraged the search for ethnic or Celtic themes. Matthew Arnold had given it a powerful impetus by his Oxford lectures on the study of Celtic literature, delivered in 1865-66, and subsequent decades had seen a growth of interest in folklore.[19] By the 1890s Yeats was the leading figure of a new Irish literary movement in English that was drawing on an amalgam of folklore and ancient Irish literature. This haphazardly selected body of material was represented as constituting a coherent tradition with prescriptive implications for true Irish literary endeavor in the late nineteenth century. The cultivation of the Irish language was a corollary of this, even if not all those concerned accepted the fact.

Since the early decades of the century, the respectables who dominated Catholic social and political life had been challenged from within on many occasions by combinations of the discontented and the ambitious under the banner of more advanced nationalism. Such was the background of Charles Stewart Parnell's Home Rule party, which by the mid-1880s had become a new political establishment allied with the bishops, the farmers, and the shopkeepers. By the 1890s a new wave of outsiders was gathering, with a large contribution coming from University College on St. Stephen's Green (the successor of Catholic University of the 1850s). Those involved with this institution around the turn of the century as either students or teachers included Eoin MacNeill, Francis Sheehy Skeffington, Patrick Pearse, Fr. Tom Finlay, Tom Kettle, James Joyce, Francis Cruise O'Brien, John Marcus O'Sullivan, Alfred T. O'Rahilly, John A. Costello, Rory O'Connor, and Eamon de Valera.

Much has been made of the impact on Irish intellectual and organizational life of the traumatic fall of Parnell, and the consequent split within the Home Rule leadership, at the beginning of the 1890s. No doubt it did drive some sensitive souls to seek alternative forms of politics and alternatives to politics, but a similar proliferation of social, political, and cultural organizations is to be found in most parts of western Europe in the quarter century before 1914. The seekers of new ways, new means, and new ends in Ireland during these decades had two establishments against which to pit their energy and intelligence. Apart from England, there was the local power bloc—identified with Home Rule—now being consolidated by the entrenchment of the farmers on their holdings and by the erection of elective institutions of local government, particularly the county councils. England could be attacked openly, the domestic powers only obliquely. The outcome was a profusion of formal and informal campaigns—sometimes dependent on one another, sometimes independent, frequently antagonistic to one another, but considerably overlapping in support—on such issues as native manufactures, native games, rural reform, agricultural cooperation, national literature, national theater, national self-reliance, anti-imperialism, dual monarchy, separatism, the curbing of clerical power, the organization of labor, de-anglicization, and the revival of Irish.

The Gaelic League made a point of declaring itself to be above and beyond political and confessional divisions. This stance was given enhanced credibility by the presence at the helm of Dr. Douglas Hyde, son of a County Roscommon clergyman and graduate of Trinity College, Dublin. But the number of Hyde's contemporaries capable of appreciating this ideal was small, and the number prepared to live by it was even smaller. Hyde himself had come to see cultural matters as being vastly more important than politics, but he did have political learnings that were decidedly nationalist. Others of the small but not insignificant number of Protestants who were prepared to embrace self-government—such as the dramatist Sean O'Casey and the writer Stephen Gwynn—were in the league also. The league attracted, too, many Protestants who by contrast were unhappy about the prospect of home rule but did not see any salvation in the militant unionist alternative. Such people saw in the league the prospect of a new beginning, the hope of moving away from the bitter politico-sectarian division that had afflicted Irish society for decades and even generations.

Captain the Honourable Otway Cuffe, son of the third earl of Desart, is an outstanding example. After a career in the army and travels in India, America, and Europe, he came in 1899 at the age of forty-six to settle near his ancestral home in County Kilkenny and set up house at Sheestown a few miles from the city. He soon joined the Gaelic League, becoming vice-president and then president of the Kilkenny branch. Like many another middle-aged convert he was unable to make much progress in mastery of the language, but under cover of the league and its philosophy of Celtic renewal he gained acceptance and prominence with the populace, becoming mayor of the city in 1907 and 1908. The donning of knee breeches and the affectation of other features of a supposed old Irish costume kept him in the public eye, but there were more substantial reasons for his popularity. With financial assistance from the dowager Lady Desart (his brother's widow), he set up factories, a theater, and a hospital.[20] Sharing a platform in

Kilkenny in August 1902 with a visiting celebrity, Fr. J.K. Fielding, president of the Chicago Gaelic League, he expressed his philosophy very simply: "Some persons thought that the learning of Irish was the only object that the League had set before it. He did not believe that was so. (Hear, hear). They knew it was the principal object of the Gaelic League. But he believed that the Gaelic League had all to do with the encouragement of all that made for beauty in the land (loud applause), for the encouragement of everything that would tend . . . to make life better and brighter with those amongst whom they lived."[21]

Even in Ulster there was recordable Protestant participation in the Gaelic League in the early years.[22] If the movement was not taken up on a large scale by unionists, that was not because it was initially deemed to be in itself politically unacceptable to them, but because it was difficult for any interest to be communicated across the barrier that separated unionism from the rest of the country long before the division was given tangible expression in political partition. Even if an interest was shared it was likely to give rise to conflict.

The difficulty of maintaining good relations across the great divide was well illustrated by the Gaelic League experience of Rev. John Owen Hannay, alias George A. Birmingham, the well-known novelist. A native of Belfast, where he learned as a toddler to proclaim "No pope, no priest, no surrender," he became rector of Westport, County Mayo, in 1892. Reading of Standish O'Grady and Douglas Hyde brought him to membership in the Gaelic League, and he gave himself wholeheartedly to the cause, even though he acquired no fuller knowledge of the language than the customary salutations and the conventional *cúpla focal* (couple of words) that have stood a few generations of nationalist politicians in good stead. It was as the result of an initiative by Hannay that the first celebration of the Holy Communion in Irish at St. Patrick's Cathedral, Dublin, was arranged. This was on 17 March 1906.[23] Meanwhile he had been elected to the central executive body (Coiste Gnótha) of the Gaelic League.

Hannay's devotion did not prevent him from becoming a sign of contradiction within the league. He was revealed in January 1906 as the author of two romans à clef—*The Seething Pot* and *Hyacinth*—that painted acerbic pictures of identifiable individuals and institutions in County Mayo. Although he had endeavored to be even-handed in his judgments, the books were interpreted as a bigoted assault on Catholicism, and Hannay was vehemently criticized in press and pulpit. At a league meeting in Claremorris in September 1906, the priest who was presiding, Canon Macken of Tuam, refused to conduct any transactions with Hannay. In the subsequent showdown within the league, Hannay was supported by many priests and by Patrick Pearse, but the Coiste Gnótha fudged the issue, leaving the minister with no choice but to drop out of prominence in the league's affairs. In this and various other crises Hyde was unashamedly pragmatic. The following explanation addressed by him to Hannay speaks volumes: "In view of the very ticklish position of the language in the archdiocese, and the certainty that to censure Macken would turn all the priests against it and kill the language, I think the C [oiste] and G [nótha] will just let things be. Not very heroic! but I am looking far ahead and want to put off any possible fight."[24] Hyde was realistic enough to know that whatever the league might aspire to in its constitution, people would bring to it their entrenched prejudices, and his main concern was not to combat these but to prevent them from wrecking the movement.

Intense prejudice on the part of an element in the Coiste Gnótha prevented the league from cooperating, as Hyde and Pearse wished it to do, with the Celtic Association, the Irish branch of the Pan-Celtic movement. The Irish Pan-Celts were predominantly Protestant and were led by an aristocrat, Lord Castletown. Much as Hyde would have liked to do business with them, he allowed them to be snubbed rather than put the internal peace of the Coiste Gnótha at risk.[25] It was not by defying political reality but by cautiously adapting to it that Hyde maintained the nominal neutrality of the league until 1915. Hyde's strongest motive for adhering to a policy of formal neutrality was the desire to facilitate the membership of young Catholic law clerks and others in official positions who might be prohibited by their employers from participating in any organization with explicitly political objectives.[26] Hyde's principal collaborator, indeed the man at whose instigation the Gaelic League had been founded, Eoin MacNeill, was a clerk in the Four Courts.[27]

Whatever Hyde may have intended or hoped, the Gaelic League had two major political consequences, related but distinct. First, it added the Irish language to the identification marks of Irish Catholic nationalism. Thus the language became politicized as it never had been in the nineteenth century. And as surely as it became identified with one of the island's political collectivities, so rejection of it became an automatic response of the other. This was far removed from what Hyde and MacNeill had envisaged, but it is seldom given to the initiators of a public campaign to foresee the ultimate outcome.

The second major political consequence of the operation of the Gaelic League was to enable the alternative leadership of the Catholic nationalist collectivity to recruit, to organize, to gain in confidence, and actually to lead in areas where the established leadership did not have the interest or the energy to operate. The Gaelic League was prime recruiting ground for

Sinn Féin and the IRB, two organizations that had explicit political objectives critical of the Irish Parliamentary party. The cadres who later took advantage of the Great War to capture the leadership of nationalist Ireland, and ultimately the political control of twenty-six counties, owed their strength, self-confidence, and cohesion in a large measure to their experience in the Gaelic League.

Patrick Pearse, executed leader of the 1916 Rising and subsequently martyr-symbol of physical force nationalism and of the demand for total political independence, had involved himself only marginally in politics for most of his career. Until the very last years of his life he had believed that Ireland was to be saved not through any political or military development but by means of linguistic and cultural revival, and education. But as soon as he did veer toward politics and armed revolution he quickly rose to eminence in that field because, through his Gaelic League work, he knew and was known to so many who were there before him. And as he prepared to lead whomever would follow him down the road of violence and insurrection marked out by the Ulster Volunteers in 1913, Pearse had before him an image from that rediscovered Celtic past that had absorbed most of his adult life, the image of Cuchulainn, the hound of Ulster, who had sworn thus as a boy: "by the oath my people swear I swear that my deeds will be told amongst the great deeds that the greatest and strongest warriors did."[28]

The outbreak of the Great War brought to a head conflict between the alternative leadership and the Home Rule establishment, particularly on the question of enlistment in the British army. Under pressure the anti-Redmondites dragged in the Gaelic League on their side. As one of their number, Ernest Blythe, was to put it later: "If the Sinn Féin or republican forces had been stronger than they were, they might have been content to allow the Gaelic League to stand neutral; but their numerical weakness and the hostile attitude of the popular majority towards them made it natural for them to seek to entrench themselves wherever they could do so."[29] At the annual convention in July 1915 the militants voted through a resolution committing the Gaelic League to support for "a free Ireland." Hyde thereupon relinquished the presidency. These developments were discouraging for any Protestant unionists still interested in the league. However, a small nucleus of mostly Dublin-based Protestant nationalists remained on as members and, with others outside the league, formed the Irish Guild of the Church (Cumann Gaelach na hEaglaise).[30]

Long before 1914, the Gaelic League had made its mark with the nationalist public, especially through its campaigns in support of the place of Irish in the education system. The breakthrough possibly began in 1899 when a vice-regal commission on intermediate education came to examine the question of Irish in the curriculum. The formidable Dr. J.P. Mahaffy of

Trinity College, who had a record of interest in secondary education, argued before the commission against the continued teaching of the language. He enlisted the support of a colleague, Dr. Atkinson, a brilliant linguist who had actually edited Irish texts. Challenged by Hyde, they resorted to derogatory criticism of the spoken language and of the ancient literature. Hyde counteracted by producing testimonials to the value of Irish obtained from a range of foreign scholars. The confrontation before the commission was dramatic and long-drawn-out, and through the newspapers it attracted widespread public attention.[31] People who had never given Irish a second thought perceived that they and theirs were now under attack from Dr. Mahaffy and identified the Gaelic League with their political community.

One episode like this would not on its own have effected a transformation, but there were to be others and in every case the Gaelic League had the propaganda advantage of being the defender of the more Irish against the less Irish or the anti-Irish. By 1910 when the Gaelic Leaguers became involved in their greatest struggle—about the place of Irish as a matriculation subject in the National University of Ireland—nationalist public opinion had come to accept that standing up for the language with no ifs or buts was, like standing up for the peasant proprietor or for home rule, one of the required postures of the true Irishman. The episode merits some detailed examination as it illustrates so well the twofold politicization of the language brought about by the league.

The Irish Universities Act[32] received the royal assent on 1 August 1908. It provided for the setting up of Queen's University in Belfast and of a federal National University with constituent colleges in Dublin, Cork, and Galway. Both universities were formally nondenominational, but everybody concerned accepted that the former was intended primarily to serve Protestants and the latter primarily to serve Catholics; indeed, there was a general acknowledgment that the National University was the answer to the generations-old demand for a university congenial to the needs of Irish Catholics. The Gaelic League leaders saw in it a means of advancing the cause of the language. Not content that it should do this simply by teaching and scholarship—something that everyone was prepared to concede—Hyde and MacNeill called for Irish to be made a compulsory subject for matriculation. That was a matter to be determined by the senate of the National University. One member of that body gave a reasoned reaction in late November 1908 as the compulsory Irish campaign got underway. He was Dr. William Delany, S.J., president of University College, St. Stephen's Green, which would give way under the new order to University College, Dublin.

Delany, who was in his seventies, had no Irish, but he was a member of the Gaelic League and had always encouraged the study of Irish in University College. At a meeting of the college's Gaelic Society on 27 November 1908, he reiterated his goodwill toward the language but declared his opposition to compulsion.[33] The league's position was argued by Patrick Pearse and Eoin MacNeill. Delany soon became an object of vituperation in the press and on the platform, and a remarkable campaign to influence the other senators was under way. MacNeill did attempt to facilitate reasonable debate, but for the most part the league's campaign was conducted without reference to the complicated educational and political issues involved. The league drummed up emotional support for "essential Irish" as an assertion of collective identity. Anyone who urged moderation or circumspection, no matter what his services to the language, was denounced as a West Briton. John Dillon, M.P., was jeered when, at a convention of the United Irish League (in effect the political organization of the Irish Parliamentary party) in Dublin on 10 February 1909, he argued against a motion calling for compulsion. On the eve of the convention a large torchlight procession through the center of the city had featured banners inscribed with the motto "No Irish, no students, no university." Dillon lost the vote, and the motion was carried by a large majority. This victory gave additional steam to the league's campaign. Its existing organization was mobilized as never before and numerous new branches were set up. Fulsome declarations of support emanated from Irish organizations in Britain and America. A most elaborate and impressive demonstration was mounted in Dublin in September 1909. It included thousands of marching children, floats featuring propagandist dramas and tableaux, and a series of platforms replete with speech makers.[34]

The Gaelic League had succeeded in convincing a significant portion of the public that what was at issue was whether Irishness would be asserted or denied. It then brought this public opinion to bear on the university through the local authorities. County and district councillors, who were manipulators of a nationalist politics that was comparatively inert most of the time, ran scared before the energy and enthusiasm of the Gaelic Leaguers. When the compulsory Irish question was posed as one of being for or against Ireland there was only one answer that they could give. By early June 1909 Hyde could claim that 19 county councils and 130 of the country's 170 urban and rural district councils had come out in favor of his demand. The county councils mattered because the 1908 act had given them functions in respect of the new university: they had the nomination of some representatives on the governing bodies of the colleges, and, more importantly, they were empowered to give scholarships to university students from their areas of jurisdiction. When a majority of county councils made clear that they would not vote money for scholarships to the National University unless Irish was compulsory there, the senate's freedom of choice was greatly diminished. After a bout of maneuvering that involved an amount of internal academic politics, the senate voted on 23 June 1910 to make Irish compulsory for matriculation beginning in 1913.[35]

A more unquestionably progressive achievement was the introduction of a bilingual program for national schools in Irish-speaking and bilingual areas approved by the national board in 1904 with the encouragement of the Gaelic League. Similarly, the league was largely responsible for the pressures that led to St. Patrick's Day becoming an official public holiday by an act of 1903.[36] A little later the post office, in response to a campaign by the league, agreed to accept letters addressed in Irish.

The Gaelic League succeeded in gaelicizing Irish nationalism. But what did that mean in practice? How much sincerity lay behind the enthusiasm? Or what kind of sincerity? Did the county councillors and urban councillors who voted for compulsory Irish in the university intend to learn Irish themselves? Did they share some vague assumption that they would acquire the language painlessly as a rising tide of Irish suffused their society?

Similar questions can be asked about the general membership of the league. In the first decade of the new century the Gaelic League had generated an enormous stir throughout the land. It had instituted a system of evening classes with peripatetic teachers which brought a new dimension to social life for many young men and women. And there was more than a language to be learned. For the league wished to give "the people" back their pastimes so that singing and dancing (of the supposed authentically Irish type) became a patriotic duty. The Gaelic League dancing session (the *ceílí*) sanctified simple pleasures that a puritanical society had for long regarded as fraught with wickedness. The success of the evening classes and of the ceílí owed much to the advent of that quintessential vehicle of revolution, the bicycle. Even more dependent on the bicycle was the *feis* (or cultural festival) organized regularly at local and county levels. All culminated in the annual national *oireachtas*.

Most revolutions are marked by paradox, and the Gaelic League was not exceptional in introducing new ways under the guise of a return to the old. One authority has estimated that in its heyday the league may have had as many as seventy-five thousand people caught up in its various activities.[37] But how many of these were attracted by the new freedom rather than by the old language? All the evidence suggests that under the league's auspices many more people learned to dance reels well than learned to speak Irish well.

The distinction between attachment to language as a symbol or a token and the intention of learning and using it was already crystal clear at the time of the essential Irish controversy. The insistence of the Gaelic League leaders on the issue may have owed something to an awareness that, for all the loud endorsements, interest in the use and study of Irish was erratic. For some years Pearse had given public lectures on elementary and advanced Irish at University College, as had MacNeill on Irish history. Dr. Delany, who made the arrangements and met the expenses, subsequently alleged that the attendances had been very disappointing.[38] Hyde and his collaborators, like so many other revolutionaries before and after them, may have come, however unconsciously, to the view that people would need to be compelled toward what was good for them.

F.S.L. Lyons, in chapter 3 of his *Culture and Anarchy in Ireland, 1890-1939*[39] explores the conflict discernible between "Irish Ireland" and "Anglo-Irish Ireland" during the period in question. What he describes, however, is a dispute between two groups of ideologues and propagandists, and while the intimations of anarchy are undeniable, no convincing picture emerges of how these warring cliques are related to anything sufficiently substantial to be called a culture. There is indeed a marvelous evocation (in chapter 5) of Ulster Presbyterian "culture," but this collectivity had its own locally based propagandist elite, and even before partition it could not care less what arguments Yeats and AE (George Russell) in Dublin were exchanging with D.P. Moran and Arthur Griffith. Outside of the northeast, the country was dominated by another "culture" whose characteristics and impulses Lyons appears to equate with those of his Dublin-based Irish-Ireland elite. In reality the Irish Irelandism that appeared to triumph in the Irish Free State was only a veneer. Irish Ireland was the preoccupation of a minority and was little more than a badge worn on the lapel of the majority, anglophone, nationalist culture that it is allowed to obscure almost completely in *Culture and Anarchy*.

This society was governed by values that related to Catholicism, land, and retailing. Internally it was neither homogeneous nor harmonious, but those without either a priest, a farm, or a shop in the family did not, with few exceptions, openly question the prevailing values. Their compliance was facilitated by a sense of nationalist solidarity, for this collectivity saw itself as "the Irish nation" and "the people of Ireland," and was accustomed to appear in these parts on the political stage. It was represented in Parliament by the Home Rule party. This Irish nation had no hereditary aristocracy and no more than a very attenuated bourgeoisie, so that it was particularly dependent on its priesthood for organizational and ideological leadership. It was clerical approval of the Gaelic League—forthcoming by 1900—that permitted the Irish language, neglected and despised by so many for so long, to be accepted as an essential element in the national identity.[40]

If John Redmond and his party had obtained home rule in 1912, they would have been obliged to make concessions to the Gaelic revival, even if many of them were unenthusiastic. All the more so was a policy of gaelicization to be expected when self-government was won by the hands of the Gaelic League generation. The 1922 constitution decreed as follows: "The national language of the Irish Free State (Saorstát Éireann) is the Irish language, but the English language shall be equally recognized as an official language." In the 1937 constitution Irish and English became, respectively, the first and second official languages.

The governments of newly independent Ireland are remarkable for how little change they tried to make in what they inherited. Almost the only radical innovation to which they committed themselves was the raising up of the Irish language. The fortunes of the national tongue were helped by making it a sine qua non for employment and promotion in almost every branch of the public service. Within its obvious limitations this was a moderately successful measure of language promotion. However, the main thrust of the revival policy was to be in the schools, and particularly the primary scools. In a variety of ways the prominence of Irish in the curriculum was advanced, so that it became not only compulsory in all schools but predominant in many.[41] The use as teaching medium (either exclusively or for some subjects only) of a language that was not the language of the home raised serious pedagogical issues. So did the fact that a sizable portion of the primary school day came to be devoted to the study of Irish itself, not counting time spent learning other subjects through Irish. Recent commentators have trenchantly criticized the policy, and in particular the way that the welfare of the child was subordinated to the political and ideological needs of the nation.[42] However, the exaltation of national imperatives and the elevation of political over pedagogical considerations in the classroom were features common to many of the newly established nation-states of Europe in the decades after the Treaty of Versailles, and Irish attitudes become more comprehensible if considered in that context.

What the framers of the constitutions and of the language policy did not realize or could not accept, and what has not been adverted to sufficiently since, was the possibility that the generality of Irish nationalists had indeed adopted the language, but merely for a symbolic role. Arguably, this society which had been de-gaelicizing for generations underwent no fundamental change of direction, no matter what its rhetoric and its gestures may have suggested to the contrary. Arguably, there was a "hidden Ireland" in existence for fifty years before 1900 and fifty years afterward where the majority of Irish people moved and had their cultural being. The idyll of the Gaelic past and the Gaelic west ("close to the gate of heaven") as promulgated by Pearse and others was the property of an elite.

In Ireland from the 1880s to the 1950s the most consistently popular book of Irish authorship was Charles J. Kickham's *Knocknagow*, a product of the early 1870s.[43] The idyll that this mid-Victorian work evokes is far removed from that of the revivalists. Here is a stratified society on the good lands where fashionably educated young ladies speak the queen's English in the strong farmer's parlor and accompany one another at the piano in renderings of Moore's melodies. And the Gaelic inheritance amounts to the occasional mangled Irish word or phrase on the lips of the less cultivated. This was unlikely fare for a society allegedly busy recovering its Celtic soul. Neither was it the kind of great literature prescribed for the new Ireland by such as Yeats, and produced by him and others for a sophisticated international audience. Small wonder that a romanticizing Irish language enthusiast like Daniel Corkery (1878-1964) should look to the eighteenth century for an Irish people to his liking, seeing that his contemporaries left so much to be desired.

The failure of the "plain people of Ireland" to modify their reading in line with their rhetoric was ominous for Irish Ireland. It has been well demonstrated that, in the Irish Free State, Catholicism and the Irish language were seized upon to emphasize national identity and justify independent nationhood. But at the popular level the working out of these twin pieties was quite dissimilar. Average citizens felt that *being* Catholic was part of their political identity. With the language, there was a difference: Sean Citizen felt obliged to *approve* of it; but as for *using* it, well— to paraphrase a French aristocrat speaking in another context—his public servants could do that for him.

Nevertheless, a useful comparison can be made between the priests and the post-1922 Irish language activists, who might be termed the Gaelic elite. The latter, consisting of teachers, civil servants, and a few writers, academics and controversialists, and a small proportion of parliamentary politicians, evoked in the popular mind something like the mixture of feelings normally reserved for the clergy—the deference and the respect certainly, but perhaps not quite the same measure of affection and perhaps a little more of the barstool skepticism. Both groups were seen as having special functions that were part of the proper order of things, and both absorbed a large share of the country's talent.

Apart from their work as teachers and public servants, the men and women of the Gaelic elite performed memorable feats. Whether working in the Department of Education, or in various learned institutions, or as free lances, they succeeded over a number of decades in the daunting task of standardizing the language and equipping it for the demands of the twentieth century. From this same small group there emanated a body of modern literature that would do credit to any small country.[44] And if the ability to laugh at oneself is evidence of maturity, then the appearance and the eventual acceptance of Flann O'Brien's satirical classic, *An Béal Bocht* (1941),[45] proved that writing in Irish had come of age. On the negative side, the collective image of the Gaelic elite was affected by the presence on its periphery of a fanatic fringe exhibiting degrees of self-righteousness and intolerance and giving the impression that attachment to the language was synonymous with adherence to the "fighting and dying" school of Irish political ideology.

How well did the schools succeed in the work of raising up Irish-speaking generations? Only to a limited extent. Obviously the great majority of Irish children leaving school in the past sixty years have had the benefit of some acquaintance with the language, and many of them have acquired competence in it. But a large proportion have acquired so little affection for Irish that they have forgotten it with all possible speed along with the theorem of Pythagoras, the chief exports of Paraguay, Keats's "Ode on a Grecian Urn," and other content learned at school to pass examinations or to ward off wrath, but not perceived as having anything to do with "real life." Even the most dedicated and talented teachers had little chance when faced with the unwillingness of the wider society to use the language, as distinct from allowing it to be taught in the schools. The average adult's contact with Irish was mainly as a ceremonial language used in the secular rituals of the politicians, the equivalent of the church's Latin.

In the 1981 census Irish speakers constituted 31.6 percent of the population of the Irish Republic, up from 28.3 percent in 1971. Interpretation of these figures is difficult, if not impossible, since they are based on a form of self-assessment uncontrolled by any threat of corrective sampling.

One trend that can be deduced from the census and from every other means of observation is that Irish is declining in the Gaeltacht, the areas where it has survived as an indigenous language. For something now approaching a century, the Gaeltacht has been successively idealized, venerated as the guardian of a flame from which the rest of the country must be rekindled, admonished as to its national duty, and latterly even given a government ministry to succor it and some special economic assistance. All in vain it seems. A recent government publication states that "it is fairly reliably estimated that no more than 25,000 of the Gaeltacht population now use Irish consistently day-to-day communication."[46] Writing in the late 1960s, another authority visualized the disappearance of the Gaeltacht by about 1990 unless something drastic could be done to save the situation.[47] The decline of the Gaeltacht suggests the consideration that we may be witnessing the final working out of a trend—the abandonment of Irish by its native speakers—that has been at work for two centuries, a piece of social history that has proved impervious to ideology, rhetoric, and politics. While for generations the ideologues of cultural nationalism taught that the Irish language was the quintessence of Irish freedom, one of the most powerful impulses to freedom operating on actual Irishmen and Irishwomen was the desire to enter the world of the English speakers. Typically it was the individual already secure in English who found liberation in Irish.

The Irish policies implemented in the schools from the 1920s onward provoked resentment on the part of some parents from an early stage, but this was muted by deference to the national pieties in an age when prescriptions from above were received respectfully, whether they were about to be observed or not. The modification of authoritarianism in the 1960s led to a vocal campaign against compulsory Irish. At another level, changing notions of authority encouraged a more purely pedagogical approach to the curriculum. The findings of a highly professional investigation published in 1966 suggested that because of the amount of school time devoted to the national language, Irish schoolchildren were considerably behind the level of achievement of their British counterparts at general subjects.[48] Not everybody agreed, but further impetus had been given to the debate. A series of changes, major and minor, in the course of the 1960s and the early 1970s considerably modified the place of the language in Irish schools. There was a new child-centered primary curriculum and the ending of the narrow state examination at the end of primary school; Irish ceased to be the sole teaching language in most of the teacher-training colleges; it also ceased to be an essential subject for passing state examinations at secondary level; and it was no longer a requirement for entry to the public service. These changes took place with a minimum of party political conflict.

The language policy modification of the 1960s and 1970s reflected a shift in the complex balance of attitudes and interest surrounding Irish. But all the indications are that basic attitudes have not changed. The majority of nationalists still see the language as a mark of their identity, feel supportive toward it, and wish it to be taught in the schools.[49] At the same time no more than a small minority is prepared to make active use of it. If there is paradox here, it is not the only paradox of contemporary Irish nationalism. In any case, far from conforming to any one model, the language dimension of each and every nationalism is different. Ireland is not at all exceptional in having its own distinctive paradoxical variant.[50]

The Irish language has survived into the late twentieth century as a precious, if burdensome, inheritance in a country not overendowed (by European standards) with either cultural or material assets. If the language's only claim to a future lay in its association with nationalism, it might have uncertain prospects in the twenty-first century. Identification with nationalism has failed to make of Irish a national language in anything except name, but at he same time has had the effect of turning it into an object of resentment for a large section of the island's population. Clearly the "first national language" is highly unlikely to become the ordinary medium of discourse in the Irish republic, much less in Ireland as a whole.

On the other hand its continued cultivation on a more modest scale seems assured in an age in which the value of conserving the unique and irreplaceable is appreciated as never before. Sean Citizen has moved on from *Knocknagow* to "Dallas" and "Eastenders," and he will quite rightly refuse to be coerced by anyone into modifying his tastes. But voluntary change is another matter. The Irish language stands as one of the many options available to those speaking ways of enriching their lives, a group growing in size and significance in most Western societies, including Ireland. This is to suggest that in the future—as has been the case in the past—the fortunes of the Irish language will depend primarily on socioeconomic and cultural trends that are little affected by nationalism or any ideological imperative whatever. The revivalists may be disappointed in their wider ambition, but it is worth remembering that the motivation of the more reflective of them has always incorporated the hope of enhancing the quality of cultural life in Ireland, and on that field there is no final victory or defeat, but endless scope for initiatives great and small that need not threaten anybody.

Mary Helen Thuente

THE FOLKLORE OF IRISH NATIONALISM

IRISH FOLKLORE, an important cultural force in Irish life for many centuries, has also been a major influence on the development of Irish nationalism. Oral traditions, especially popular stereotypes and horror stories of sectarian atrocities, played an important role in the 1798 uprising, for example. Nationalists throughout the nineteenth century, most notably Daniel O'Connell, tapped the folk memory of great historical injustice. The revival of traditional Irish games by the Gaelic Athletic Association (GAA) in the 1880s was of major political significance. Douglas Hyde's popularization of Irish folklore fostered both a literary revival and a political revolution. Indeed, it was fitting that Hyde, a folklorist, became the first president of Ireland. Most importantly, folklore was central in the evolution of cultural nationalism into political nationalism during the nineteenth century when nationalists repeatedly tried to reflect as well as to recreate the oral traditions of the people.

This transformation of cultural into political nationalism involved folklore in several ways. Popular oral traditions, especially songs and legends, had been the main channel for whatever primitive national consciousness had existed in the native Irish culture. The study of Irish folklore by patriotic eighteenth-century antiquarians (the term *folklore* was not coined until 1846) and the popularization of Irish folklore by poets such as Charlotte Brooke and Thomas Moore inspired later literary and political nationalists and bequeathed an iconography to them. Attempts by the United Irishmen in the 1790s, by Daniel O'Connell in the 1820s and 1840s, by the Young Irelanders in the 1840s, and by the Fenians in the 1860s to speak for "the people," to represent the popular mind, all involved the creation of what is best termed a pseudofolk tradition.

The United Irishmen produced a songbook, *Paddy's Resource*, and innumerable songs and ballads. O'Connell's campaigns for Catholic emancipation and for repeal also produced their share of ballads. Irish newspapers, the most important vehicle of nationalist propaganda in the nineteenth century, were filled with songs. *The Spirit of the Nation* (1843), a collection of patriotic song-poems by Young Ireland writers originally published in the *Nation*, and Charles Gavan Duffy's anthology, *The Ballad Poetry of Ireland* (1845), each went through more than fifty editions in the course of the century. Irish nationalism thus created its own folklore, because the songs and poetry it produced exemplify all the definitive characteristics of folklore: traditional oral texts subject to variation and possessing a common stock of motifs and ideas. This folklore of Irish nationalism evokes two questions. The first concerns the relation between Irish folklore and the folklore created by the nationalists: to what extent did the nationalist folklore resemble the popular attitudes expressed in the indigenous oral tradition? Because the interpretation of Irish history was central to both traditions, the second question that arises is how accurately do either of these folklores mirror history? This essay addresses these questions by identifying some of the major motifs and ideas propagated by the folklore of Irish nationalism, comparing them to the indigenous folk tradition, and considering their interpretation of Irish history.

Twentieth-century folklorists, historians, and literary scholars have questioned the claim of nationalists to have represented the popular mind in their writings, speeches, and political actions. For example, Seamus Deane has declared that Irish nationalism is a potent example of a rhetoric that imagined as true structures that did not exist or were never to exist outside language. To what extent the nationalists were actually mirroring, interpreting, or creating the popular mind is a more complex question than any blithe dismissal of the unreal dimensions of nationalist propaganda admits. Moreover, the folklore of Irish nationalism, most especially its imaginative and mythical dimensions, had and continues to have a major influence on Irish history. Historical events may be distorted by folksongs and by nationalist songs, but their versions of history have been important historical forces, often more important than the historical events themselves.

The power that a folklore's memory of an event can have is suggested by the ending of Lady Augusta Gregory's play *The Canavans*: when the mayor requests an old Irish washerwoman, who feels that she has been unjustly treated, to be loyal to Queen Elizabeth I, she replies, "We are well able to revenge ourselves. Whatever may be done in this district, it's the telling of the story is with us."[1] The oral versions of Irish history remembered by the people were often inaccurate or oversimplified; nationalists offered still other versions, which often replaced the earlier popular memories of events. Like the old washerwoman in Lady Gregory's play, nationalists were well aware of the emotional power and the potential for propaganda that resided in "the telling of the story." Thomas Davis expressed the creed of many nationalists when he declared that the "exact dates, subtle plots, minute connections and motives" found in the most superior prose history did not serve what he identified as "the highest ends of history": "to hallow or accurse the scenes of glory and honour, or of shame and sorrow; to give to the imagination the arms, and homes, and senates, and battles of other days; to rouse, and soften, and strengthen, and enlarge us with the passions of great periods; to lead us into love of self-denial, of justice, of beauty, of valour, of generous life and proud death; and to set up in our souls the memory of great men who shall then be as models and judges of our actions—these are the highest duties of history."[2]

Efforts by nationalists to represent and to mold the popular mind began with the United Irishmen who published a songbook in three volumes (1795-98) entitled *Paddy's Resource: Being a Select Collection of Original and Modern Patriotic Songs, Toasts and Sentiments Compiled for the Use of the People of Ireland.* This declaration that the songs were "original and modern" and "for the use of the people of Ireland" admitted that *Paddy's Resource* was political propaganda rather than authentic songs from oral tradition; later nationalists would be less forthright about their intentions. The songs in *Paddy's Resource* were significantly different from Irish folksongs in style, subject matter, and attitude.

The majority of the songs use a third-person imperative voice to preach abstract philosophical messages. Words and phrases such as "Freedom," "Liberty," "Unity," and "The Rights of Man" recur throughout the collection. The preface to *Paddy's Resource* praised the person who "dares the stroke of death defy, for virtue and for liberty," and even the most abstract songs frequently celebrated the martyr whose death represented a moral victory against the forces of tyranny and injustice. The song "The Rights of Man" (sung to the tune of "God Save the King") declared, "Death in so just a cause, Crowns us with loud applause."[3] Songs such as "Edward," commemorating the death of Lord Edward Fitzgerald, embodied abstractions in a powerful if pathetic emotion:

> What plaintive sounds strike on my ear!
>   They're Erin's deep-ton'd piteous groans,
> Her harp, attun'd to sorrow drear,
>   In broken numbers joins her moans.

> In doleful groups around her stand
> Her manly sons (her greatest pride),
> In mourning deep, for by the hand
> Of ruthless villains Edward died.[4]

The melancholy and melodrama celebrated in that opening stanza fore-shadow Thomas Moore, whose debt to the poetry of the United Irishmen has not been duly recognized. The poem's tone of moral righteousness and outrage against the "assassin horde," its praise of manly virtues, and its call to revenge would all reappear in poetry of the Young Ireland poets in the 1840s. Indeed, the poem "Edward" was included in R.R. Madden's influential *Literary Remains of the United Irishmen of 1798* in 1846.

Another political ballad from 1798 which was frequently anthologized during the next century was William Drennan's "Wake of William Orr," which commemorated Orr's unjust trial and execution. Its opening lines celebrate martyrdom, moral virtue, manhood, and unity:

> Here our murdered brother lies—
> Wake him not with women's cries;
> Mourn the way that manhood ought;
> Sit in silent trance of thought.
> Write his merits on your mind—
> Morals pure and manners kind;
> In his head, as on a hill,
> Virtue placed her citadel.
> . . . .
> Countrymen, UNITE! he cried,
> And died—for what his Saviour died.[5]

The concluding song in the first volume of *Paddy's Resource*, "Ierne United," portrayed ancient Ireland as united, civilized, free, and happy. This image of an idyllic and idealized early Ireland was also to become standard in nineteenth-century nationalist poetry.

Two of the major images inaugurated in political poetry by the United Irishmen—the hero as martyred victim and a melancholy nostalgia for the past—did echo popular attitudes in Irish folksongs, but the imperative first-person plural or third-person voice and the philosophical abstractions in the political ballads were foreign to the native tradition. Songs in the oral tradition had generally used a singular first-person voice to sing of the particular not of the abstract. For example, the Irish songs about the outlaw heroes known as *rapparees,* such as those which Douglas Hyde translated and published in his *Songs of Connacht,* are notable for their expression of personal sorrow rather than of national loss. According to Irish folksong authority Donal O'Sullivan, Gaelic poetry sang not of great events in a general way, but of the results of events seen and experienced by individuals.[6] Seán Ó Tuama has also noted the strong personal feeling that attached itself to public issues in Irish poetry between 1600 and 1900.[7] The folk lyrics usually focused on concrete, immediate experiences; they were more likely to be concerned with one hero or victim rather than the fate of the community; and they expressed emotion rather than preached a message.

Even the most allegorical of Irish folksongs had a powerful personal dimension. For example, the Jacobite song "The Blackbird," which was immensely popular in oral tradition since the eighteenth century, was at once a political allegory about the Stuarts and a moving lament in a first-person voice by a woman for her lost lover. Indeed, considering the low opinion popular tradition had of King James after the Boyne (he was commonly referred to by epithets such as "dirty Seamus who ran from the Boyne"), one suspects the popularity of "The Blackbird" was due more to its personal than its political frame of reference.

"The Blackbird" was typical of the passivity apparent in numerous songs in Irish. Many of the folk poems and remnants of bardic poetry contained in Seán Ó Tuama and Thomas Kinsella's definitive collection, *An Dunaire: An Irish Anthology 1600-1900: Poems of the Dispossessed* and the materials in Donal O'Sullivan's *Songs of the Irish* are notable for their melancholy fatalism and passivity and their nostalgia for the material pleasures of the past. For example, even the two enormously popular folksongs that commemorated two of the most renowned outlaw heroes who had actively defied English oppression remember "Seán Ó Duír A' Ghleanna" and "Éamonn an Chnuic" in a passive state. "John O'Dwyer of the Glen" voices a passive first-person lament of the outlaw of that name for all the *chreach ar maidin* (woe and ruin) that have befallen him. O'Sullivan has pointed out that the patriotic note which George Sigerson injected into his translation is alien to the original Irish lyrics.[8] O'Sullivan's translation of the last lines of "Ned of the Hill," who also was in hopeless flight, echoes O'Dwyer's despair:

> But it grieves me for more
> Than the loss of my store
>   That there's none who would shield me from danger,
> so my fate it must be
> To fare eastward o'er the sea,
>   and Languish amid the stranger.[9]

Another example of passivity and of nostalgia for concrete sensual pleasures would be the eighteenth-century song, "The Jail of Clonmel," in which a grieving and lonely Whiteboy bewails his approaching fate on the gallows with self-pity rather than heroic defiance. O'Sullivan's translation of that song accurately reflects the Irish original in which the young man was "languishing in chains."[10] A very different translation of the same song by Jeremiah John Callanan, whose accuracy as a translator has frequently been questioned by modern scholars, was popularized by nationalists in the nineteenth century under the title "The Convict of Clonmel."[11] Callanan infused his version with what the United Irishmen and the Young Ireland poets referred to as a "manly" tone by having his convict remember his active days at hurling and dancing.

The image of the hero as a martyred victim of treachery in the songs in *Paddy's Resource* echoed attitudes in popular folksongs and would continue to be a standard motif in popular songs of the people and in folksongs by nationalists. However, although the celebration of manly behavior and the call to action in songs which the United Irishmen wrote for propaganda contradicted the passivity and fatalism so obvious in songs in Irish, the manly vigor of a hero like Callanan's convict would become a dominant motif in the folklore create by nineteenth-century nationalists. Nationalist songs frequently transformed the personal and pathetic dimensions of even an actual martyred hero's plight. For example, the original 1798 ballad "Roddy McCorly," which was very popular in oral tradition after 1798, bears little resemblance to the version written a century later by the nationalist poet Ethna Carbery. In the original ballad the prisoner himself laments the perjury that betrayed him and looks to his Christian resurrection in a tone of self-pity rather than heroic defiance.[12] Carbery tells his story in the third person: as he "marches to his fate on the bridge of Toome," he steps "smiling proud" and "there's never a tear in his blue eyes, / Both glad and bright are they." Such heroic and joyous defiance of one's fate resembles Yeats's heroes more than the pathetic heroes celebrated in the popular ballads. Carbery's concluding stanza injects a national note which echoes the songs in *Paddy's Resource* rather than the people's folksongs about '98 which had been sectarian and provincial: "Because he loved the Motherland / Because he loved the Green, / He goes to meet the martyr's fate / With proud and joyous mien."[13]

Such manly behavior on the part of Irish heroes, common in nationalist songs throughout the nineteenth century, represented a major difference in attitude between the native folklore and the nationalist folklore. The passive resignation to their fate displayed by the speakers in the original versions of the songs just discussed express a fatalism and a passivity which are common in Irish oral tradition. A strong belief in the role of the supernatural in human affairs is a major theme in both early Irish narratives and in the oral traditions of recent centuries. Alan Bruford has demon-

strated that the helper motif is common in the older Irish folktales, such as
those in which a supernaturally gifted being arrives to help the Fenians
against giants or witches who try to harm them, and is "one of the most
popular stock motifs in modern Gaelic folklore."[14] James MacKillop's
recent study of the Fenian legends in oral tradition also shows that the
ancient hero Fionn, whose most celebrated heroic role was the defense of
his country, usually needed supernatural assistance.[15] Legends about the
fairies, one of the oldest and most popular traditions among the people, also
credit a powerful influence to supernatural forces. Popular millenarianism
is still another manifestation of the people's deeply ingrained fatalism.
Prophecies, especially those attributed to St. Colmcille who predicted the
liberation of Ireland by foreign help, were immensely popular among the
people. A reliance on God's help in the form of His grace to save frail
humans who sin was a common theme in popular religious songs in Irish
during the late eighteenth and early nineteenth century.[16] A vengeful God
who would rout Ireland's enemies was also a stock motif in songs and in
curses. Roger McHugh's study of the famine in oral tradition, which
showed that the postfamine peasantry saw even that as an act of God rather
than a political act of mass murder on the part of the English, suggests a
fatalism that was probably even stronger earlier in the century.[17] Even
Daniel O'Connell regarded the famine as an act of God.

Even the popular and most overtly patriotic songs, *aislings* such as
"The Blackbird," were characterized by a tone of fatalism. The aisling was a
vision poem in which the poet dreamed that Ireland, in the form of a
beautiful lady, appeared to him. After describing herself as the bride of the
exiled Stuart king and her present woes, she predicted the expulsion of the
foreigner as a process of divine vengeance, as in Owen Rua O'Sullivan's
aisling "The Mower":

> But God is good and, by the rood on which He died for men,
> He soon will chase the foreign race from out our land again,
> . . . .
> As ancient seers and prophets tell,
> Who con and read the omens well,[18]

Edward Walsh's "translation" of another aisling by Owen Rua O'Sullivan,
which the *Nation* published on 27 April 1844, injected a tone of energy,
optimism, and self-reliance into the lady's address to the poet which is
totally foreign to the aisling tradition:

> "Arise," she cries, "let joy possess thee,
> Ere harvest's golden glories bless thee,

Thine ear hears the battlecry loud!
Go tell the bards who pine in sadness
To teach their harpstrings songs of gladness,
And rise strains of victory proud."

The ideal of manly behavior, like the philosophical dimensions of the songs in *Paddy's Resource*, deviated from the local and practical concerns characteristic of the people's world view. F.S.L. Lyons has argued that even repeal was "too abstract a question for the peasantry."[19] The popular attitudes expressed in the very popular folksong, "The County of Mayo," illustrate the major ways in which the vision of the United Irishmen and of later nationalists differed from that of the people. The song was common in Irish since the seventeenth century and is best known today in George Fox's nineteenth-century translation in which the speaker is "sailing, sailing swiftly from the county of Mayo." The speaker is a victim, as are the heroes celebrated in the folklore of nationalism, but his passive resignation to his fate was seldom echoed in nationalist songs. He describes himself thus: "On the deck of Patrick Lynch's boat I sat in woeful plight, / Through my sighing all the weary day and weeping all the night."[20] He expresses the nostalgia for the past which became a common motif in nationalist poetry, but his sense of loss is very personal, local, and concrete. He mourns for specific local leaders, and for the very sensual pleasures of drink, women, and money.

The emphasis on the individual, the local, and the particular, so common in Irish folksong, was also mirrored in the social and political milieu. Indeed, studies of nineteenth-century political and social history, such as Thomas Garvin's *The Evolution of Irish Nationalist Politics* (1981), K. Theodore Hoppen's *Elections, Politics and Society in Ireland, 1832-1885* (1984), Fergus O'Ferrall's *Catholic Emancipation: Daniel O'Connell and the Birth of Irish Democracy* (1985), and R.V. Comerford's *The Fenians in Context: Irish Politics and Society 1848-82* (1985), have demonstrated that localism was a crucial force in the evolution of Irish nationalism. Local and concrete grievances generated agrarian violence in the eighteenth and nineteenth centuries. Contemporary accounts of the 1798 rebellion claimed that the expectation of immediate local and practical benefits were central to popular support. An eyewitness account of Wexford in 1798 declared the rebels believed "they were to possess the estates of different gentlemen and that they would only have to draw lots for their possession."[21] George Cornewall Lewis reported that the peasantry in 1798 expected liberty to include freedom from tithes and taxes.[22] Daniel O'Connell's success in unifying the people in a common cause was largely

due to his shrewd appeal to their very local and practical concerns. He repeatedly told his audiences that emancipation and later repeal would make
them free *and* prosperous. Not surprisingly, according to Fergus O'Ferrall, the "great expectation of practical benefits at the local level" resulted in widespread popular disillusion after 1829.[23] Although Thomas
Davis and Charles Gavan Duffy tried to popularize the idea that the Irish
were the least sensual and most spiritual people on earth, even the inaugural issue of the *Nation*, on 15 October 1842, declared that "National
feelings, National habits, and National government are indispensable to
individual prosperity." Another editorial in the *Nation*, on 4 May 1844,
declared that self-government would "ennoble souls" and bring "bodily
comforts."

Another major motif in the songs in *Paddy's Resource*, the celebration
of the glories of ancient Ireland, had wide popular appeal because it echoed
the nostalgia so common in the people's traditional literature, such as "The
Old Woman of Beare" and the popular dialogues between St. Patrick and
the hero Oisin who lamented the glories of the pagan past. However, the
idealistic image of ancient Ireland polpularized by nationalists must also be
seen in the larger cultural context of the Celtic revival. The supposedly
Celtic emotion expressed in James MacPherson's Ossianic fragments in the
late eighteenth century had been largely spurious, but he inspired literary
nationalists all over Europe to turn to their country's past and to native
literary traditions. In Ireland in the early nineteenth century Catholic
historians labored to reveal the magnificence of ancient Celtic Ireland,[24]
and Thomas Moore celebrated the glories of ancient Ireland in his *Irish
Melodies* (1808-15).

Moore's songs echoed the melancholy nostalgia of many Irish folksongs. However, the more overtly national note in Moore's *Irish Melodies*,
his repeated addresses to Erin, and his celebration of "the days of old" and
"the long faded glories," represents an important development because the
cultural nationalism so evident in the oral tradition now begins to assume
political overtones in Moore's repeated references to sleeping heroes and to
reawakening. Although passive melancholy pervades most of Moore's
songs, even he has the Irish warriors who are fighting the Danes in "The
Wine Cup Is Circling" cry "On for liberty."

The Young Ireland poets of the 1840s heeded Moore's call to "Let Erin
Remember the Days of Old." As Charles Gavan Duffy explained later in the
century, Moore's "wail of a lost cause" became "virile and passionate hopes"
in the poems of the *Nation*.[25] Moore's harp may have "hung mute on Tara's
walls" as if its "soul were fled," its "pride" asleep, and glory's thrill—o'er,"
but the *Nation* sought to reawaken the glory and pride and thus reactivate

the national soul. Significantly, the two poems by Moore which Duffy
included and thus emphasized in his *Ballad Poetry of Ireland* are among
the least melancholy of Moore's Irish melodies. Moore's "The Desmond"
expresses the violent passion that a Desmond had for the daughter of one of
his followers, whom he married. He draws an image of a man of the people
far different from the artistocratic distance and self-interest that modern
historians argue characterized the Desmonds in their rebellions against the
Crown. The speaker in Moore's "The Return of O'Ruark" is the husband of
the infamous Devorgilla whose infidelity, according to legend, caused the
betrayal of Ireland into Norman hands. The concluding stanza is too strong
to be typical Moore, yet it fits the political mood Duffy sought to inspire in
his anthology:

> Already the curse is upon her,
>   And strangers her valleys profane;
> They come to divide—to dishonour,
>   And tyrants they long will remain!
> But onward! the green banner rearing,
>   Go, flesh every sword to the hilt;
> On *our* side is VIRTUE and ERIN!
>   On *theirs* is the SAXON and GUILT.[26]

Those last two lines were used by Daniel O'Connell as the epigraph to his
history of Ireland, *A Memoir on Ireland, Native and Saxon* (1843). O'Connell, whose own pragmatic nationalism was a far cry from the mystical
Irishness popularized by Moore, frequently quoted Moore's poetry in his
speeches for the violence that Moore celebrated was safely in the past and
his nostalgic tone appealed to O'Connell's audiences.

Moore's highly successful popularization of Irish history and culture inspired the Young Ireland writers in the 1840s. Their politics of repeal
involved the delineation of the mind and heart of the people in song, and
their songs are among the most popular and influential in the folklore of
Irish nationalism. The inaugural issue of the *Nation* claimed that its aim was
"to reflect the popular mind." The verbs used in the *Nation's* motto—"To
create and to foster public opinion in Ireland"—suggest, however, that the
Young Ireland writers created more than they expressed the popular mind.
Indeed, they were to be no more successful in that regard than the United
Irishmen had been, but like the United Irishmen the ideas and motifs
propagated in their songs were to be major influences on later generations
of nationalists.

The national identity which Thomas Davis and his associates created
rested on precarious theory and procedure. Presumably because his peas-

ant and middle-class audiences were already "Irish," David announced in his foreword to *The Voice of the Nation* that the purpose of the Young Ireland writers had been "to create a race of men full of *a more intensely* Irish character and knowledge" (italics added). Additional "knowledge," especially of Irish history, could understandably make one "more intensely Irish," but intensifying the Irishness of a people's character was another matter entirely.

Having accepted Moore's theory that Irish music in itself revealed the Irish soul, the *Nation* poets like Moore created their own verse for the music, verse which they contended was inspired by the emotion and spirit of the music. Their response to the logical question of why they did not use the original words was twofold and contradictory. On the one hand, they argued in the *Nation* on 26 November 1842: "The words of the national songs to which Ireland has narrated her long tale of suffering have for the most part perished; the music alone has been saved. This music paints the inside of souls, as well as narrative paints actions." Songs in Irish seemed alive and well according to other essays in the *Nation*. The *Nation* for 21 December 1844 declared that Irish speakers had "thousands of songs" but they were "too despairing." In the *Nation* of 4 January 1845, an essay entitled "Irish Songs" said of songs composed in Irish during the last century: "Their structure is irregular, their grief slavish and despairing, their joy reckless and bombastic, their religion bitter and sectarian, their politics Jacobite, and concealed by extravagant and tiresome allegory." Rather than accept that very accurate description of the Gaelic song tradition which contradicted their own image of the true Irish soul, later in the same essay they presented such songs as debased and unrepresentative: "Ignorance, disorder, and every kind of oppression weakened and darkened the lyric genius of Ireland."

Because centuries of oppression had stunted the flowering of that soul in song, the Young Irelanders thus conferred upon themselves the right to transform or "restore" the national character to its true state. Irish history was their source for examples of the real Irish soul. If the bards and peasant poets had not interpreted Irish history correctly, the *Nation* would.

Samuel Ferguson's example gave Thomas Davis and his fellow writers a program for doing just that. The martial energy and moral seriousness that Ferguson injected into his "translations" of poems in Irish and his ideas about the national identity he believed was inherent in the originals influenced Davis. Ferguson argued, quite correctly, that Irish songs reached the heart not the head; that the soul of a song revealed Irish sentiment which he characterized as "languishing savage sincerity" and pathos. Irish song and, by implication, the Irish soul consequently needed judgment, control, moral seriousness, knowledge of the past, and masculine energy.[27] Davis obviously took Ferguson's dictums to heart because those were the very qualities he sought to engender in the Irish people and their literature. Nevertheless, as Terence Brown has pointed out, Young Ireland's literary nationalism differed significantly from that of Ferguson whose nationalism had envisioned "a flowering of the Irish intellect rather than a violent assertion of her spiritual identity."[28]

Another inconsistency in Young Ireland's literary nationalism centered on language. They repeatedly argued that the Irish language, which Davis said was a "wild liquid speech" in his essay "Our National Language," was fundamental to the national character—"A people without a language of its own is only half a nation."[29] Yet, despite their many denunciations of how anglicization corrupted the Irish soul, they insisted that soul could be expressed in poetry in the English language, a language which Davis had called "the mongrel of a hundred breeds which creaks and bangs about the Celt who tries to use it."[30] Furthermore, in his essay "Ballad Poetry of Ireland," Davis said he preferred Anglo-Irish ballads written during the last thirty years and Samuel Ferguson's poems to old Gaelic ballads or to peasant ballads in English.[31] Davis supported that preference by quoting Duffy's defense of those same Anglo-Irish ballads in his introduction to his collection of them, *The Ballad Poetry of Ireland*: "Many of them, and generally the best, are just as essentially Irish as if they were written in Gaelic."[32] Later in the century, even Douglas Hyde argued that the people should read the works of Moore and Davis until Irish was revived and their native heritage was thus accessible to them again.

Yet the songs of the literary nationalists, though they often had titles in Irish, generally represented a transformation of Irish folksong. Two of the most popular songs in the nationalist canon, "The Shan Van Vocht" and "Dark Rosaleen," originated in oral tradition wherein they had had no political meaning. Although Irish folk tradition displayed a strong consciousness of cultural identity and superiority, its poets had not been especially attracted to patriotic themes.[33]

"The Shan Van Vocht" was originally a scurrilous eighteenth-century love song in Irish about a young man married to an old woman. The political song in English, popularized in the late 1790s and first printed in the *Nation* on 29 October 1842, about the poor old woman expecting help from her troubles from overseas kept the tune and refrain of the original. Only by coincidence then does the nationalist version echo the motif of the land as a hag transformed into a beautiful woman through her marriage to her rightful king which was popular in early Irish mythology. Interestingly, the numerous political songs in oral tradition, sung to the tune and using the

refrain "says the Shan Van Vocht," occasionally reverted to the coarseness of
the original version, as in these lines from an 1828 ballad about Daniel
O'Connell and Vesey Fitzgerald: "O'Connell has an Ass, says the Shan Van
Vocht / And Fitzgerald may kiss his arse, says . . ."[34]

The optimistic, assertive tone of this 1798 song appealed to the nationalists for it contrasted favorably with the image of Ireland as a beautiful
woman languidly mourning her departed Stuart savior in the aislings which
were so popular among the people. A version of the song by Young
Irelander Michael Doheny of later Fenian fame further improved upon the
original. Doheny gave his version a title in Irish, "An T-Sean Bhean
Bhochd" and created a storyline about how in 1176 the Gaelic chieftains
banded together to expel the Normans as they had the Danes.[35] Of course,
the Irish had not united against the Danes or the Normans; indeed, in their
celebrated defeat of the Danes at Clontarf, the Munster forces of Brian
Boru had faced an army composed of Danes and Leinstermen. Likewise,
Doheny's idyllic images of early Ireland—"the sainted isle of old" and "the
parent and mould of the beautiful and bold"—were also metaphor not fact.

James Clarence Mangan's "Dark Rosaleen," first published in the
Nation on 30 May 1846, was inspired by the Irish folksong "Róisín Dubh,"
an impassioned love lyric which probably originated in the seventeenth
century. Mangan's note to his "translation" is sheer fiction. He claimed the
original song had been "an allegorical poem from Red Hugh O'Donnell to
Ireland on the subject of his love and struggles for her, and his resolve to
raise her again to the glorious position she held before the interruption of
the Saxon and Norman spoilers.[36] However, according to Seán Ó Tuama,
the poet's beloved was not a pseudonym for Ireland.[37] Donal O'Sullivan
claims that the only possible allegory in the original—the references to
friars, Rome, and Spain in the oening stanza—was not national but religious, for the allusions could have referred to the hoped-for triumph of the
Catholic church in Ireland.[38] Indeed, the power of Mangan's song is
derived from its personal dimension and the passionate, intimate tone he so
masterfully retained from the original: "O my dark Rosaleen! My own
Rosaleen!"

A comparison of the lament which Turlough O'Carolan wrote in Irish
for Owen Roe O'Neill with Thomas Davis's "Lament for the Death of
Eoghan Ruadh O'Neill" demonstrates several major differences beteen the
way the people had remembered Irish history in song and the way the
literary nationalists retold the same history. A sense of immediacy, of deep
personal loss, of resignation, and of nostalgia pervades Douglas Hyde's
translation of O'Carolan's lament. O'Neill and the other Irish heroes who
could have defeated the now-ascendant Clann Cromwell are dead; no

person and no thing can replace O'Neill. He is mourned in vivid, concete, sensual terms as the speaker stands on the hero's silent grave. That the speaker laments the loss of drink and sport, along with the passing of victories over foreigners, typifies the down-to-earth concerns of the people. [39] Davis's poem begins as a dialogue between a member of O'Neill's clan and a messenger about the circumstances of O'Neill's death and then becomes a lament in which the speaker, using the plural *we*, commands his audience to weep. Rather than the personal dimensions of O'Carolan's song, which was a soliloquy, the speaker in Davis's poem focuses on the fate of the community when he uses phrases like "our dear country," "we're slaves," "sheep without a shepherd," and "we're orphans." The aggressive sense of outrage in the opening line—"Die they dare, did they dare, to slay Eoghan Ruadh O'Neill?"—has replaced O'Carolan's tone of resigned melancholy and personal loss. [40]

Davis and his fellow writers transformed the despair with which the people remembered their history with a new note of gladness, and joy, and the "strains of victory proud," such as Callanan had injected into his free translation of Owen Rua O'Sullivan's aisling. Davis declared that "Irish political songs are too desponding or weak to content people marching to independence as proudly as if they had never been slaves." [41] Young Ireland writers repeatedly criticized Ireland's passivity, referring to the "sickening sense of destiny" in the *Nation* on 4 May 1844 and the policy of "sitting down and waiting for freedom" in the *Nation* on 16 December 1843. The *Nation* followed the example of Father Matthew who had met with great success in transforming the Irish habit of drinking, which the *Nation* labeled the "luxury of despair" and "the saturnalia of slaves" on 28 January 1843, into a temperance movement that exhibited the people's capacity for self-control and discipline. If the temperance movement could replace the despair, which had led the Irish to drink, with hope and freedom through a process of education and organization, the *Nation* announced it would do likewise with the mournful poetic expression of the same despair.

The *Nation* relentlessly preached the doctrine that traditional Irish fatalism must be replaced by self-reliance. The poem "Ourselves Alone" appeared in one of the first issues on 3 December 1842 and declared: "Too long our Irish hearts were school'd / In patient hope to bide; . . . Our hope and strength, we find at last, / Is in OURSELVES ALONE. . . . 'Twas long our weakness and our curse, / In stranger aid to trust." In a similar vein, the despondence which Davis found so objectionable in Irish songs was reinterpreted as the positive virtue of endurance, "the discipline to forbear," in the *Nation* of 30 March 1844. The courage, the perseverance, and the discipline manifested in the endurance that the Irish had displayed throughout the centuries became components of the image of manhood popularized by the *Nation*. "Men," "manly," and "manhood" were among the most popular words in the *Nation's* vocabulary. If Irish history had not provided adequate examples of manhood, the *Nation* did. M.J. McCann's song, "O'Donnell Abu," first published in the *Nation* 28 January 1843, typifies the martial and national dimensions of the manhood which the *Nation* sought to inspire. In the song, which purports to be the marching song of the O'Donnells in 1597, the local dimensions of the rebellion are conveniently forgotten as the "warrior-clans" fight to the rousing national battle cries of "On for old Erin!" and "Strike for your country!"

In a similar manner later in the century, Canon Sheehan's ballad "After Aughrim's Great Disaster" celebrated Sean O'Dwyer's vigorous and gory defiance of "the hungry Saxon wolves" in the plural voice typical of nationalist songs—"with our swords and spears we gored them."[42] Sheehan's rousing ballad presents a vastly different portrait of Sean O'Dwyer than the song in Irish mentioned earlier in which a broken Sean O'Dwyer lamented his woes. Nationalists in the twentieth century continued to celebrate Irish manhood. Patrick Pearse declared in his famous speech at Wolfe Tone's grave that the memory of '98 had given manhood to Ireland. Arthur Griffith praised John Mitchel as Ireland's manliest man and argued that Ireland failed Mitchel because it lacked manhood.[43]

The reinterpretation of Irish history was central to the nationalist's attempt to reawaken Ireland, to inspire the people to manly action. An allusion to "warfare of six hundred years" in Drennan's "Wake of William Orr" was to become a common motif in the folklore of Irish nationalism, despite the historical fallacy of depicting earlier Irish rebellions and uprisings as one ongoing struggle of national dimensions. Nationalists even transformed the passive and personal dimensions of the aisling in order to present images of heroism and national unity. Instead of the languishing lady who appeared to the poet in traditional aisling, the speaker in "McKenna's Dream," a ballad very popular in the 1850s and 1860s, has a dream-vision of a vast army of heroes such as Brian Boru and Sarsfield who completely rout the enemy and avenge Ireland before he wakes and discovers it was only a dream.[44] A similar ballad of 1867 entitled "Burke's Dream" envisions the Fenian men battling the "proud Saxon," who flee their terrible vengeance until the speaker awakes.[45] Although the image of a continuous national struggle for freedom was spurious, the apocalyptic motif in such vision poems echoed the millenial note common in Irish folklore.

In calling upon the people to emulate such heroic models from Irish history, the nationalists transformed another motif from oral tradition, the resurrection of the sleeping warrior. However, they sought to awaken an entire nation. Drennan's "Wake of William Orr" had commanded the men of 1798 to: "Conquer fortune—persevere! / Lo! it breaks, the morning clear! / The cheerful cock awakes the skies, / The day is come—arise!—arise!" Thomas Moore's repeated allusions to Erin slumbering were echoed in many Young Ireland songs such as "Awake, and Lie Dreaming No More" and Thomas Davis's "The West's Asleep." The charter song of the *Nation*, "Fág An Bealach" ("Clear the Way"), published in its third issue and placed first in *The Spirit of the Nation* anthology, declared: "We preach a land awoken." James Clarence Mangan's poem "The Nation's First Number" in the inaugural issue commanded: "Arise! fling aside your dark mantle of slumber." "Arise" and "awake" were among the most numerous of the many imperative verbs used in the *Nation's* verse. John Mitchel used the motif repeatedly in both his *Jail Journal* and his *History of Ireland*.

As part of their attempt to reinterpret Irish history as a source of pride rather than tears and shame, nationalists celebrated daring heroes whose defeat nevertheless represented a moral victory against English treachery, whose courage should be imitated, and whose defeats cried out for revenge. One of the most famous and influential nationalist poems, John Kells Ingram's "Who Fears to Speak of Ninety-Eight?" which was published in the *Nation* on 1 April 1843, epitomizes this new version of Ireland's story. Those who feared to speak and blushed in shame at the memory of '98 were knaves, slaves, and cowards. True men would remember the brave of '98 with pride and be inspired by their memory to act as brave a part, to unite, even if it meant death.

Such a heroicizing of 1798 had not been the people's immediate response to the failure of the uprising. Contemporary observers and folklorists such as Patrick Kennedy, who collected oral traditions about 1798 later in the century, have noted how demoralized the people were. One of the few popular songs in Irish about 1798 to have survived, "Sliabh na mBan," suggests the popular response was far different from the one Ingram's poem called for half a century later. The song commemorates a local insurrection in which yeomen defeat badly armed rebels who are scattered like a herd without a drover on the slopes of Slievenamon. The speaker in Frank O'Connor's translation laments that "Our major never came to lead us, / We had no orders and drifted on" and that the French promise "to set the Irish free" did not materialize. The despair and poignancy of the lines, "Little children burned to ashes, / Women in holes and ditches hid," eclipses any hope in the poem's call for revenge.[46]

Daniel O'Connell's practical successes and the literary propaganda of the romantic nationalists were largely responsible for transforming such

despair in the decades after 1798. Nationalists, whether of the constitutional or the physical force variety, would have their greatest successes
when, like O'Connell and Parnell, their political aims paralleled the people's practical and immediate concerns about religion and land such as were
expressed in these lines from a popular nineteenth-century ballad:

> The labourers and the tradesmen that's now in poverty
> —They'll have mutton beef and bacon with butter eggs and tea,

> Then Luther's generation must take a speedy flight
> And go to Hanover from the lands of sweet delight,
> All hereticks must cast their sticks and leave this fertile land,
> For it was decreed that Harry's breed should fall by the old command.[47]

But constitutional and physical force nationalists alike confronted an ambiguity and equivocation at the heart of popular attitudes about violence
when they tried to mobilize the people. John M. Synge's *Playboy of the
Western World* immortalizes the ambiguity about violence so central to the
Irish consciousness: Synge's Mayo peasants celebrate violence when the
deed is committed elsewhere or in the past; they recoil in horror when they
see it firsthand. So, too, have the Irish people often celebrated violence
when it was safely in the past or prophesied as an apocalyptic future event.

No one incarnated this ambiguity about violence more than Daniel
O'Connell. Indeed, he transformed the people's equivocal attitudes about
physical force into effective political action.[48] He reflected the people's
abhorrence of violence, such as had been expressed in the folksong "Sliabh
na mBan," when he repeatedly exhorted them to remember 1798 with
horror. That he often made sure there were veterans of '98 on the platform
with him when he spoke demonstrates he was shrewdly aware that the
people heroicized violence once it was safely in the past and, more importantly, that much of the political success attributed to his doctrine of nonviolence was due to the threat of violence such as had occurred in 1798.

Gearóid Ó Tuathaigh's translations of the songs in Irish about O'Connell indicate that there was a significant gap between O'Connell's philosophy of nonviolence and the people's equivocal attitudes about violence.[49]
The Irish lyrics often celebrated physical force and many of the people
expected O'Connell to lead them in an armed revolt. In a similar manner,
although official political ballads in English about O'Connell (such as those
in the collection of chapbooks from the 1830s in the National Library of
Ireland) often used an abstract rhetoric reminiscent of *Paddy's Resource* to
celebrate O'Connell's nonviolence, popular street ballads often gave a
different portrait of O'Connell. For example, some nationalist ballads such
as "O'Connell's Health" proclaim O'Connell's "glorious name" is "dear to

freedom's cause" and praise how "in the bloodless field of glory" he "flung th' oppressor down." However, even that final image depicts his bloodless victory in terms of physical force.

Other ballads explicitly celebrated violence. The popular broadside ballad "Slieve Na Mon," which demonstrates O'Connell's success in transforming the post-1798 despair so evident in the earlier song of that title in Irish ("Sliabh na mBan") into militant nationalism, presents antithetical attitudes about violence. The ballad celebrates O'Connell's nonviolence in millenial terms when it refers to the prophecy that "One true Catholic, without a weapon, would banish the legions from Slieve na Mon," and proclaims the typical reliance on supernatural help, "The hand of Providence will surely aid us." However, the song, which was written to commemorate one of the bloodiest battles of the Title War when peasants armed with scythes and pitchforks had killed a tithe proctor and at least twelve policemen at Carrickshock in December 1831, also praises the people for having used violence: "Who could desire to see better sport, / To see them groping among the loughs, / Their sculls all fractured, their eyeballs broken, / Their great long noses and ears cut off?"[50] O'Connell's doctrine of nonviolence had obviously not succeeded in, as John Mitchel put it, emasculating Ireland.

Indeed, despite attempts by physical force nationalists to discredit O'Connell, he is by far the most popular folk hero. The way he is remembered in oral tradition also suggests the gap which existed between O'Connell's philosophical principles and what mattered most to the people. They preferred to remember him as the indomitable counsellor, the cunning lawyer whose tricks outmaneuvered English law and brought practical, concrete benefits, rather than as the liberator who won abstract political rights.[51] The people's expectations about O'Connell are immortalized in the words of one of William Carleton's characters in *Traits and Stories of the Irish Peasantry*, who threatens his jailers with these words:

Did yees ever hear of a man they call Dan O'Connell? Be my sowl, he'll make yees rub your heels together for keepin' an innocent boy in gaol—I tell yees, that if a hair o' my head's touched—ay, if I was hanged tomorrow—I'd lave *them* behind me that ud put a bullet, wid the help an' blessin' o' God, through anyone that'll injure me! So lay that to your conscience, an' do your best. Be the crass, O'Connell 'ill make you look nine ways at wanst for this! He's the boy can put the pin in your noses! He's the boy can make yees thrimble, one an' all o' yees—like a dog in a wet sack! An, wid the blessin' o' God, he'll help us to put our feet on your necks afore long![52]

Ó Tuathaigh's translations of songs about O'Connell and many popular street ballads in English exemplify another gap in attitude between folksongs of the people and those written by literary nationalists. A blistering sectarianism was central to the popular mentality and was to remain largely untouched by the liberal principles of nationalist leaders. Although the songs in *Paddy's Resource* had preached religious toleration, popular ballads of the day displayed fierce sectarian animosity.[53] Louis Cullen, in the course of arguing that race and class were basic to the development of Irish nationalism, has declared that the 1798 uprising was "a sectarian civil war."[54] Neither the nonsectarian cultural nationality preached by Thomas Davis nor the liberal religious principles of Daniel O'Connell were successful in transforming popular sectarian attitudes. Moreover, O'Connell and the Young Ireland writers frequently used epithets like "Celt" and "Saxon," the racial connotations of which could only have aggravated the racial and sectarian biases of their audiences.

Although nationalist poets wrote many songs extolling religious toleration, this idea unfortunately never achieved the popularity of other ideas and motifs which they propagated in their folklore of Irish nationalism. Davis expressed the hope of the few rather than the sentiments of the many when he wrote in his poem "The Penal Days" that "All creeds are equal in our isle." Nationalists oversimplified and misrepresented popular opinion and Irish history, but some aspects of their vision, especially their call for national unity, deserve to become more than myth and metaphor. The Fenian John O'Leary's declaration in 1886 that the Irish could never go astray in thinking and feeling with Thomas Davis, has been echoed by modern historians.[55] In *Ireland Since the Famine* F.S.L. Lyons wrote, "If the reality of Irish life came to bear little relation to Davis's dream, the fault may be in the reality not the dream."[56] Fergus O'Ferrall concludes his recent study of O'Connell with the hope that the comprehensive Irish nationalism of Davis and O'Connell will be rediscovered.[57]

Today's attempt to demythologize Irish nationalism must grapple with the images and ideas propagated in the folklore of nationalism. Too often the images of historical events and of popular opinion propagated by nationalists have been accepted as historical fact, most notably their myths of a glorious and united ancient Ireland, and of an unbroken, centuries-old national struggle for independence between the Gaels or Celts and their Saxon oppressors. However, myths can inspire and influence history as well as distort it. Although nationalist myths about the Irish past and about the popular mind at various periods have obscured history, nationalist myths, especially the image of manly behavior which challenged traditional passivity and fatalism, have inspired important constitutional and violent agitation. In separating the myths in the folklore of nationalism from reality, we should not lose sight of those myths which represent higher truths, especially the call for a national unity transcending sectarian differences, which indeed deserve to become reality.

Thomas Flanagan

NATIONALISM:
THE LITERARY TRADITION

> *Oh! quench'd are our beacon lights—*
> *Thou of the Hundred Fights!*
> *Thou on whose burning tongue*
> *Truth, peace, and freedom hung!*
> *Both mute,—but long as valour shineth,*
> *Or mercy's soul at war repineth,*
> *So long shall ERIN's pride*
> *Tell how they liv'd and died.*
> —Thomas Moore, *Irish Melodies*

IN 1868 a history of Ireland was published that might have presented a minor problem to an overly scrupulous librarian.[1] Its title page declares it to be, "a continuation of the History of the Abbe MacGeoghegan," and so in a sense it is. It opens where MacGeoghegan's book closes—with an account of the Treaty of Limerick—and carries forward the narrative to the years immediately after the Great Famine. In all else, however, it would be difficult to imagine books less complementary in style, method, attitude, purpose, or type of historical imagination.

The Abbe MacGeoghegan published his three-volume history between the years 1758 and 1763, in the Paris of Louis XV.[2] The continuation was written by John Mitchel, fresh from his experiences in Paris as financial agent for the Irish Republican Brotherhood on the eve of the 1867 Rising. The century that lies between the composition of the two books suggests a multitude of differences, but one that is both specific and definitive—the development of an Irish nationalism in the modern meaning of that term. Mitchel himself was a formidable shaper of that nationalism, and as a shaping instrument, his *History* is second only to the *Jail Journal*. He and MacGeoghegan have in common only that they are Irishmen writing in exile.

MacGeoghegan was born near Uisnech, in Westmeath, in 1702, and into a family of the Catholic gentry.[3] They had produced Richard Mac-Geoghegan, the defender of Dunboy at the time of the O'Neill rebellion, and had been active in both the cause and the army of James II, despite which they had contrived to hold small, scattered properties in their native country. James MacGeoghegan was educated and ordained in France and became one of the clergy of the Church of Saint Merry in Paris. Patrick O'Kelly, who in the next century translated MacGeoghegan's history into English, speaks of him as the chaplain of the Irish Brigade: certainly the history is dedicated to the brigade, and members of the family had been attached to it from the days of Sarsfield. When the first volume was published, MacGeoghegan reminded his readers that General Lally and his regiment were embarked for Pondicherry, there to seek "amidst the waves of another hemisphere the eternal enemies of King Louis." Alexander MacGeoghegan, James's kinsman, was embarked with him, and was to acquit himself in India more handsomely than did his luckless commander.

MacGeoghegan's is a history with a purpose, written, as its preliminary discourse makes explicit, to establish the Irish as one of the most ancient of peoples, rather than the barbarous and unhistoried race described by their enemies and traducers, from Giraldus Cambrensis to Hume and Voltaire. The final volume of Hume's *History of England* had appeared the year before; at the moment he was in Paris with the embassy, enjoying the friendship of D'Alembert and Turgot. As for Voltaire, his casual gibes and sneers still rankled MacGeoghegan and his compatriots in France. In the caste-ridden world of court and army, it was at the least mortifying to be seen lumbering about as the living vestiges of a barbarous and primitive people.

As a history, or to speak more properly, as an apologia, Mac-Geoghegan's joins with others of the later eighteenth and early nineteenth centuries to form a distinct genre, and is one of the earliest. Of its kind, it is neither the worst (a palm that should be awarded to Sylvester O'Halloran's) nor the most fluent (that one left unfinished by Thomas Moore). Almost without exception, they have a political purpose that is openly avowed or, in some instances, very thinly submerged. And, again almost without exception, they are written without any useful knowledge of the sources in Irish upon which an actual or, for that matter, a traditionally mythological history could be constructed.

Eugene O'Curry relates that when Moore was in Dublin collecting material for his history, he encountered O'Curry at the Royal Irish Academy. After inspecting some of the annals upon which O'Curry was at work and attending to O'Curry's description of these exotic and impenetrable artifacts, Moore exclaimed that clearly they were works of learning, and without their help it was foolish of him to attempt a history of Ireland. But, of course, this did not stop him, any more than it stopped MacGeoghegan, who relies, with but a single exception, on sources in Latin and English. The exception offers equivocal evidence as to whether he could read Irish: the *Book of Lecan* was then conveniently to hand at the Irish College in Paris, but he remarks a bit peevishly that he found it "difficult to read."

This places him in the awkward position, so far as the early part of his narrative is concerned, of relying for his authorities upon the very writers whom he is in the process of refuting. Fortunately, he possessed an almost effortless skill in casuistry, although at times the facts are too intractable to yield to it. Thus, as he tells us at the outset, "the nation which forms the subject of this history is without doubt one of the most ancient in Europe," with arts, sciences, and letters borrowed "from the most polished people of their time, the Egyptians and the Phoenicians," and with a system of government founded upon the laws of nature and humanity. The valor of its arms carried it into the very heart of the Roman Empire, and later it was to be the one bright beacon in a world of Gothic superstition. But if the ancient Irish had been possessed of so coruscating a brilliance, why had no one save themselves ever heard of them, much less been stimulated by greed or envy into invading them? To be sure, they are given passing references by Strabo, Ptolemy, and other ancient geographers, but not much by way of praise. MacGeoghegan is at a loss to explain this on grounds other than a fathomless malignity, and he rushes forward to the twelfth century, where Giraldus Cambrensis awaits him.

For MacGeoghegan, as for all contemporaries of his persuasion, Giraldus is the chief and originating villain, the earliest historian of Ireland and the most vicious. All later historians, Hanmer, Harris, Spenser, Campion, Camden, and the others, accept his judgments and follow his example "like the asp that borrows the venom of the viper." Among moderns, he admits that Clarendon possesses great virtues as an historian, but his hatred alike of Catholics and of Irishmen, to the extent that he distinguishes between them, has clouded his judgment. As for Bishop Burnet, to his scholarly defects may be added the personal ones of avarice and simple dishonesty.

But by the time MacGeoghegan has reached the events of the preceding century, which is the core of his history and its most rewarding volume, he has a variety of sources among which to choose, and he marshals his narrative with skill. Now the pattern not only of his narrative but also of its apologetic purpose becomes clear. The "nation" for which he acts as advocate is that of the Catholic nobility and gentry of Ireland, Gaelic and Old English. It is a defeated nation, and if its defeat has been anything other than entire and permanent, he exhibits no awareness of this. His stance might be described as chivalrous, as befits a chaplain of the brigade.

As a matter of strict, pedantic fact, at the time of his writing, James III, the Old Pretender, was still alive and, being recognized as the legitimate sovereign by the Pope and more fitfully by Louis XV, had a claim upon the loyalty of that "nation." But it was a claim that each passing year rendered more shadowy and sentimental. When James died, three years after the publication of MacGeoghegan's history, the Pope pointedly did not recognize the claims of his son, the Young Pretender. Thus was removed one impediment at least which had prevented Irish Catholics from swearing allegiance to King George and the Protestant House of Hanover. By 1778, Daniel O'Connell, an officer of the brigade (and the Liberator's uncle), writing home to Kerry in response to the recent relaxation of the Penal Laws, remarks that "One step more remains to be made—I mean the Liberty of spilling their blood in defence of their King and Country." Although he adds, with hasty O'Connellite prudence, that "no motive cu'd induce me to bear arms against France."[4]

MacGeoghegan is not writing on behalf of Ireland, as that word was to be given romantic definition by nationalists of the next century, but as spokesman for the nation of Irish Catholics, an ancient people who suffered an honorable defeat and then a dishonorable spoliation, and who could look only to the Crown for relief from the crushing disabilities under which they labored. It was at this exact time that Charles O'Conor of Belnagare and Dr. John Curry were publishing their antiquarian and historical researches into the chronicles of the Irish past and the condition of the Catholic community, the form being in each case scholarly but the purpose that of advancing the relief of the Catholic gentry from penal legislation.[5] And, indeed, it is now that there begins the series of whining protestations of loyalty on the part of Catholic peers and "respectable" tradesmen that were to be such an embarrassment to later generations.

Unlike MacGeoghegan, the Catholic historians who succeeded him made it their prudent habit to close, as does Sylvester O'Halloran, with the coming of Strongbow and the end of the ancient kingdom.[6] When they do venture into more recent centuries, however, they almost invariably pause to denounce, as he does, those Protestant writers who "stigmatize with the name of rebellion the efforts of the Catholics of Ireland on behalf of their legitimate sovereign." The sovereign to whom MacGeoghegan refers is James II, and he has there, of course, a very strong case. But writers of his school were able, by strenuous verbal gymnastics, to argue that loyalty to a legitimate monarch was a hereditary trait of the Gael, apparent instances to the contrary being attributable either to duplicitous lords deputy or else to what would now be called failures in communication. At any event, the native Irish were to be shown as an ancient, polite, and loyal people, entitled by nature if not by law to those privileges enjoyed by King George's more fortunate subjects.

But whether such historians as MacGeoghegan and O'Halloran knew it or not, they were constructing a myth of origins, a sacral history, which could be put to quite different purposes. By a twist of the kaleidoscope, it would be possible to dispose the same brightly colored bits of glass into a very different pattern. Into, as Terence Brown has said, "a myth of the indestructible Irish people permanently betrayed by traitorous informers and national apostates." Before the hand of history could change that pattern, however, a slight but crucial shift was necessary in the modes by which the past is understood.

Brown, in the passage which I have just quoted from, is discussing a remarkable essay in which Oliver MacDonagh examines the histories of the country produced between 1790 and 1820 by Catholic writers and their refutations by Protestant critics. To borrow Brown's summarizing language, "Catholic historians labored to reveal the magnificence of ancient Celtic Ireland while their protestant contemporaries were assiduous in anti-Romantic reductionism of the same period. What they shared however was a predeliction for eliding time, foreshortening historical chronology, even in a sense annulling it, so that 'the character of druidical Ireland was being treated as validating or otherwise, in some significant degree, the early nineteenth century political and social order.' "[7]

In fact, the grandiloquent creation of an ancient, splendid, and absurd antiquity had preceded the period with which MacDonagh deals. O'Halloran had conjured up a hazy world, half-barbarous, half-chivalric, a world of poets, kings, priests and high-priests, palaces, "elegant public works," "silver chariots" and emblazoned with coats of arms, and a five-fold chivalric order, clad in helmets and corselets "cased with the gold of Spain and Africa." The great festival of Samhain was celebrated with sacred odes set to a great variety of musical instruments, and "in the days of Saint Patrick this meeting in the presence of Laogaire the monarch, was compared for grandeur and magnificence to that of Nebuchadnezzar king of Babylon, on the plains of Dura."[8]

With the history of Ireland in such hands, it was not unreasonable of the Edgeworths to protest in their *Essay on Irish Bulls* that it was to them a matter of indfference "whether the Irish derive their origins from the Spaniards, or the Milesians, or the Welsh. . . . We moreover candidly confess that we are more interested in the fate of its present race of inhabitants than in the histories of St. Patrick, St. Facharis, St. Cormuck; the renowned Brian Boru; Tireldach, king of Connaught; MacMurrough, king of Leinster. . . ."[9] But in describing this faerie kingdom of the imagination as the work of Catholic apologists and cryptapologists, MacDonagh slights the equally influential fabrications of such dilettantes as Charlotte Brooke, Joseph Cooper Walker, Edward Ledwich, and Charles Vallencey, Protestants all, and the last named of them not merely a British general but an Eton man.

Catholics, that is to say, were interested in antiquity and Protestants in antiquities. It was a first instance of that unspoken covenant, coming to full flower in the Victorian period, by which Catholics took up political nationalism and Protestants, cultural nationalism. Walker and Brooke, in particular, sought to imbue the surviving ruins of the antique past, whether of melody or of stone, with that melancholy fascination made fashionable by Grey with *The Bard* (1757) and by MacPherson with *Fingal* (1761) and his other Ossianic poems.[10] The pastness of that past, its irrecoverableness, its present impotence, was crucial to that particular mode of romantic sensibility.

It is true that fleeting references to Ireland's ancient glories adorn the speeches of Grattan and Curran and the other parliamentary orators, but for a reason specified by Owen Dudley Edwards with sardonic accuracy: "Irish triumph in pre-Christian days, and Irish misfortunes in medieval and Tudor times, simply added an aura of distinction to the 'nationalist' pretensions of the day, suggesting on the part of those who alluded to them that they themselves were of ancient lineage and title, and not the newly-rich money-minded profiteers from confiscations achieved by superior military force in the preceding century."[11] It was, that is to say, an entirely sentimental allegiance, in the full range of the pejorative meanings of that word, including the Meredithian one favored by Stephen Dedalus in *Ulysses*: "The sentimentalist is he who would enjoy without incurring the immense debtorship for the thing done."

At any rate, by the turn of the century, the atmosphere and sensibility which Thomas Moore was to exploit had been created and thickened: the theater of feelings; the landscape of ruined towers; shimmering, vanished glories; sighs and softly breathed avowals and protestations—all were in place for the creation of the *Irish Melodies*. And the importance of the *Melodies* to the shaping of nineteenth-century nationalism should never be underestimated, whether by those who mistakenly think they know his politics or by those whose ears are deaf to his marvelous songs.

Professor MacDonagh has noted, in the debates between the magniloquent Catholic historians and their antiromantic, reductionist opponents, a shared predilection, as Brown puts it, "for eliding time, foreshortening historical chronology, even in a sense annulling it," and this kind of atemporality, infusing Irish historiography at its very outset, has continued to shape "the historical assumptions of most ordinary Irish people." It has not been remarked upon, I think, that a specific variation of this process of elision lies at the heart of the *Melodies.*

It was in 1807 that Power proposed to Moore a series of songs to be set to music arranged by Sir John Stevenson, but his interest in the native music of Ireland was of long standing and had begun during his student days at Trinity. He was entirely familiar with Bunting's collection (only too familiar, Bunting was later to claim), and Hudson, another collector and enthusiast, was his friend. But so, too, was Robert Emmet his university friend, and his memoir carries a vivid account of Emmet leaping up with fiery enthusiasm as Moore played for him the air to which "Let Erin Remember" was later set. If the story is apocryphal, so much the better, for it would then suggest the association which had come to exist in this memory and imagination between the "native music" of Ireland and the political drama which began with the recall of Lord Fitzwilliam and swept through the rebellion to the collapse of Grattan's nation and the passage of the Act of Union.

Moore did not play, nor did he ever claim to have played, an active role in those events, but the memoirs and, later, his biography of Lord Edward Fitzgerald make clear and vivid the atmosphere of the times and the sentiments of young liberals like himself, leaving little doubt as to where his own sympathies lay. The singular success of the *Melodies,* judged purely as a contribution to a developing nationalism, is at once specific and complex, and is bound up in events that he had moved beyond, politically, but which held his emotions in delicate solution.

In 1844, when Patrick O'Kelly republished his translation of Mac-Geoghegan's history, he embellished the title page with two lines of verse with which all literate Irishmen had become familiar: "Let Erin remember the days of old / Ere her faithless sons betrayed her."

"Oh, breathe not his name" and "The harp that once" appear in the first number of the *Melodies,* and "Let Erin remember" in the second: together they set the political key—a melancholy sign for a vanished music, a vanished kingdom, a hero slain but slain so recently that it is not yet safe to speak his name. The second verse of "Let Erin remember" is the less familiar one, but is revelatory of Moore's strategy of feeling and sentiment:

> On Lough Neagh's bank as the fisherman strays,
>   When the clear cold eve's declining,
> He sees the round towers of other days,

> In the wave beneath him shining;
> Thus shall memory often, in dreams sublime,
> Catch a glimpse of the days that are over;
> Thus, sighing, look through the waves of time
> For the long-faded glories they cover.

Giraldus (of all people!) has provided Moore with an Irish model of one of the great romantic images, the sunken city, submerged by a sudden, catastrophic wave. Moore's note, paraphrasing Giraldus, supplies context: "He says that the fishermen, in clear weather, used to point out to strangers the tall ecclesiastical towers under the water." By means of that resolute atemporality which is central to the *Melodies*, those temporal elisions and foreshortenings of which we have spoken, he can hold within a single moment of feeling the fall of Tara and the fall of Grattan's nation. King Brian is lost to Mononia and Emmet is lost to Ireland; it matters not at all that Brian was killed in the eleventh century, and Emmet hanged a bare half-dozen years before the song which discreetly mourns him was written. The submerged city, for Moore as for those other romantics who were drawn to the image, creates a deathly, pleasurable moment of irremediable defeat, irrecoverable loss, absolute immobility.

A passage in Moore's journal for August 1823 reveals in a manner almost touching his lack of any genuine relationship to a living Gaelic culture. In that year he accompanied Lord and Lady Lansdowne, his patrons, to their estates in Kerry. They set off from Kilkenny to Lismore, and along the road passed the ruined castle and demesne of Kilcash. It is, of course, the subject of not merely one of the loveliest but also one of the most familiar Gaelic songs, mourning the death, early in the eighteenth century, of Margaret Butler, the Lady Iveagh. "What shall we do for timber? / The last of the woods is down." His journal entry reads: "The ruined house of Killcash, on the road, that once belonged to a Mr. Buller [*sic*], struck me both from the appropriateness of its name (Kill-cash), and the dreary, shaven look of the country round it: not a bush left standing. These recent ruins tell the history of Ireland even more than her ancient ones." This Pooterish notation places him in relation to the older tradition with unhappy precision: Kilcash is no more to him than an indifferent pun.

But if critics from his own day to our own, beginning with Bunting himself, have deplored the changes wrought by Moore and Stevenson upon the "authentic" airs, they are right only in part. At the least, as he makes clear in the letter to Lady Donegal that he prefixed to the third number, he knew what he was about, and reshaped by design and not out of ignorance. If Stevenson has "spoiled the simplicity of his airs, by the chromatic

richness of his symphonies, and the elaborate variety of his harmonies,"
then so has Haydn (and, Moore could have added, Beethoven) in his
arrangement of Scottish airs. Giraldus himself, and every historian who
followed him, including Spenser, had allowed that the Irish were skilled in
music and song, if in little else. And those who played and sang, those who
heard the *Melodies* did so with a feeling, misplaced or not, that they were
touching the spirit of their people. Moore had either restored a national
feeling or else he had created one.

By the 1830s, Moore was established in the Irish popular mind as the
national poet, his occasional visits back to the country of his birth the
occasion of civic displays of bad taste surpassed only by those accorded
O'Connell, whom he detested. And, at just this time, a dispute as to the
nature of native poetry and, by extension, the quality of Gaelic, Catholic
civilization arose. It offers so uncanny a parallel to the earlier histo-
riographical controversies that it may reasonably be considered as their
exact continuation in cultural and literary terms. For many years, James
Hardiman, the antiquarian and historian of Galway, had been collecting the
Gaelic poetry of his province, songs ranging back, a few of them, to the
sixteenth and seventeenth centuries, and most of them still known and
sung. Now, in 1831, he published his *Irish Minstrelsy* in an elaborate
edition, with Gaelic verses faced, on the opposing page, by English "translations."

Hardiman's purpose was twofold, as his introduction and occasional
annotations make clear. He was concerned to preserve the poetry, but he
was also a Catholic and an O'Connellite writing in the immediate wake of
emancipation, and notes of triumph, ranging between the peevish and the
bellicose, enter his prose. He is writing on behalf of a people battered by
history until yesterday and a poetry unknown to its enemies, yet nevertheless derided by them. His fatal error, however, was not political but
editorial, although it was an editorial decision informed by cultural politics.
To demonstrate the civility, in some instances the daintiness, of Gaelic
verse, he thought it necessary to turn over his literal translations to Dublin
poetasters who would recast them in the meters and stanzas of fashionable
magazine verse. The collaborators whom he chose were uniformly abom-
inable: Samuel Ferguson has claimed that Thomas Furlong was the most
wretched of them, as I do myself, but this is a matter requiring great
niceness of judgment.

Ferguson made his extended and celebrated response, under the
general title, "Hardiman's *Irish Minstrelsy*," in the April, August, October,
and November 1834 numbers of the *Dublin University Magazine*. It is
remarkable that this essay, crucial to the cultural history of Ireland, has

never been reprinted and must be consulted in the now-brittle pages of the
DUM. On at least three occasions, however, it has been quoted from
extensively and toward tendentious ends. Lady Ferguson, in her rambling
biography of her husband, reads it as an ecumenical document, asking the
Protestants of Ireland to embrace "a thorough knowledge of the genius and
disposition of their fellow-citizens," and occasioned by Ferguson's wish to
be "the first to tell the world what genius, what bravery, what loyalty, what
pious love of country and kind, have been vindicated to the mere Irish by
Mr. Hardiman. . . ."[12] But Ferguson had closed his first number with the
ominous words, "We have now done with the adulatory."[13]

   That number itself had addressed "the vicious vulgarity of Hardiman's
politics," and Malcolm Brown, in his book on Ferguson in the Bucknell
series (one of the slimmest entries in that enterprise) takes an impish pride
in demonstrating the tone and color of the whole as a flaming Orange.[14]
Hardiman, Ferguson says, "disfigures his book and disgraces himself by
flinging in the teeth of his manumission, the whole boardings of his hatred
when a slave." "Oh, ye fair hills of holy Ireland," he has begun, "who dares
sustain the strangled calumny that you are not the land of our love? Who is
he who ventures to stand between us and your Catholic son's good will?"
The immediate answer is the hapless Hardiman, but the actual target is
O'Connell, and all that he represents, his "directory of knaves and scoun-
drels," specified by Ferguson in a sentence far too long to be quoted in full
as "the bankrupt and fraudulent demagogue, the crawling incendiary, the
scheming, jesuitical, ambitious priest—that perverse rabble on whom the
mire in which they have been wallowing for a quarter of a century, has caked
into a crust like the armour of the Egyptian beast. . . ."

   Robert O'Driscoll, in his monograph, *An Ascendancy of the Heart*,[15]
seeks to accommodate the two Fergusons to one another, and if he does so
by playing down the passages which give Brown such impish glee, and if his
own sense of cultural history seems to me somewhat shallow, it should be
said that his own heart, like Ferguson's, is in the right place. Because the
astonishing thing about Ferguson's essay is that it moves beyond political
and sectarian diatribe to a disquisition on Gaelic poetry which rises to
imaginative heights and an informed sympathy of which Hardiman is
incapable. And Ferguson, properly to display to his readers the poetry
which Hardiman's translators have travestied, offers translations of his own
which have become classics of Anglo-Irish verse. Some of them were to be
included later (1864) in his *Lays of the Western Gael*, a volume which for
several generations of English-speaking Irishmen would carry, with conviction, the odors, colors, and rhythms of the other tradition.

   "Seven hundred years of disaster," writes Ferguson in language which
might have been Thomas Davis's, "as destructive as ever consumed the

vitals of any country, have each in succession seen our people perishing by famine or the sword in almost every quarter of the land; yet at this day there is neither mountain, plain, nor valley that is not rife with generations of the unextinguishable nation. . . ." That two such contrary impulses can exist within a single essay might seem to border upon schizophrenia, and it had been preceded five months earlier by an essay whose title might seem to sustain the diagnosis: "A Dialogue between the Head and Heart of an Irish Protestant."

The young Ferguson and his essays (he was then in his midtwenties) should be seen within the context of that witty and supple group of Orange writers who flourished within the triangle formed by Trinity, the *DUM*, and the Royal Irish Academy who in the 1830s and 1840s were at work upon a cultural nationalism which in the long run was to prove as powerful in its subterranean effects as the more obvious and more public achievements of Thomas Davis and Young Ireland. To remember their names is to make the point—Ferguson himself, Petrie, Charles Lever, Isaac Butt, Sheridan LeFanu. To these names may properly be added those of their allies and colleagues on the Ordnance Survey, O'Donovan and O'Curry, Catholic by creed, but barely O'Connellite in politics, and not at all allies of Young Ireland. Poor James Clarence Mangan may even be enrolled, for he published far more often in the *DUM* than in the *Nation*, and even, perhaps, Bunting, who in the 1840s was ending his days as organist in a Dublin church.

The *DUM* was the organ of Orange Young Ireland, of which Owen Dudley Edwards has written wittily and well. Isaac Butt, its first editor, defined it as the "monthly advocate of the Protestantism, the intelligence, and the respectability of Ireland." Whatever its respectability, it did a remarkable job, under Butt and with Ferguson's help, of defining a cultural nationalism capable not merely of standing apart from political nationalism, but of subverting it. Thus "Heart," in Ferguson's dialogue, could in 1833 define the plight of Anglo-Ireland with a precision that was never to be equaled:

Deserted by the Tories, insulted by the Whigs, threatened by the Radicals, hated by the Papists, and envied by the Dissenters, plundered in our country seats, robbed in our town houses, driven abroad by violence, called back by humanity, and, after all, told that we are neither English nor Irish, fish nor flesh, but a peddling colony, a forlorn advanced guard that must conform to every mutinous movement of the pretorian rabble—all this, too, while we are the acknowledged possessors of nine tenths of the property of a great country, and wielders of the preponderating influence between two parties; on whose relative position depend the greatest interests in the empire.

In short, no petty people, but one of the great stocks of Europe. Fergson's cultural nationalism issues, ultimately, from this passonate definition of a social and political entrapment, but, far from being formulated as a program of separatism, it is being placed, at whatever hazards, in the service of Union and the Crown. There are moments, as I have said, in which the prose of Ferguson seems indistinguishable from that of Thomas Davis. "We hail," Ferguson writes, "with daily increasing pleasure, the spirit of research and liberality which is manifesting itself in all the branches of our national literature, but chiefly in our earlier history and antiquities—subjects of paramount importance to every people who respect, or even desire to respect themselves." And thus Davis:

> The Irish antiquarians of the past century did much good. They called attention to the history and manners of our predecessors which we had forgotten. They gave a pedigree to nationhood, and created a faith that Ireland could and should be great again by magnifying what she had been. They excited the noblest passions— veneration, love of glory, beauty and virtue. They awoke men's fancy by their gorgeous pictures of the past, and imagination strove to surpass them by its creations. They believed what they wrote, and so their wildest stories sank into men's minds. To the exertions of Walker, O'Halloran, Vallencey, and a few other Irish academicians of the last century, we owe almost all the Irish knowledge possessed by our upper classes until very lately. It was small, but it was enough to give a dreamy renown to ancient Ireland, and if it did nothing else it smoothed the reception of Bunting's music, and identified Moore's poetry with his native country. [16]

But the differences, which are as much of tone as of substance, are crucial though submerged. It is not merely that Ferguson probably and Petrie certainly would have found this defense of Vallencey's foolishness and Walker's giddy fabrications one which carried toleration too far. Ferguson's lyrics and Petrie's drawings and watercolors offer moving and attractive evidence of their own romantic sensibilities, but they were also, like Stokes and Sir William Wilde, hard-headed antiquarians, distrustful of Ireland's dreamy renown. Beyond this, however, they would have been suspicious of the meanings with which Davis was endowing such a phrase as "pedigree to nationhood," and still more suspicious as to the meaning which it was carrying to readers of the *Nation.* "Young Ireland," Yeats was to write, "had sought a nation unified by political doctrine alone, a subservient art and letters aiding and abetting." [17] He would seem to have forgotten (for the moment) that to young romantics of the 1840s, whether in Ireland or on the Continent, political doctrine was a mode of poetry.

A pardonable forgetfulness, for by the 1890s, a full half-century later, that mode had ossified, with one of its shapers, Sir Charles Gavan Duffy, returned from Australia for the sole purpose, so it seemed, of plaguing Yeats. There were many at that time, Yeats writes, who "found it hard to refuse if anybody offered for sale a pepper-pot shaped to suggest a round tower with a wolf-dog at its foot, who would have found it inappropriate to publish an Irish book that had not harp and shamrock and green cover, so completely did their minds move amid Young Ireland images and metaphors." The harps and the pepper pots came in the end to achieve a lurid iconographic status in his prose: he had but to speak of them to evoke certain specific ways of feeling about Ireland.

Yeats's chief summarizing statement upon Young Ireland, however, is not only balanced and accurate but surprisingly precise: "The movement of thought, which had in the 'fifties and 'forties at Paris and London and Boston, filled literature, and especially poetical literature, with curiosities about science, about history, about politics, with moral purpose and educational fervor—abstractions all—had created a new instrument for Irish politics, a method of writing that took its poetical style from Campbell, Scott, Macaulay and Beranger, with certain elements from Gaelic, its prose style—in John Mitchel, the only Young Ireland prose writer who had a style at all—from Carlyle." And he makes a nice distinction between that generation of nationalists and the preceding one: "Old men who had never accepted Young Ireland, or middle-aged men kept by family tradition to the school of thought before it arose, to the Ireland of Daniel O'Connell and of Lever and of Thomas Moore, convivial Ireland with the traditional tear and smile." Convivial is a well-chosen word, suggesting the sounds of the *Melodies*, voices and pianoforte, heads gathered about a punch bowl, Lever's fox hunters roistering in a battered Connaught big house.

Convivial Ireland was Whig Ireland (Moore's exact political position), and however matters may have looked to Yeats, it was in substantial cultural alliance with the respectable semiseparatist legatees of Young Ireland. By a process with which Irishmen were becoming familiar, each rebel generation, the danger that they presented having dissipated itself, was absorbed into what was by his day a century-old tradition of nationalism. It was a nationalism thick-textured and thick-skilled, capable of producing such prodigies of flexibility as T. D. Sullivan, who contrived to be at once the unyielding enemy of Fenianism and its poet laureate. And it was overwhelmingly Catholic, both as a political movement and as a fabric of sentiments, aspirations, and familial alliances. To be sure, it sincerely regarded itself as nonsectarian, indeed antisectarian, faithful in this to the example of Tone and the teachings of Davis. Cordial welcomes were given to occasional, eccentric Protestant recruits, a Yeats, a Rolleston.

"Oh, ye fair hills of holy Ireland," Ferguson begins his essay, address-
ing not the inhabitants of the island, but rather its mountains, lovely and
time-hallowed.[18] It was a shrewd choice of audience, for as we have seen,
few within any of the factions of actual Irishmen would have attended him
with full sympathy. And certainly not the Catholics, for all his protestations
of affection. "If Catholic emancipation produce repeal, so surely will repeal
produce ultimate separation; and so sure as we have a separation, so surely
will there be war levied, estates confiscated, and the Popish church established." So Head, with considerable percipience, had cautioned Heart,
and Heart, like many another kindly Protestant who followed him could
only protest: "I love this land better than any other. I cannot believe it a
hostile country." (Heart does in fact have a plan: the conversion of the
peasantry into "free, loyal, and united Protestants," but we need not
concern ourselves with such flights of fancy.)

The Abbe MacGeoghegan would no doubt have savored as poetry an
apostrophe to the fair hills of holy Ireland, but as a fact of political discourse
it would have baffled and perhaps repelled him. In his century political
argument, whether sincere or disingenuous, was addressed to particular
groups of people, or to the common judgment of mankind, but not to
aspects of landscape. Ferguson, like Davis and other nationalists, was
drawing from the deep well of romantic sentiment, which would have
seemed alien and exotic alike to MacGeoghegan and to Hume and Voltaire,
his rationalist antagonists. Romantic nationalism had come into flower on
the Continent from a soil enriched by disparate elements—an enthusiasm
for the Revolution and a revulsion against Napoleon, the enthusiasms of
Herder and the researches of the Grimms, German idealistic philosophy, a
cult of the folk and an allied if not quite identical cult of the nation, new and
powerful modes of the historical imagination. It had created ways of feelings, a climate and a culture, in which such phrases as "the inextinguishable
nation" could come easily to Ferguson's pen or to Davis's, and in which hills
rather than people could be addressed as its representative.

I once wrote of certain of Yeats's poems that their image of Ireland "is
totally autonomous, a Platonic form of which the actual island is but a
smudged and imperfect copy."[19] Red Hanrahan, although the second
stanza of his song displays a foot fetishism which I trust is idiosyncratic,
expresses it perfectly: "But purer than a tall candle before the Holy Rood /
Is Cathleen, the daughter of Houlihan."[20] But Yeats was shaping in Irish
terms, and of course in a singularly powerful and compelling manner, that
process of simultaneous abstraction and reification that, defiant of logic, is
the heart of nationalism.

For the very young Yeats, Ferguson was "the greatest poet that Ireland has produced, because the most central and the most Celtic," one "who was made by the purifying flame of National sentiment. . . ."[21] He was therefore distressed when two members of the West Briton scholarly establishment, J. P. Mahaffy and Margaret Stokes, writing on the occasion of Ferguson's death in 1886, stressed his loyal unionism. "There was never a more loyal or orderly British citizen," Mahaffy declared with an evident and faintly malicious pleasure, while Miss Stokes noted that, as Yeats was forced to admit, he had suppressed some early poems "lest, by any means, the Nationalists should claim him for their own." In a footnote, Yeats properly objects that there was a time in 1847 when Ferguson had served as chairman of the Protestant Repeal Association and had delivered in that capacity "a speech so national in tone that Emmet might have owned it." This puts matters a bit strong, but the fact remains: in that year, at the height of the famine, English mismanagement of the disaster had driven even loyalists into a rage. It was short-lived. It is more to the point that Yeats claims Ferguson for Irish nationalism through every line of verse that he wrote: "Irish singers, who are genuinely Irish in thought, subject and style, must, whether they will or no, nourish the forces that make for the political liberties of Ireland."[22]

This is generously if strategically argued, and characteristic of the suppleness with which Yeats was to conduct his politics of culture. Ferguson, Yeats tells us, "was like some aged sea-king sitting among the inland wheat and poppies—the savour of the sea about him, and its strength." It is disconcerting to turn from these words to a photograph of Ferguson, a prim, bespectacled barrister. There is more instruction to be derived from a consideration of the four cultural figures of Victorian Ireland of whom Yeats writes with respect—John Mitchel, John O'Leary, Ferguson, and Standish O'Grady. Not Davis, whom he held in a distant and ambiguous admiration, sweet-tempered and magnanimous, but whose "Ireland was artificial, an idea built up in a couple of generations by a few commonplace men."[23] Far closer to him in temperament and attitude were Ferguson and O'Grady, the one a staunch and the other a ferocious loyalist.

But of three of them—Mitchel, O'Leary, and O'Grady—it must be said that their several relationships toward Ireland were, if not artificial, then surely histrionic. When Yeats writes of them, his imagery comes as though by instinct from the arts of performance. Mitchel is the only man of Young Ireland "who had music and personality, though rancorous and devil-possessed." The more outrageous O'Grady became, in argument and metaphor, the more did "we" murmur " 'We do it wrong, being so majestical, to offer it the show of violence.' " O'Leary's "long imprisonment and longer exile, his magnificent appearance, and, above all, the fact that

he alone had personality, a point of view not made for the crowd's sake, but
for self-expression, made him magnetic to my generation."[24]

In Ireland, "personality, if it be but harsh and hard, has lovers," and
with these three, harshness took the form of a hatred of "every form of
democracy," and a Yeatsian detestation of such abstractions as philanthropy
and humanitarianism. How Mitchel and O'Leary contrived to combine
their aristocratic hauteur with their Fenianism, a mass movement composed largely of working-class men with a fondness for lachrymose ballads,
is far less a mystery than it might on the surface appear. But with O'Grady
there is no shadow of contradiction, for as Yeats says, "he had given all his
heart to the smaller Irish landowners, to whom he belonged, and with
whom his childhood had been spent, and for them he wrote his books, and
would soon rage over their failings in certain famous passages that many
men would repeat to themselves like poets' rhymes. All round us people
talked or wrote for victory's sake, and were hated for their victories—but
here was a man whose rage was a swan-song over all that he held most dear,
and to whom for that very reason every irish imaginative writer owed a
portion of his soul."

Swan song: again a theatrical image. But although those passages in
which O'Grady turns with scorn and a palpable nobility of being upon his
own class were indeed famous for a time, one wonders if Yeats, for one, did
not repeat to himself passages of a different tenor, of which an example is of
course provided by the irrepressible Malcolm Brown. Was Ireland,
O'Grady asks, to be surrendered by its feckless gentility to "this waste,
dark, howling mass of colliding interests, mad about the main chance—the
pence-counting shopkeeper; the publican, the isolated, crafty farmer; the
labourer tied to his soil, or tramping perhaps to the polling booth, as an
enfranchised citizen, a member of the sovereign people, a ruler in the land,
with the wolf on his right hand, and the poor house on the left, and in front,
at his *disposal*, the whole property of the island."[25]

O'Grady's prose style, although like Mitchel he is much in Carlyle's
debt, deserves to be called inimitable. As an expression of mood, however,
his pamphlets may be placed beside three poems exactly their contemporaries by the now-aged Ferguson, "The Curse of the Joyces," "At the Polo-
Ground," and "In Carey's Footsteps."[26] The first, supposedly set upon the
day of the Maamtrasna hangings in Galway on 15 December 1882, is a curse
uttered upon the Land League leaders, "panders and apologists of crime,"
who have coached unlettered peasants like the Joyces through "these three
awful years." The other two, Browningesque dramatic monologues that
take up the murders of Cavendish and Burke by the Invincibles in May
1882, is more complex in its assessments but equally implacable. Like

O'Grady, Ferguson saw that political nationalism lacked even a Cairbre-Cathead.

There had been a time, so he wrote to a friend in 1885, when he had sympathized with Young Ireland's aspirations toward "a restoration of Grattan's Parliament in which all the estates of the realm should have their old places. But I have quite ceased to sympathise with their successors who have converted their high aspirations to a social war of classes carried on by the vilest means."[27] Ferguson had taken his place in the long, winding procession of literary patriots who discovered that nationalism was much messier than they had supposed. At the head of that procession, Maire and Conor Cruise O'Brien have placed William Drennan, United Irishman and patriot, who found himself apprehensive as to his plans to "commit arms and rights to such savages as these Catholics?" His sister, Mrs. McTier, writing to him a few years after the collapse of their cause, speaks of a "singing procession" of Catholics: "I begin to fear these people and think, like the Jews, they will regain their native land."[28]

In the eighties, with Ferguson gloomy and O'Grady in full song, youthful ardor was carrying Yeats into nationalist circles peopled by "medical students and shop assistants," the great-grandchildren, it may be supposed, of Mrs. McTier's processional Catholics. It was, as Yeats would tell such men of birth and education as he could persuade to support him, a baptism "of the gutter," and from there a straight line would carry him, decades later, to the leaders of the crowd and their "abounding gutter."

Seamus Deane has written:

> Cultural nationalism is thus transformed into a species of literary unionism. Sir Samuel Ferguson is the most explicit supporter of this variation, although, from Edgeworth to Yeats, it remains a tacit assumption. The story of the spiritual heroics of a fading class—the Ascendancy—in the face of a transformed Catholic "nation"— was rewritten in a variety of ways in literature—as the story of the pagan Fianna replaced by a pallid Christianity, of young love replaced by old age (Deirdre, Oisin), of aristocracy replaced by mob-democracy. The fertility of these rewritings is all the more remarkable in that they were recruitments by the fading class of the myths of renovation which belonged to their opponents. Irish culture became the new property of those who were losing their grip on Irish land. The effect of these rewritings was to transfer blame for the drastic condition of the country from the Ascendancy to the Catholic middle classes or to their English counterparts. It was in essence a strategic retreat from political to cultural supremacy.[29]

A bold move, and characteristic of Deane's cavalryman's approach to the wars of culture, and yet, despite the heavy burden which it rests upon poor Deirdre's graceful shoulders, an arguable thesis. By suggesting that

Yeats may have been a literary unionist, however, Dr. Deane has contrived
what is probably the only generalization about him upon which Dr. Do-
noghue and Conor Cruise O'Brien would join forces in opposition. But
this, fortunately, has not been my subject, or at least, not quite.

My purpose rather has been to argue that nationalism, a creation of
romanticism, provided writers (and ordinary people) of the nineteenth
century with new ways of thinking and feeling about their country, and set
the terms of discourse. The spiritual heroics of a fading ascendancy class
required the vocabulary of that discourse no less than did a Pearse or a
Corkery. "Who dares sustain the strangled calumny that you are not the
land of our love?" young Ferguson had asked the hills of holy Ireland.
Occasionally, and in the tart accents of his native Belfast, a Mrs. McTier has
answered him.

James S. Donnelly, Jr.
THE LAND QUESTION IN
NATIONALIST POLITICS

THIS ESSAY is primarily concerned with the ways in which Irish
nationalist leaders, both constitutionalist and revolutionary, viewed the
land question, as they defined it, in relation to their political goals from the
late eighteenth to the early twentieth century. It would have been difficult
at almost any time between 1790 and 1921 for nationalist leaders to ignore
the land question altogether, even if they had wanted to do so. In one form
or another, and sometimes in several forms at once, the land question was
nearly always there, demanding attention. Widespread, organized agrarian
discontent was admittedly discontinuous, with a pronounced tendency to
rise and fall in accordance with economic fluctuations, particularly in prices
and crop yields. But even during the intervals between outbreaks of
agrarian unrest, nationalist chieftains could still feel the heat of the land
question.

From the perspective of nationalist leaders and organizations, the
persistence of agrarian discontent created both opportunities and difficulties. On the one hand, the prevalence of intense agrarian grievances
provided enormous possibilities for mass mobilization behind nationalist
goals, at least as long as the leaders could convincingly demonstrate that the
redress of such grievances hinged upon making progress toward larger
political objectives or upon actually achieving them. It was not always
necessary for nationalist chieftains to advocate radical agrarian reform in
order to achieve mass political mobilization, much less to orchestrate a
genuine agrarian agitation. The career of Daniel O'Connell showed abun-
dantly how much could be accomplished without doing either. But it was
necessary to take account of and to channel agrarian grievances in practical
ways. This required much more than the simple advocacy of radical agrar-

ian reform. As the Fenian leaders of the 1860s discovered, it was not a winning position in the countryside to propound peasant proprietorship as the solution to the land question while insisting that this was impossible to achieve under existing political conditions and so ought to be postponed until the connection with Britain was ended. The events of 1879-86 showed the wisdom of the New Departure strategy of coupling agrarian and nationalist demands and pressing them in tandem. Yet the concessions of successive British governments to Irish agrarian demands eventually came to be seen by most nationalist leaders as threatening rural support for Home Rule. Instead of hastening the progress toward peasant proprietorship, they hindered it.

If effective exploitation of the land question opened up tempting vistas, agrarian unrest could also pose grave political risks for nationalist leaders and organizations. By long tradition Irish agrarian rebels were addicted to the use of violence and intimidation. In the early nineteenth century there were several great bursts of agrarian violence, which were usually sustained for a few years at a time, as in 1806-11, 1813-16, 1821-24, and the early 1830s. Agrarian movements after 1850 exhibited less violence, but it was still a salient feature of nearly all of them. For the leaders of constitutional nationalism especially, the association of violence with agrarian discontent caused a variety of difficulties. The government repression that violence invited could curb the operations of nationalist political organizations; moderate allies or potential supporters could be frightened away from nationalist movements whose leaders excused or seemed to encourage agrarian crime. There was also the danger that nationalist chieftains might not be able to control the forces of agrarian discontent if they actually sought to direct such forces toward agrarian as well as political goals.

Several kinds of class conflict were also inherent in Irish rural unrest. It was impossible for nationalist leaders to become serious agrarian reformers without alienating the vast majority of Irish landowners, but many leading nationalists, especially in the early nineteenth century, ardently hoped to attract substantial landlord support for their political goals and were consequently reluctant to place their organizations at the service of agrarian radicalism. Even after 1880 some nationalist leaders, including several of the most illustrious, entertained a vision of the new Irish political order in which landlords as individuals would continue to make major contributions to public life. This vision prompted them to seek a settlement of the land question on terms that were relatively advantageous to landlords as a class.

Whatever their attitudes toward landlords, nationalist leaders also faced the additional problem that other class conflicts were imbedded in the land question. In pursuing nationalist goals, political leaders generally sought to construct mass movements that overrode or subordinated class differences and antagonisms, such as those between graziers and large farmers on the one hand and smallholders and landless laborers on the other. But such antagonisms repeatedly broke out of the safe channels into which nationalist leaders tried to direct them, and in tending to the interests of one side or the other, leaders ran the risk of dividing their movements.

The survey of nationalist movements that follows examines how leaders tried to resolve the various political dilemmas posed by the land question, with particular emphasis on their responses to the problems of violence and class conflict. In the prefamine period nationalist leaders enjoyed the advantage of being able to draw upon and to stimulate the extremely widespread notion among Catholics at the popular level that the achievement of nationalist aims would be followed more or less immediately by a completely new and just solution of the land question. Whether it was the republic sought by the United Irishmen after 1794, the drive for Catholic emancipation under O'Connell in the 1820s, or O'Connell's campaign for repeal and the restoration of the Irish parliament in the 1840s, each of these was associated in the minds of Catholic peasants and farmers with wholesale agrarian change: sweeping reductions in rents, tithes, and taxes, or even (when the millenarian mood prevailed) the total abolition of all three.[1] As the writer of a Rockite notice posted in Tipperary declared in December 1821, "English laws must be curbed in, for we will never be satisfied until we have the Irish parliament and [the] king crowned in Ireland as there formerly was; the sword is drawn and the hand of God is with us and tyranny will be soon swept away."[2]

The national leaders of the United Irishmen in the 1790s never committed themselves to anything so revolutionary as the abolition of rents or a general redistribution of land. They did advocate the abolition of tithes, perhaps the most burning of all agrarian grievances up to the late 1830s, but in other respects their ideas about property rights were safely orthodox.[3] They did not proclaim this message to the world, however, nor did they try to restrain their local agents, who often whetted the appetites of new recruits for the confiscation of estates and the sweeping redistribution of land.[4] The case has been made that the national leaders of the United Irishmen were deeply afraid of social revolution and that their alliance with the French was partly designed to forestall it: professional military assistance from France would enable them to gain a relatively quick victory and to control popular pressures for the wholesale division of landed estates.[5] But they were not so fearful of the rural masses that they refused to ride the tiger of agrarian discontent. Had they succeeded with French help in establishing their republic, it appears likely that the tiger would have carried them much farther than they wanted to go.[6]

How utterly different was the position and the practice of Daniel O'Connell! Such was his fear of, and acute distaste for, the violence of Irish rural society in his day that he always refused to ride the tiger. Though he had long denounced the Irish tithe system, he declined to place himself at the head of the Tithe War in the early 1830s because he was convinced that he could not control the agitation or the violence surrounding it. Writing to a highly placed Whig friend early in 1833, O'Connell disclosed his revulsion over the alarming state of affairs:

There is an almost universal organisation going on. It is not confined to one or two counties. It is, I repeat, *almost universal.* I do not believe there is any man in the rank of a comfortable farmer engaged, not one man, probably, entitled to vote. But all the poverty of our counties is being organised. There never yet was, as I believe, so general a disposition for that species of insurrectionary outrages. . . . All I can add in the way of advice is that the more troops are sent over here, the better. In every point of view it is best to increase the king's troops.[7]

If volumes of words are the measure, no other Irish nationalist leader of the nineteenth century denounced agrarian secret societies more vehemently or more frequently than O'Connell. And these denunciations were backed up by "O'Connell's police"—a succession of organizational devices at the local level designed to quell Whiteboys, faction fighters, and other disturbers of the peace.[8]

This strenuous opposition to agrarian violence must have alienated many of O'Connell's rural supporters. But the political costs were partly offset by the fact that O'Connell acted as defense counsel for more Whiteboys than any other barrister of his day. Among the cases which he adopted were some of the most gruesome and chilling agrarian crimes ever committed in Ireland.[9] Though such a pattern of professional activity, pursued most intensely in the early 1820s, hardly made O'Connell a Whiteboy sympathizer, it must have helped his standing with those who were. The rich folklore that came to surround O'Connell in his role as the Counsellor, a folklore that attested to his technical legal prowess and to his ability (much exaggerated) to save Whiteboys from hanging or penal banishment to Botany Bay, was extremely useful politically.[10]

But this was only the beginning of O'Connell's capacity to attract broad rural support while denouncing agrarian secret societies and their violence. As a nationalist agitator, O'Connell's most remarkable talent was his ability to channel a rich assortment of popular grievances—agrarian and otherwise—into his mass political organizations. "Grievance letters," as they were called in the 1820s, poured into the offices of the central body in Dublin from branches throughout much of the country, and though the central body did nothing about most of these complaints, the perception was created and fostered that the national leadership wanted to see these grievances redressed. In the case of agrarian grievances this perception was encouraged by strong rhetoric about landlord oppression and by endless assurances that the achievement of emancipation or repeal would bring utopia to pass.[11] What his political enemies perhaps hated most about O'Connell's agitations was the way in which he and his colleagues converted the Catholic and Repeal associations into vast storehouses of popular grievances and then proceeded to claim that these organizations were all that stood between the maintenance of social order and popular insurrection. After taking note of nineteen agrarian murders in 1844 in just two counties, all reportedly preceded by "the wholesale slaughter of the clearance system," O'Connell intoned his usual refrain: "It is the Repeal Association and the hopes it excites which prevent a rebellion."[12]

As much as O'Connell wished to excite and channel the hopes of Catholic peasants and farmers, he was almost equally concerned with how he and his repeal movement were regarded by the Protestant gentry. In the early and mid-1840s, O'Connell placed great importance on the task of breaking down the general resistance of the Irish Protestant gentry to the idea of repeal.[13] He believed it possible to win over at least a significant section of the landed elite to his cause. This was an aim that he shared with the Young Irelanders, who after the showdown at Clontarf in 1843 became increasingly disenchanted with his leadership of the repeal movement. Among other things, the adhesion of many of the Protestant gentry would legitimize the social respectability of the repeal cause, which had always been treated as a cryptorevolutionary movement in British political circles. In 1844 O'Connell was even prepared to offer the leadership of the movement to some of the nobility and gentry who were not thoroughgoing repealers, namely, the federalists. In a confidential letter to one of them in October of that year, O'Connell declared: "It is perfectly certain that the aristocratic federalists, if they came forward *now*, would be allowed to lead and conduct the cause. . . . At all events you may rely on my *discretion* as well as my anxiety to place the property and rank of Ireland at the head of the Repeal cause—federalist or otherwise."[14]

This intriguing letter was part of a short-lived attempt by O'Connell to chart a new political course by moving to the right, away from simple repeal of the Union. He quickly retreated when his indefinite federal proposals were coldly received not only by other nationalists, especially the Young Irelanders, but also by the Whigs and the federalists themselves.[15] For our purposes, what is interesting about this and other examples of O'Connell's persistent wooing of the Protestant gentry is its connection in his mind with erecting barriers against agrarian rebellion. In the same letter of October 1844 he told his federalist friend, "You know that if the people were not kept in hopes and under control, their natural tendency would be to a revolutionary convulsion; . . . and you must feel how incumbent it is upon *us* to save the country from any convulsion and give it the benefits of a resident nobility and gentry."[16]

This tenderness toward the Protestant landed elite, however, did not prevent O'Connell from becoming a pronounced agrarian reformer in the mid-1840s. The extent of his shift in position can be exaggerated; it had a conservative basis, though O'Connell realized that it reduced his hopes of attracting landlord support for repeal. The agrarian program that he and the Repeal Association formally advanced in 1845 was a mixture of diverse elements that varied greatly in their social significance and political contentiousness. Some elements were not likely to raise the hackles of Irish landowners. Included in this category were the establishment of country agricultural schools, the promotion of public works on a limited scale through grants and loans, the sale of holdings on crown estates to the occupying tenants in small lots, and a scheme for creating peasant proprietors on reclaimed wasteland. Graziers could not have been enthusiastic about O'Connell's proposal for compulsory conacre plots on pasture farms, but since the compulsion would not have applied to ranches of less than two hundred acres, many graziers would have been exempt, and thus O'Connell was far from advancing a laborers' charter. On the other hand, several elements of the program were highly contentious and were bound to arouse widespread landlord opposition. In this category were the legalization of tenant right in Ulster, the payment of compensation for tenants' improvements, and restrictions on the landlords' power of ejectment. "This was," as Joseph Lee has declared, "the most radical land reform programme proposed by any major public figure at that date."[17]

What explains the timing of these radical proposals, and what was their political purpose? The O'Connellite program was largely an outgrowth of profound disappointment among repealers over the conclusions of the famous Devon Commission. After exhaustively examining the subject of landlord-tenant relations for more than a year (November 1843–February 1845), the commission decided to recommend no fundamental changes in the law. Like other repealers, O'Connell was dismayed by the extreme modesty of the commission's recommendations, and he offered his own far more ambitious program in order to underline their complete inadequacy.[18] In addition, the attractions of pursuing substantial but piecemeal reforms within the existing constitutional structure had gradually been regaining the ascendancy in O'Connell's mind ever since the setback at

Clontarf in 1843 seemed to demonstrate that the basic strategy of the repeal movement had failed. This full-scale return to pragmatism in O'Connell's thinking and behavior, with its obvious implications for a resumption of the Whig alliance, was of course the central element in O'Connell's quarrel with the Young Irelanders. And it was no accident that as that quarrel reached its climax in 1846, O'Connell formally reiterated his commitment to radical changes in landlord-tenant relations.[19] This tactic was partly designed to cast doubt on the readiness of the troublesome Young Irelanders to press for such changes.

Yet too much ought not be made of O'Connell's belated conversion to agrarian radicalism. Joseph Lee has called attention to O'Connell's parliamentary declaration of June 1846 in favor of fixity of tenure. His motivation, according to Lee, was his fear of social revolution in the context of the threat of famine.[20] But for O'Connell, this dread was hardly new, and a loose endorsement of fixity can be found in O'Connell's correspondence more than a year earlier. In April 1845 he had warned that unless real remedies were applied to the land question, there might soon be "such a servile war in Ireland as has been unknown since the days of [the] French *Jacoterie* or of the English *Jack Cade*." "Nothing will do," he then declared, "but giving some kind or other of fixity of tenure to the occupiers; and especially an absolute right of recompense for all substantial improvements. I am ready to take (as to the security of tenure) as mitigated a measure as is consistent with the principle."[21] The obvious indeterminacy of O'Connell's position in April 1845 makes his ambiguous parliamentary endorsement of June 1846 look like an advance, but the declaration involved only a few words, and the looseness and equivocation of 1845 probably still applied.

Moreover, demands voiced in Conciliation Hall or declarations made at Westminster were very different from stirring land demonstrations in the Irish countryside. When the Whigs (not to mention the Tories) showed no inclination to embody any of his agrarian proposals in legislation, O'Connell allowed them to pass into oblivion. To stump the country for his agrarian program, to lead a grass-roots agitation of that kind, never entered his head. In his view, while monster meetings on behalf of repeal prevented a rebellion, monster meetings on behalf of radical land reform would have sparked a conflagration.

The approach of the Young Irelanders to agrarian issues was more complicated than is usually realized. In a significant essay entitled "Udalism and Feudalism" published in 1841, Thomas Davis argued on economic and cultural grounds for turning Irish tenants into peasant proprietors. His essay breathed deep hostility to the landlords as a class. "While the people remain serfs," he declared, "they will be trampled beggars. Free the

peasantry from the aristocracy. All else is vanity and vexation of spirit."
Davis also addressed himself to the question of which had priority—
nationality or proprietorship. He asserted that because the issue of tenure
was a life-or-death matter for the people, it should not be postponed until
Ireland had won its national rights. But he also rejected the idea of
deferring the struggle for national rights until the tenure issue had been
solved, since Irish landlords, "while supported by a foreign army," would
never yield to a demand for peasant proprietorship. In the end he resolved
the question by advocating that the social end of peasant proprietorship be
sought through the prior struggle for national rights. Davis was not only a
radical in theory but also a militant by inclination. "At all events," he
concluded, "let the question [of land and its relationship to the national
struggle] be spoken of, written of, taught, preached, agitated, in fairs and
markets, in churches and by the fireside (for it is a solemn subject and
worthy to engross us). . . ."[22]

Davis's hostility to Irish landlords and his agrarian militancy were also
reflected in the early issues of the *Nation* newspaper. The inaugural issue of
15 October 1842 contained the following lines from a poem by James
Clarence Mangan: "We announce a new era—be this our first news—
/ When the serf-grinding landlords will shake in their shoes."[23] In another
early number a discussion of Ribbonmen, or agrarian rebels, led to the
startling conclusion that "though the laws of man are against them, they are
justified in the sight of God." O'Connell must have been appalled. He had
intended that the *Nation* would win Protestants to the repeal cause, a
strategy that could hardly succeed if Davis continued to indulge in this kind
of poetry and editorializing. O'Connell forcefully indicated his displeasure.
To this was added the view of Charles Gavan Duffy, whose conviction was
that, apart from a military situation involving "mortal peril" to England, the
Irish national struggle could be won only through a political "combination
of all classes." Under the joint pressure of Duffy and O'Connell, Davis
became an enthusiast for the original mission of the *Nation* as O'Connell
conceived it, and agrarian radicalism quickly disappeared from its pages.[24]

Indeed, by the time that the Young Irelanders split away from O'Connell and the Repeal Association in mid-1846, it could fairly be said that they
had no agrarian policy at all. For this there were two main reasons. First, in
the firm belief of the Young Irelanders and especially at that political
juncture, repeal—the full measure of it—was a holy cause that could not
cede priority, even in the short run, to the advocacy of land reforms or other
subsidiary issues. Second, even more than the O'Connellites, the Young
Ireland leaders until late in 1847 were addicted to the illusion of a pan-class
nationalist coalition that would embrace a substantial section of the Protes-

tant gentry. Wedded to this illusion were not only the risk-averse landlord William Smith O'Brien, one of the few landed Protestant converts to Duffy's "combination of all classes," but also the adventurous militant John Mitchell, though by late 1847 Mitchel was fast shedding his old faith, partly under the influence of the radical agrarian theorist James Fintan Lalor. Unlike O'Connell, who was belatedly willing to risk foreclosing the possibility of landlord support for repeal when he espoused radical agrarian reform in 1845, the Young Ireland leaders long sought to avoid divisive social issues as they solicited the gentry backing that never came. In the end, of course, the Young Irelanders were forced to abandon their grand illusion by the relentless logic of tragic events, including the great clearances of 1847-48. They could either join fully in the general denunciation of the appalling conduct of "exterminating" landlords, or they could forfeit any claim to be regarded as Irish nationalists.[25]

Still, it cannot be said that the Young Irelanders had ever committed themselves to an agrarian program before the farcical Rising of 1848. When such a program was offered to them, they spurned it. In the pages of their own newspaper James Fintan Lalor set forth a theory, goals, and a strategy. According to his theory, the land of Ireland, though privately owned, belonged ultimately to the whole community, and the current occupiers of the soil had rights that were the practical equivalent of co-ownership with the proprietors. Endowed with such rights, the tenants were entitled at a minimum to fair rents and security of tenure. To achieve these goals, Lalor advocated what he called "moral insurrection," that is, a national strike against the payment of rent until the British government and Irish landlords instituted a new agrarian order that would provide tenants with economic security.[26] Lalor's strategy wildly assumed that in a country prostrated by famine the tenants still possessed the discipline and energy to engage in an organized rent strike. This assumption provoked Charles Gavan Duffy's biting comment that Lalor's "angry peasants, chafing like chained tigers, were creatures of the imagination—not the living people through whom we had to act."[27] Only a few members of the Irish Confederation, the organization founded by the Young Irelanders to rival the O'Connellite Repeal Association, were prepared to endorse the kind of agrarian campaign that Lalor advocated.

But for politicians, whether revolutionaries or constitutionalists, defeats are the crucibles from which fundamental reassessments come. Just as O'Connell and the Repeal Association shifted to a more radical agrarian position in the wake of their setback at Clontarf, and just as many Fenians sharply altered both their posture and their practice after the abortive Rising of 1867, so too did some of the Young Irelanders who escaped transportation or self-exile decide after the Rising of 1848 that harsh realities required a fresh start on a new basis. By no means all of the Young Irelanders who remained in the country and resumed their political careers took this approach, but among those who did was Charles Gavan Duffy. Soon after his release from jail in 1849, Duffy publicly repudiated what had been an axiom of the moderate Young Irelanders in the years before the Rising, namely, their belief that it was essential to avoid becoming embroiled in class conflict between landlord and tenant. In effect, the new doctrine, proclaimed by Duffy in the revived *Nation* newspaper in September 1849, was pragmatically O'Connellite in giving primacy in the short term to something other than the holy grail of repeal. Temporarily, the struggle for independence must be superseded by strenuous efforts "to bring back Ireland to health and strength by stopping the system of extermination."[28] But Duffy raced ahead of O'Connellite orthodoxy when he also declared it to be "the first duty of a national association to assault" the existing land system.[29]

No doubt the political circumstances of 1849-50 were quite different from those of 1845. Instead of monopolizing popular politics, as in 1845, the Repeal Association was virtually extinct by 1849-50. And during the interim spontaneous local activity had brought into existence many tenant-protection societies in the south and tenant-right bodies in the north. These were open and legal organizations in contrast to the secret and violent societies of traditional Whiteboyism. Thus they were amenable to much greater control from the top and could conceivably be yoked to a parliamentary campaign for agrarian reforms. This is what the leaders of the tenant-right agitation of the early 1850s soght to achieve.

Insofar as the agrarian demands of the tenant-right movement went beyond those of the O'Connellites in 1845-46, they were extensions of earlier claims: all tenants, not just those in Ulster, should be allowed to sell the interest in their holdings at the highest price they could obtain, and tenants were to be made more secure in the occupation of their holdings by having their rents determined by independent valuators. Coupled with the further demand for security of tenure as long as the rent was paid, this position amounted to what was later denominated as the "three Fs" of fair rents, fixity of tenure, and free sale. Yet the distinctive contribution of those nationalist leaders who helped to guide the movement, in association with nonnationalists, was less the program they enunciated and more their readiness to put themselves at the head of a popular agrarian campaign. It was this characteristic which marks the tenant-right movement of the early 1850s as the real beginning of an agrarian political tradition in which local, national, and parliamentary activities were closely intertwined.

The intertwining was far from perfect, much too far to ensure success. The most glaring weaknesses were located at the parliamentary level. The new Liberal party of Gladstone and Bright had yet to be born, and none of the three major British political parties of the 1850s was at all inclined to curb landlord power. In addition, the number of Irish M.P.s willing to support the demands of the Tenant League was embarrassingly small. Even apart from the sectional and religious divisions that plagued and distracted the movement, the harsh parliamentary realities were alone sufficient to doom it to failure.[30]

The Tenant League's failure, and the sources of that failure, were hardly calculated to encourage the early Fenians to repeat the experiment or even to view Ireland's agrarian problems as the vehicle by which to achieve an effective mobilization of the countryside. In his highly revisionist analysis of Fenianism in Ireland between the late 1850s and the early 1880s, Dr. R.V. Comerford has argued, with reference to the period before 1867, that "criticism of the Fenian leadership along the lines that it was too engrossed in doctrinaire republicanism to formulate an agrarian policy and attract the hard-pressed tenant farmers is . . . both mistaken and seriously misconceived."[31] I agree with Dr. Comerford that the Fenians before 1867 "in the eyes of friend and foe stood for both expropriation of the landlords and for a redistribution of land," with the result that Fenianism "was by its nature anathema not only to the landlords but to the generality of farmers."[32] The common talk in the 1860s about the Irish exiles' return from across the sea and the accompanying assumption that they would claim or be rewarded with places on the land now held by others must have been disquieting to many graziers and large farmers. This is a point that was not at all appreciated by historians before it was effectively developed by Dr. Comerford.[33]

But if Dr. Comerford is correct in asserting that the Fenian organ, the *Irish People*, "had much to say about the land question," was its agrarian policy designed to attract strong tenant-farmer support? Like their nationalist predecessors, the Fenian leaders were aware that sharp divisions existed in the countryside below the landowning elite. Unlike the Young Irelanders, whose ideas they adopted in some other respects, the Fenian leaders harbored no illusions about the gentry,[34] but like the Young Irelanders, the shrank from exploiting class differences and antagonisms for political purposes. Insofar as they did take sides, they were against the larger farmers and the Catholic clergy, two groups whose political weight in rural areas it was costly to lose.[35] But to gain the solid allegiance of the small farmers or the laborers, it was not enough to discuss their distinctive needs in the columns of the *Irish People*. Instead, it was essential to demonstrate that their local and immediate concerns deserved and would receive priority of attention. In charting the shift in the geographical and social composition of Fenianism in the late 1860s and 1870s, Dr. Comerford seems to make exactly this point.[36]

The remarkable success which the Fenians enjoyed in building up their organization in the west and the northwest during the 1870s was mainly the result of their readiness not only to identify themselves rhetorically with the interests of the small farmers, but also to engage in agrarian agitation. Besides being the enemies of rack-renting or evicting landlords and the proponents of peasant proprietorship, these so-called Ribbon Fenians were also the loudest critics of graziers and the grazing system. They called repeatedly for the breaking up of the great grass farms and for the redistribution of the land among the smallholders. This stance largely explains the local electoral appeal of John O'Connor Power, who in 1874, while still a member of the Supreme Council of the IRB, was returned to Parliament as a Home Rule M.P. for County Mayo, and who became an ally and then a rival of Charles Stewart Parnell in the militant wing of the Irish parliamentary party of the late 1870s. Matt Harris, another Fenian, who served as O'Connor Power's election manager in 1874, was instrumental in the establishment two years later of the Ballinasloe Tenants' Defence Association.[37] And as Samuel Clark has shown, many local Fenians took an active part in organizing the demonstrations that led to the formation in 1879 of the Land League of Mayo, the forerunner of the Irish National Land League.[38]

But the agrarian radicalism of western Fenianism, and especially its fairly uninhibited use of the rhetoric and tactics of class warfare directed against graziers, caused it to be viewed as a disruptive and dangerous force by other sections of the Land League coalition. For the IRB and the Clan na Gael, the prominence of O'Connor Power was an enormous irritant because he was regarded as a traitorous parliamentarian even after it became officially permissible for Fenians to participate in the agrarian and parliamentary campaigns headed by Parnell. But the root source of dissension stemmed from the desire of national Land League leaders, Parnellite M.P.s, and Fenian chieftains to build a broadly based coalition embracing nationalists of all social classes. The national executive of the Land League, though largely controlled by Fenians or ex-Fenians, increasingly viewed its mission as the creation of a truly national movement that would bridge the differing interests of large and small farmers, graziers and laborers, townsmen and country people, by focusing on common objectives and the common landlord enemy. Parnell had early won the political support of large farmers and graziers, as represented, for example, by the Central

Tenants' Defence Association, and he was determined to retain their allegiance while he bid for the backing of smallholders in the west and elsewhere. Even James Daly, whose *Connaught Telegraph* was frequently given over to vehement denunciations of graziers and the grazing system, was willing for a time to restrain the rhetoric of class warfare in the interests of nationalist unity.[39]

Not only did the national leadership of the Land League refuse to lend any support to a Fenian-inspired antigrazier agitation in the west, but it also shifted its tactics in 1880 and 1881 in a way that was clearly advantageous to the interests of large farmers and detrimental to those of small ones. Under the direction of the national executive, the emphasis of the League's policy changed from frustrating the eviction of small farmers to encouraging tenants to refuse to pay unjust rents unless they were immediately faced with dispossession. Large farmers strongly preferred the new policy, known as "paying rent at the point of the bayonet," because it allowed them to exert maximum pressure on their landlords without the pain of having to surrender their holdings as part of a common sacrifice. Small farmers, with fewer resources, fared better under the original policy, by which the holdings of some of them were surrendered to the landlord and then boycotted, a tactic known as "letting the farms go to the emergency men."[40] As a result of the shift in policy and of the accompanying reduction in legal assistance provided by the national executive of the League to embattled small tenants, evictions in Mayo soared in 1880 and 1881. The unity of the Land League coalition was badly strained by this shift in policy, and in Mayo the Fenians were so outraged by the central League's neglect of the smallholders that they repudiated their allegiance to it.[41] Demobilization is not too strong a word to describe what happened in Mayo in 1881, and the inability of the Parnellites to secure protection in the Land Act of 1881 for tenants in arrears only increased the disenchantment and alienation of western smallholders.[42]

The passage of the Land Act in August 1881 initiated a series of events—the imprisonment of Parnell and his chief lieutenants, the issuance of the No Rent Manifesto, the suppression of the Land League, and an upsurge in agrarian violence—that necessitated a general political reassessment among nationalists. In this reassessment the relationship between the land question and nationalism was bound to figure prominently. The 1881 Land Act obviously had not solved the land question in the way that nationalist leaders wanted it solved, namely, through the establishment of peasant proprietorship. Even within its own terms of reference, as a measure designed to pull the rug from under the agrarian agitators by appeasing their followers, the act was grossly inadequate. Probably about half of all Irish tenants were excluded from its provisions, either because their rents were seriously in arrears or because they were leaseholders. On the other hand, the act and the events which it set in train deeply divided the nationalist-agrarian coalition headed by Parnell. Even if the League's policy of testing the act had not been rendered impossible by the jailing of nationalist leaders, it would have been difficult to stem the tide of eager eligible tenants into the land courts. The No Rent Manifesto had gravely alarmed the more conservative members of the Parnellite coalition, especially the Catholic hierarchy and clergy, and even many moderates and radicals opposed it or refused to take it seriously. At the grass roots it was widely ignored and quickly discredited. Above all, the suppression of the Land League by the government, coupled with the return of agricultural prosperity and the sweetener of court-mandated rent reductions, foreclosed many political options on the agrarian front. Even if Parnell had wanted to restart the engine of agrarian agitation, the prospects for success were dismal. [43]

In this context Parnell, ever the resourceful opportunist, always mindful of the diverse elements of his coalition, decided to lurch to the right, not only subordinating agrarian issues to nationalism but to what was, in the eyes of many, a rather debased form of nationalism at that—Home Rule. The essence of this rightward lurch was the Kilmainham "treaty" of April 1882 with Gladstone, in which Parnell undertook in effect to halt agrarian agitation in return for the admission of leaseholders and tenants in arrears to the benefits of the 1881 act and the extension of the facilities for land purchase provided in that measure. "The accomplishment of the programme" thus outlined, declared Parnell in a famous letter, "would, in my judgment, be regarded by the country as a practical settlement of the land question, and would, I feel sure, enable us to cooperate cordially in the future with the Liberal party in forwarding Liberal principles. . . ."[44]

What is perhaps most surprising about Parnell's rightward repositioning in 1882 was how little opposition it aroused, even in those quarters from which opposition might have been expected. [45] The general support of Irish America and in particular of the Clan na Gael was hardly a foregone conclusion. After all, Home Rule was not the self-government of John Devoy's New Departure proposals of 1878-79, nor was the extension of the purchase clauses of the 1881 Land Act the equivalent of peasant proprietorship, though Devoy and other American Fenians eventually persuaded themselves that Parnell was on the right track. Partly, this was because most of them were interested in forging a united Irish-American political movement and because the revived emphasis on a political goal appeared to offer the best prospects for unity. [46]

The main reason Irish Americans did not oppose Parnell's position was the highly negative reaction of Devoy and other Irish-American leaders to Michael Davitt's ill-timed and ill-judged scheme for land nationalization, which was an adaptation of the ideas propounded by Henry George in his famous book, *Progress and Poverty*. Almost from the time that he unveiled his scheme in May and June 1882, Davitt found himself excoriated by nationalists of all shades. In effect, what he was proposing was a continuation of the agrarian struggle with the goal now defined not as individual ownership of Irish farms by their current tenants, but as state ownership of the land, with Irish farmers holding as tenants of the state and paying not rent but rather a tax whose total amount Davitt estimated at a sum only half that of current rents. Since under Davitt's scheme the industrial and commercial classes would have paid no tax, and since the state would have provided agricultural laborers with plots of land, presumably cut out of farmers' holdings, this was not a plan with automatic general rural appeal, quite apart from its abandonment of individual ownership. Though Davitt explicitly denied that his scheme represented a challenge to Parnell, it was generally regarded as such, and its socialist humanitarianism and implicit internationalism obscured its nationalism. As a result, Davitt not only marginalized himself politically, both in Ireland and in Irish America, but he also drove Irish-American extremists much closer to the rightward-leaning Parnell than many of them would have gone on their own.[47]

In Ireland as well, Parnell's shift to the right was accepted with remarkably little opposition. The Phoenix Park murders of May 1882 were of great importance in this respect: the general revulsion over these grisly killings discredited political extremism, sanctioned moderation, and legitimized Parnell's retreat from agrarian militancy into the quieter path of respectable constitutional nationalism. Only a handful of Parnell's old land war allies were really capable of effectively challenging his new line, but none of them made a serious, sustained attempt to do so. John Dillon, an agrarian militant who hankered for a continuation of the struggle and rejected the new policy, retired temporarily from politics. And Michael Davitt, while disagreeing with Parnell on numerous issues, settled for concessions on certain social questions and accepted service under Parnell in the new Irish National League founded in October 1882. Even as he moved to the right to construct a centrally dominated, tightly controlled, national political organization capped by a disciplined, partly salaried parliamentary party almost slavishly loyal to himself, Parnell did not abandon the interests of many of those on his left. He helped to secure passage of the important Arrears Act in 1882, which brought the weakest Irish tenants—perhaps a quarter of the total—within the scope of the 1881 Land

Act. And he publicly advocated the claims of agricultural laborers to allotments and improved housing as well as to the parliamentary and local franchises.[48]

Nevertheless, under Parnell, agrarian issues, even those of the greatest magnitude, were firmly subordinated to the quest for Home Rule. This was clearly demonstrated by his handling of the question of land purchase. Gladstone coupled his Home Rule bill of 1886 with a large measure of land purchase. Initially, as much as £120 million of government credit was to be used to finance the sale of Irish estates, although Gladstone was soon obliged to cut the figure to £50 million. Even though the measure was only optional and offered terms that were highly favorable to Irish landlords, Parnell, unlike most of his party colleagues, was disposed to accept it. "We think," he declared, "that by giving up as much as we can to the landlords, we shall clear the way for the settlement of the difficult and complicated question of Irish autonomy."[49] Fully subscribing to the political and social logic of Gladstone's coupling of the Home Rule and land purchase bills, Parnell believed that tenant sacrifices were necessary to the achievement of something that was much less than complete autonomy.

Once he had forged the political alliance with the Gladstonian Liberal party in 1886, Parnell became resolutely wedded to what he understood to be its implications. Until the Gladstonian Liberals returned to power, nothing must be done to jeopardize the alliance or weaken the Liberals' commitment to Home Rule. In Parnell's view, the maintenance of the alliance precluded the renewal of agrarian agitation in Ireland. When the worsening of economic conditions there led to its revival in the form known as the Plan of Campaign beginning in 1886, Parnell tried to dissuade William O'Brien and others from fanning the flames. Violence and intimidation, occurring under the aegis of the National League, would, he feared, severely strain the all-important union between Liberals and nationalists. Parnell's attempt to subordinate the land question to his quest for Home Rule was rejected by a substantial section of his party, especially by William O'Brien and John Dillon, who widened the operation of the plan to almost 120 estates. On the other hand, they conducted the new campaign in such a way as to limit greatly not only the amount of violence but also the extent of the zones of organized combat, thus reducing the danger of straining the Liberal-nationalist alliance. Indeed, the heavy-handed weapons of coercion used by the Conservative government to combat the plan tended to strengthen the bonds of union between Irish nationalist and Liberal M.P.s, while at the same time deepening the hold of nationalism and its symbols in rural Ireland.[50] Parnell's studied aloofness from the Plan of Campaign was a serious miscalculation for which he was made to pay a heavy price at the time of the famous split in the Irish parliamentary party in 1890 and during its bitter immediate aftermath.

In the wake of the disastrous split, followed by the Lords' overwhelming rejection of a second Home Rule bill in 1893 and Gladstone's retirement from the Liberal leadership in 1894, the prospects of constitutional nationalism were about as bleak as they could possibly be. Although the land question was far from settled in the 1890s, whether or in what form it could play a constructive role in the revival of nationalist fortunes was generally an unanswered—indeed an unasked—question. A realistic appraisal of agrarian politics would have indicated that the social groups whose concerted actions had once made the Land League coalition so formidable could again be harnessed together only with great difficulty, if indeed they could be harnessed together at all. In many districts the agricultural cooperative movement sowed division between the small farmers who benefited from it and the shopkeepers and traders who steadfastly opposed it. Among small farmers and laborers, the land-grabbing activities of shopkeeper-graziers had made this social element particularly hated, and in the west this conflict was part of the larger and long-standing antagonism between ranchers and those with too little or no land. Even before the Wyndham Land Act of 1903 heightened the awareness of western smallholders that peasant proprietorship was not the answer to their economic problems, they realized that the graziers had lost interest in further agrarian reform. For obvious reasons, however, the warring nationalist factions of the 1890s could see no political potential in the sectional grievances of western smallholders.[51]

The special grievances of these small farmers were therefore ignored by almost all leading nationalists until William O'Brien carried off the remarkable feat of organizing a Connacht-based antigrazier agitation and of using it to lay the basis for both a reunion among nationalists and a wider agrarian movement. The luster of this accomplishment, however, was soon dimmed by fresh disagreements, some of which echoed old conflicts over the relationship between nationalism and the land question. In theory, the United Irish League of O'Brien's creation was committed to the breakup of the grazing ranches and land redistribution in the west and to compulsory land purchase for the country as a whole. But once the UIL struck deep roots outside Connacht, the sectional and politically difficult goal of redistribution was in practice overtaken by the national and politically manageable aim of comprehensive land purchase. In one important respect O'Brien's hopes for the UIL were disappointed. Instead of remaining an independent body capable of giving direction to the reunited party, it quickly came under the party's domination, in contrast to the Land

League, but like the National League. Yet, in another respect O'Brien's hopes were rewarded with an offer from progressive unionist landlords to settle the terms of a comprehensive measure of land purchase. Their agreement provided the basis for what became the Wyndham Land Act of 1903, which enormously speeded up the whole business of land sales to the tenants.[52]

The terms of this legislation, and the implications of the land conference that preceded it, exposed the conflicting attitudes of nationalist leaders. Though the terms of the bill were generous to the landlords, with high upper limits in sale prices allowed, O'Brien's attitude was similar to that of Parnell in 1886. Some sacrifice of tenant interests was needed to win over the landlords, first to an agreed scheme of land purchase and then to wider nationalist political aims. Like Parnell, whose ideals he saw himself adopting, O'Brien had no wish to drive landlords out of the country or even out of politics, but rather hoped that they would contribute to Irish public life in various ways. Men of public spirit, though rich and Protestant, would find a secure if limited place in O'Brien's Ireland of the future. With the successes of the land conference and the 1903 act under his belt, he became an addict of what he called "conference plus business," which he perceived as an instrument for escalating political cooperation between nationalists and progressive unionists.[53] When Parnell had shown a similar concern for Irish landlords in 1886, he had possessed the advantage of the direct and immediate linkage with Home Rule, which forced his reluctant party colleagues to swallow what would otherwise have been inedible. O'Brien completely lacked this advantage.

Davitt and Dillon were highly critical of Wyndham's bill when it was under discussion at Westminster, and they continued their fire after the act became law. Davitt had, of course, long been a lonely advocate of land nationalization, the root-and-branch method of abolishing landlordism, albeit with compensation. But he insisted that this solution, or the more likely one of peasant proprietorship, should be deferred until after independence had been achieved. As Davitt proclaimed as early as 1887, "The settlement of the land question must be made between the Irish state and the Irish landlords."[54] The idea that Irish tenants should be the ones to make sacrifices to become the owners of their own farms was abhorrent to him, partly because it violated his canons of justice, but even more because he feared that if the land question were resolved, after a fashion, prior to the realization of self-government, it would have the effect of weakening popular support for independence.

This view of the relationship between nationalism and the land question actually had a long pedigree. As Thomas Davis put it as early as 1841,

"Some men may think that agitated alone, the demand for proprietorship would end in some paltry and unprincipled compromise, but that if kept as an ulterior result of nationality, and agitated as one of its blessings, it will be won by the same effort."[55] What some repealers ruminated about in the early 1840s had become by the 1880s political doctrine with many Home Rule leaders. As Tim Healy told a meeting of the central branch of the National League in September 1888, "Until a great treaty of peace had been made between England and Ireland, no Irish farmer ought to make a treaty of peace on his own account, and the man who purchased under Ashbourne's act [of 1885] was making a treaty of peace behind the backs of the nation as a whole."[56] Coming from Conservative hands, conciliatory land legislation was widely regarded as a poisoned chalice designed to "kill Home Rule with kindness."

This remained the dominant view after the Irish party was reunited in 1900, and apart from Davitt, its most notable spokesman was John Dillon. It was on precisely this issue that Dillon became permanently estranged from O'Brien, his old Plan of Campaign comrade-in-arms. Dillon, like Davitt, was afraid that many overeager tenants would foolishly agree to pay the high land prices that the Wyndham Act permitted and, what was worse, that satisfied owner-occupiers would not be enthusiastic supporters of Home Rule. He confided his opinions privately in May 1903 to William Scawen Blunt, who recorded them in his diary: "His view is that it is useless trying to get the landlord class on the side of nationalism, that they would always betray it when the pinch came, that the land trouble is a weapon in nationalist hands, and that to settle it finally would be to risk Home Rule, which otherwise *must* come. For this reason he was opposed to the conference [of 1902] with the landlords, and he was opposed now in principle to the bill [of 1903]."[57]

In sharp contrast to O'Brien, Dillon clearly viewed landlords as permanent political enemies whose departure from the country should not be the occasion for lamentation or regret. His hopes for Home Rule, and those of most members of his party, were firmly fixed on the Liberals, and unionists, however progressive in other respects, were in his judgment beyond conversion. Nor could he agree with O'Brien that coquetting with unionists would not endanger the Liberal alliance.[58] The quarrel deeply embittered O'Brien, who chose to regard all this as a rejection of an Irish nationalism that reached out to members of all classes and creeds. History, he later insisted, had vindicated the correctness of his approach since the settlement of the land question by the acts of 1903 and 1909 did not rob the quest for Home Rule or independence of popular support.[59]

The land question, then, was always a vexing issue for Irish nationalist leaders. Their preferred method of dealing with it was by one or another kind of subordination. The precise motives varied enormously. For O'Connell and the Young Irelanders in the early and mid-1840s, the primary motive was the forlorn desire for Protestant landlord support. For the Fenians in the 1860s, the reason was (as the *Irish People* declared in 1864) "the utter hopelessness of all efforts to get rid of special grievances as long as Ireland continued to be ruled by a foreign parliament."[60] With Parnell after 1881, the motive was almost the reverse—the seemingly realistic prospects of gaining the prize of Home Rule and a clutch of agrarian concessions into the bargain.

Rigid subordination of the land question was neither always possible nor always considered desirable. The new agrarian militancy of many Fenians in the 1870s was predicated on the view that tenant farmers could be converted to revolutionary nationalism by enlisting them in an agitation that had peasant proprietorship as one of its main goals, a goal that would be maddeningly refused by the British parliament, thus convincing outraged tenants of the necessity of prior political revolution. This was the strategy that inspired John Devoy's New Departure proposals of 1878-79.[61] The strategy was foiled by the limited but substantial agrarian successes of the Land and National Leagues and by the willingness of the British Parliament to promote a prolandlord version of peasant proprietorship. At that point, in the mid-1880s, the dominant nationalist view shifted to the proposition that no British government would grant an *acceptable* measure of peasant proprietorship. The terms would always unduly favor the landlords and unduly prejudice the prospects for self-government.

It would be quite unhistorical to believe that nationalist leaders after 1880 could have addressed themselves to the land question in isolation from their political strategies. But it is not unhistorical to suggest that one critical unintended result of their preoccupation with the terms and supposed dangers of peasant proprietorship was to distract their attention from other instruments for securing higher agricultural incomes and a fairer distribution of rural wealth. Too few of them agreed with Parnell's dictum, "The better off the people are, the better nationalists they will be."[62] And fewer still really understood that the abolition of landlordism was not the end but only the beginning.

Emmet Larkin

THE IRISH
POLITICAL TRADITION

ALL POLITICAL SYSTEMS are indigenous and therefore unique. Some, however, are more unique than others, and the modern Irish political system would appear to be a very rare specimen, which, if taken in the context of the liberal democracies of Western Europe, has defied all classification.[1] Indeed, one imaginative Irish political scientist has gone so far as to suggest, unfortunately without attempting to pursue the idea further, that the modern Irish political system might be better compared to the recently emerged postcolonial states of the Third World, or even to the states of Eastern rather than Western Europe.[2] There is, in fact, a great deal to be said for thinking about the modern Irish political system in terms of the recently emerged Indian, or the emerging Polish political system. The chief difficulty involved in comparing such systems, however, is that they all have been a very long time in the making, and even when they may be said to have been made, they are still continually evolving, for constitutions, when they embody the aspirations and will of a people concerned about their political process, are living things, and as such are also subject to change. Before any attempt at a meaningful comparison can be made, however, one would want to be sure that one actually understood the integrities of the systems to be compared, and that task, in the last analysis, is essentially historical.

Because the modern Irish political system has been very much misunderstood, this essay will attempt to clear up that misunderstanding by explaining its uniqueness in terms of the complex relationship between religion, nationality, and the Irish idea of freedom. Religion and nationality, however, are relatively simple terms when compared with the more subtle notion of the Irish idea of freedom. Implicit in any discussion of the idea of freedom in the modern world is the interesting assumption that the earliest and perhaps the most exquisite flower of that rare plant is English. If beauty does indeed lie in the eye of the beholder, first may not be, no matter how lovely, necessarily best. Nearly thirty years ago, for example, Leonard Krieger, in his seminal book, *The German Idea of Freedom*, pointed out that "the Germans shared so much of and so internally in western norms and practical arrangements that they named their own values and action in western terms and saw in their divergence only their positive cultural creation within the common western pattern."[3] "Thus," Krieger added, providing students of modern Irish history with considerable food for thought, "the limited efficacy of individual rights in their political system during the 19th century was for most Germans an indication not of a defect in freedom but of a distinctive German dimension to freedom." Like the German, the Irish idea of freedom depended on a perception of having made a positive cultural contribution to freedom, and it was a creation with a considerable difference. For the Irish, their political genius was that they were able to integrate to an unusual degree the various dimensions of liberty—personal, civil, political, and religious—into a longer-term communitarian ethos, and eventually harmonize both to produce a distinctive Irish political tradition, communitarianism. How religion and nationality contributed to this tradition, and were in turn accommodated by it, without essentially impairing the legacy of liberty that was ironically an English gift, is then the story of the modern Irish political system and the constitution in church and state it has produced.

Because the formative period of the Irish political experience was basically a colonial one, Irish political rhetoric in regard to freedom was both strident and aggressive in maintaining that their idea of freedom was morally superior to that of the English because it was not tainted with the besetting sin of the English version, hypocrisy. In writing to congratulate Fr. P.E. Moriarty, an Augustinian, in the summer of 1864, about a recent lecture on "English Rule in Ireland," the celebrated nationalist archbishop of Tuam, John MacHale, maintained that seldom had the rights of subjects to the enjoyment of good government been so clearly placed within the rule of strictest orthodoxy.[4] "Yet it would seem," MacHale added, "as if the duties and rights of the governors and governed were to be regulated by the varying meridians of the countries they inhabit. For whilst our rulers extend to all subjects of all the other governments of the world the right to revolt beyond what religion or reason would sanction, so jealous are they of the superior excellence of their own government that to arraign it of tyrany or injustice would be deemed wickedness or infatuation." MacHale concluded ironically, "Such is the practical result by which the fine theories of the British Constitution are often illustrated."

In his lecture, Father Moriarty delivered up what had become by 1864 the pure milk of Irish constitutional theory.[5] He had argued that because all authority and power of civil governments are derived from God, and because God had communicated that authority and power directly to the people, they as his instruments and ministers had bestowed it in turn on the ruler of their choice, who governed in their interest and for their good. When the ruler or government became tyrannical, however, the people not only had a right but a duty to rebel. After thus establishing the relationship between popular sovereignty and the right to revolution, Moriarty then proceeded to argue that the English had no right to rule in Ireland for two reasons. First, that the Irish people had never given their consent to English rule in Ireland, and that this was what gave real significance and meaning to Irish nationality; and second, that the history of the English occupation of Ireland over some seven hundred years, which he elaborated on at great length, was a long and brutal record of oppression, exploitation, and extermination, which could be summed up in a single word—tyranny. "All that is native to Ireland, all that is social, loyal, moral is essentially Celtic and Catholic," Moriarty further maintained. "Whatever *Charter*, Bill of Rights, or Act of Settlement, she may pretend for legal government," he concluded, referring to English misrule, "its clauses are such as I have enumerated—printed with type of blood and tears."

Before the end of the 1860s, therefore, and on the eve of the emergence of the modern Irish political system, the crucial constitutional concepts about sovereignty, consent, and rights had settled in the Irish mind in a way that was basically inimical to the English Victorian Constitution.[6] The Irish had not only evolved a doctrine of popular as opposed to parliamentary sovereignty, but they had opted for a radical rather than a liberal view of the nature of consent as being delegatory rather than representative. Finally, there were also fundamental rights of a people at least, if not of inividuals, which a law-making body, or parliament, could not infringe without risking the ultimate sanction of a people—the right to revolution. In regard to their basic constitutional concepts about sovereignty, consent, and rights, the Irish might appear to be at first sight a good deal closer to the American political tradition than to the English, but there was that other fundamental difference that distinguished the Irish political system from either the English or the American. The Irish tradition was communitarian rather than individualistic and in its practical workings functioned by consensus rather than majority. The Irish political system, therefore, and the idea of freedom that informed it, was essentially communal, and the needs of the community, or nation, took precedence over those of the individual.

The roots of this communitarianism lie deep in the social order of the Irish past. The sense of wholeness, or the concept of unity, on which the idea of community depends is certainly derived in great part from the aristocratic Gaelic order, and has been sustained over time by the Catholic church in Ireland. In understanding the contribution of the Gaelic order to the concept of unity, it is essential to realize that while that order was politically decentralized it was culturally homogeneous, and what sustained the cultural homogeneity was a learned and priestly class. In posing a fascinating analogy between the early societies of India and Ireland, Proinsias MacCana, the Celtic scholar, has maintained:

> In both India and Ireland, then, culture—in the sense of belief, ritual and general tradition—was the transcendent force operating towards unity, but it was able to do so effectively only because there was in both countries a learned and priestly class which could assert the claims (broadly speaking) of orthodoxy. The druid or *file* had his local affiliations but at the same time, he and he alone, had free and untrammelled passage across tribal boundaries, throughout Ireland. He had therefore, like the brahmin, the mobility as well as the professional status and cohesion to propagate an accepted culture to all parts of the land and all segments of the population, irrespective of ethnic origins. It might indeed almost be said of him, as has been said of the brahmin, that "the destruction of tribal culture was a logical outcome, if not the conscious goal, of his ideology."[7]

It was this cultural homogeneity, more than anything else, that eventually allowed Irish society to absorb the incursion of the Vikings and the Normans as indeed India, on a larger scale over an even longer period of time, has been able to absorb an endless variety of peoples and traditions in a way that is virtually unparalleled elsewhere in the world. In the late sixteenth century, however, the expansion of English power in Ireland aimed not merely at military conquest, but at cultural suppression as well, and the result was the destruction of the aristocratic Gaelic order and the learned class, the bards, who had sustained its ideology.

With the fall of that aristocratic order in the early seventeenth century, and its final liquidation during the course of the century, the Irish people became, as Daniel Corkery has so aptly put it, "the residuary legatees of a civilisation that was more than a thousand years old."[8] Corkery has further maintained, "With that civilisation, they were still in living contact, acquainted with its history; and such of its forms as had not become quite impossible in their way of life, they still piously practiced, gradually changing the old moulds into new shapes, and whether new or old, filling them with a content that was all of the passing day and their own fields."[9] Indeed, it was one of those "residuary legatees," who, in support of Daniel O'Connell's struggle for Catholic emancipation, articulated the basic Irish sense of otherness in conjunction with the historic Irish experience of inequality that lies at the root of modern nationalism, and who discovered in that symbiosis the original sin of the Gael in this struggle with the Gall— the lack of unity. As Humphrey O'Sullivan, the diarist and schoolmaster of Callan, explained in Irish to a meeting at Ballyhale, County Kilkenny, on 8 July [1826]:

Children of the Gael, I wish to address you to-day to explain to you how you have come under the "tooth of the harrow" at the hands of the children of the foreigners; and, with the help of Almighty God, to tell you how best to rise out of the miserable plight in which the Catholics of Ireland find themselves.

It is now well nigh seven hundred years, since, through our own fault, we came under the dire tyranny of the foreigners. The Irish clans failed to help one another; and, accordingly, they were plundered and hanged and tortured.

When the children of the foreigners abandoned the Catholic Faith, they banished the Catholics from six counties of the Province of Ulster, and then from a large part of the other Provinces, telling their victims to go to hell or Connaght. The Catholic rose in arms against their deadly enemies, the Protestants, but without success, they lost their lands. They had no Brian Boru or Washington or other stout warrior, to keep them fighting hand in hand. Then the Protestants tried to do to the Catholics as the Jews did to the Canaanites—to leave unslain not a single person of the children of the Gael, man woman nor boy, weak nor strong, rich nor poor, in this land flowing with milk and honey.[10]

"Catholic Emancipation," O'Sullivan then pointed out, "means this, that all power and honours now enjoyed by Protestants should be within the reach of Catholics on equal terms. . . . Accordingly, fellow Catholics!" he then concluded, "let us help one another and God will help us, and we shall no longer be harried by the proctors of the Protestant clergy, and by others of that ilk, and grace and good fortune will again well forth from God on the Catholics of Ireland."

O'Sullivan's exhortation on behalf of Catholic emancipation is interesting in a number of ways, but in none perhaps more than his equating Gael with Catholic. Not only was it obvious in 1826 that the tradition of the "seven hundred long and weary years of English tyranny" was already deeply embedded in the historical memory of the residuary legatees of the old Gaelic order, but even more importantly that the dispossessed Gael had now been unconsciously metamorphized into the disenfranchised Catholic. Because the Catholic church became the most important institutional element in sustaining the ongoing Irish identity after the collapse of the aristocratic Gaelic order, it was inevitable that Irish and Catholic over time would become virtually interchangeable terms.[11] But if the church reinforced the Irish sense of otherness and deepened the Irish awareness of the inequality of Catholics, it also contributed profoundly to the idea of an Irish-Catholic community by insisting not only on the unity, but the orthodoxy of that community. Indeed, in the early 1820s, and simultaneous with Daniel O'Connell's efforts to launch his Catholic Association, the future archbishop of Tuam, John MacHale, under the pseudonym of Hieropolis, sounded the tocsin by announcing that the faith of Irish Catholics was in danger. Inveighing against the Kildare Street Society for proselyting Irish Catholics while providing them with a primary education, MacHale, who was then a lecturer in dogmatic theology at Maynooth, in a letter to the Catholic clergy of Ireland, regretted "that some uniform system of defense has not been hitherto adopted. . . . It is not by desultory efforts, however ably conducted, that the enemy is to be defeated, but by a compact, well-regulated plan originating with the bishops, and adopted by the great body of the clergy. The exertions of the societies cannot be any longer contemplated with indifference," he maintained. "It is then," he said, squarely laying the responsibility, "the duty of those whom the Holy Ghost has placed as bishops, to rule the Church of God, to provide for its defence."[12]

Both MacHale and O'Sullivan diagnosed their respective problems, proselyting Protestantism and political inequality, as being the result of a lack of unity in the face of the enemy. The one thing necessary, therefore, was to achieve unity, and that required, above all, effective leadership. For MacHale, the leadership was to be provided by the bishops as a body, and for O'Sullivan, a leader comparable to Brian Boru or Washington had already emerged in the person of Daniel O'Connell. Indeed, by the time that O'Sullivan spoke at Ballyhale in 1826, O'Connell had given the communitarian instinct for unity concrete form in the Catholic Association, and had thereby laid the foundations of the modern Irish political system. In the meantime, MacHale had been promoted in 1824 to the episcopal body as the coadjutor to the bishop of Killala and had become a firm supporter of O'Connell and the association in the effort to secure Catholic emancipation. MacHale and O'Connell, moreover, were representative of a new generation of Irish Catholic leadership in that they not only gave the Irish political system form in terms of its constitutional elements in church and state, but they also gave it its tone and content in regard to its values. They appreciated above all the profound political and psychological truth that a man who does not know that he is equal does not deserve to be free. "How I smile," O'Connell explained to his wife from London on 17 March 1825, in the midst of his negotiations with English politicians on behalf of Catholic emancipation, "at the folly which surrounds me. Darling, they think themselves great men, but the foolish pride of your husband would readily make him enter into a contest with them. I have not the least fear of being *looked down on* in Parliament. This is miserable vanity—but darling, it means that I have a poor opinion of them and a greater one than I ought of myself."[13]

In retrospect, it is now very clear that O'Connell's supreme political achievement was the Catholic Association, and that the unity he realized through it by effectively combining large and small tenant farmers, high and low clergy, city merchants and country shopkeepers, liberal Protestants and ecumenical Catholics, and the large, though less respectable class, men of no property was to prove to be the essential formula in the eventual creation of the modern Irish state. In a word, the real significance and importance of O'Connell is that he was the first to give Irish communitarism concrete political expression, and to identify that communitarism at the same time with the radical and liberal ideas of his day. He was the first, in fact, to create the governing consensus of leader, party, and bishops, which in the long run would be the cornerstone of the emergent modern Irish political system. But O'Connell did more than furnish the constituent elements of the Irish political system and give it its tone—he also helped to provide that system with its basic libertarian values. How and when he acquired those values, therefore, is crucial to understanding not only the radical nature of that system, but also the complex relationship of religion, nationality, and the idea of freedom that informs it. O'Connell's radical political and religious creed was acquired during his law student days in London and Dublin between 1794 and 1797.[14] By his twenty-first year, in the spring of 1797, he was already a democrat in politics and a Deist in religion. For O'Connell, the end of all government was the happiness of the governed whom he was prone to universalize as mankind, and the means to that end was a moderate and rational liberty, whereby a government governed best when it governed least. Because those governed included all, they should be governed by all rather than by the few, and aristocratic privilege must therefore give way to democracy. O'Connell's views on the nature and purpose of government were profoundly influenced at this time by his reading of William Godwin's *Inquiry Concerning Political Justice*.[15] In Godwin he found confirmed that abhorrence of violence that was always to remain such a prominent feature in his political and constitutional creed. While he was reading Godwin's *Inquiry*, O'Connell also read Tom Paine's *Age of Reason* and was converted to Paine's God of nature.[16] In truth, after reading Paine, he could not believe that a good God would punish him for a lack of faith, which was the unbiased conviction of this soul confirmed by right reason. Though in time O'Connell sincerely resumed the practice of Catholicism, the tolerance he had acquired for honest doubt as a Deist in matters of religious belief was to remain a basic tenet of his religious convictions for the rest of his life.

In understanding the timing of the forming of O'Connell's radical

convictions about civil, political, and religious liberty, however, it is important to realize that they were not only formed early in a highly charged
political environment, but they were also firmly in place several years
before the passing of the Act of Union between Britain and Ireland in 1800.
Before that political trauma took place, O'Connell had, in effect, been
inveighing against bad government both as a radical and as an Irishman. As
a radical he was protesting universally about all bad government and calling
for its reform everywhere, while as an Irishman he was complaining
particularly about his bad government for denying him civil, political, and
religious equality. The abstract nature of his radicalism, therefore, was
given particular point through his grievances as an Irishman, which he soon
expected to be able to remedy by taking part in the reform of that bad
government. "I have this day been thinking on the plan to be pursued *when
I come into Parliament,*" he confided to his journal on January 28, 1797. "If
to distinguish myself was the object of my exertions, that could be best
done by becoming a violent oppositionist. But as it will be my chief study to
serve my country, moderation will be the proper instrument for the purpose. Moderation is the character of genuine patriotism, of that patriotism
that seeks for the happiness of mankind," he wrote. "There is another
species," he added, making an interesting distinction in regard to the forms
of patriotism, "which is caused by hatred of oppression. This is a passion.
The other [moderation] is a principle."[17]

The Act of Union, therefore, came as a profound shock to both O'Connell's political career and his moderation. Instead of perhaps entering the
Irish Parliament in his middle twenties, he had to wait some thirty years
before he was able to force his way into the British Parliament in his middle
fifties. In those thirty years, moreover, the principle of patriotism that he
had early announced as moderation was soon transformed into that passion
he had defined as hatred of oppression. By mobilizing that hatred as
righteous anger, furthermore, O'Connell was eventually able to fashion an
indigenous Irish political system that was a function of his fusion of religion,
nationality, and the Irish idea of freedom. The Act of Union gave him a
country to recover, and in his first public speech on the subject, he
responded nobly to the challenge. "Let us show to Ireland," he proclaimed
on 13 January 1800, protesting the Act of Union, "we have nothing in view
but her good; nothing in our hearts but the desire of mutual forgiveness,
mutual toleration, and mutual affection; in fine, let every man who feels
with me proclaim that if the alternative were offered him of union, or the re-
enactment of the penal code in all its pristine horrors, that he would prefer
without hesitation the latter, as the lesser and more sufferable evil; that he
would rather confide in the justice of his brethren, the Protestants of

Ireland, who have already liberated him, than lay his country at the feet of foreigners."[18]

What O'Connell was referring to by preferring all the pristine horrors of the penal code, of course, was that in order to persuade Irish Catholics to acquiesce in the Act of Union, the English government had promised to grant as its quid pro quo Catholic emancipation. After the union, therefore, the continued refusal of successive British governments to grant emancipation allowed O'Connell to turn that religious grievance into a successful national agitation. "Desiring as I do," O'Connell pointed out gleefully to a large meeting in Dublin on 29 June 1813, "the Repeal of the Union, I rejoice to see how our enemies promote that great object. Yes, they promote its inevitable success by their very hostility to Ireland; *they delay the liberties of the Catholic, but they compensate us most amply, because they advance the restoration of Ireland; by leaving one cause of agitation, they have created and they will embody and give shape and form to a public mind and a public spirit.*"[19]

Indeed, because emancipation was delayed for yet another sixteen years, it was O'Connell who finally did most to give shape and form to that raised political consciousness he forecast in 1813. Because he was obliged, however, to mobilize that consciousness with the goad of religious ine-quality, the identity which eventually emerged was undoubtedly a good deal more Catholic than he had originally intended it to be. For, in winning emancipation, O'Connell had to incorporate the Catholic bishops and clergy in such a way and to such an extent in his association, that they became and would remain an essential element in Irish politics. The dangers to the Irish idea of freedom of an ascendant Catholicism, especially in its intolerant, ultramontane, nineteenth-century variant, were all too apparent in an exclusiveness that would destroy the unity of the communi-ty. In the long run, however, the reality of a Catholic ascendancy did not materialize because O'Connell's communitarian and libertarian vision was ultimately consolidated by his successors in the 1880s in a constitutional system that successfully contained the very considerable power and influ-ence of the church in politics.

The continued vitality of O'Connell's communitarian vision, for exam-ple, was well illustrated in 1875 on the occasion of celebrating the centen-ary of his birth. When the lord mayor of Dublin, Peter Paul MacSwiney, attempted, with the approval and assistance of the archbishop of Dublin, Paul Cardinal Cullen, to turn the celebration into a purely Catholic and religious demonstration, the reaction of the Catholic nationalist press and politicians was as interesting as it was instructive. In a pastoral letter to his clergy on 23 July 1875 announcing the three-day celebration in the first

week of August, Cullen had deemphasized the nationalist and patriotic
dimension of the proposed fesitivites by concentrating on O'Connell's role
as a Catholic in securing emancipaton in 1829 and ignoring his life-long
effort on behalf of repeal.[20] Typical of those Catholic nationalists and
prominent Home Rulers, who were furious with Cullen and MacSwiney for
their attempt to turn a national festival into a purely Catholic one, was W.J.
O'Neil Daunt, who had been a friend and staunch supporter of O'Connell
in his efforts to win repeal. In his diary Daunt complained that Cullen had
attempted to set the tone of the celebration "with what he calls a 'Pastoral',
eulogizing the deceased patriot as a tremendous Catholic and champion of
Catholic liberties, but saying not one word of his merits as a Nationalist or as
an earnest agitator for the Emancipation of Dissenters."[21]

Two days after the celebration closed, MacSwiney, who was unable to
leave well enough alone, decided to write a circular letter to a large number
of prominent Catholics, including all the Irish bishops. "A feeling largely
prevails," MacSwiney explained on 8 August, "that the spirit of piety and
patriotism, awakened by the centenary celebrations, should be availed of to
give practical effect to the principles of O'Connell."[22] Their motto in such
an endeavor should be "Faith and Fatherland," MacSwiney said. "In order
that O'Connell's principles with regard to questions affecting not merely
the temporal but the eternal interests of the people he loved so well, may
be carried out to their full development, it is deemed advisable to establish
in Dublin a National O'Connell Committee." When the circular was finally
published in the press some five weeks later, the Dublin *Freeman's Journal*, the largest and most influential Catholic nationalist daily paper in
Ireland, wasted not a moment in assailing the lord mayor's sectarian
views.[23] "What does this talk about 'Faith and Fatherland'," the editor of
the *Freeman* expostulated, "about temporal and eternal interests,' mean? If
it means anything, in the first place it means this: It means that the Lord
Mayor proposes to degrade the Centenary to sectarian ends—to found in
connection with that event and under the shadow of the great name of
O'Connell a political association to which none but Catholics are to be
admitted and from which the Protestant Irishman is to be excluded. . . .
When Ireland forgets the past—when she forgets the glorious services of
her Protestant patriots, of men who pleaded and prayed, who lived and
died, for her—then indeed the cup of her shame will be filled up, the doom
of an apostate nation written on the wall. No political enterprise, can
succeed in Ireland which seeks to galvanise the dead bones of Sectarian
hate. . . . Such an attempt is an act of high treason against the nation, and
deserves universal condemnation."

In the next week, the condemnation called for by the *Freeman* was not delayed, as the Catholic nationalist and liberal press was virtually unanimous in congratulating the *Freeman* on its stand against sectarianism. When the London press, led by the *Times*, then attributed the circular to the inspiration of the Irish bishops, the *Freeman*, apparently with Cullen's approval, immediately and authoritatively denied the charge.[24] The upshot of the lord mayor's indiscretion in issuing the circular was that it not only resulted in finis being written to his own career in Irish politics, but because he had also been regarded as Cullen's factotum in local politics, the cardinal's unenviable, if sometimes undeserved, reputation for being antinationalist and even reactionary in Irish politics was further confirmed in the public mind.

This episode has been treated at some length because it is representative of the inability of purely Catholic or clerical political formations to make any real headway in Ireland since O'Connell's day. Not only was some Protestant presence necessary to the respectability of any nationalist political formation, but when Catholic nationalist public opinion perceived that the effective weight of the clergy in a political organization was greater than it ought to be, that public opinion uniformly withheld its approval. This had, in fact, been the case of the Repeal Association under the aegis of John O'Connell after the death of his father in the late 1840s as well as that of the Catholic Defence Association, the National Association, and the Catholic Union, all of which were launched, respectively, under the patronage of Cullen in the 1850s, 1860s, and 1870s. It is even more interesting and ironic that in all these Cullen-sponsored organizations the element of Catholic public opinion most conspicuously absent in the end was that of the bishops and priests. The lesson to be learned, of course, was that the clergy were Irishmen as well as bishops and priests, and this augured well for the Irish idea of freedom.

The real challenge to the Irish idea of freedom, in fact, has come less from the dangers of a clericalist-inspired Catholic ascendancy than it has from the fanatic adherents of an intolerant nationalism. How this challenge has been met and contained over time was well illustrated in a characteristic incident during the struggle for Home Rule in the 1870s. In November 1873, in a great national conference in Dublin, all the various shades of nationalist opinion, from the moderate constitutionalists on the right to the physical force enthusiasts on the left, decided to sink their differences with regard to means and join together under the leadership of Issac Butt to win Home Rule for Ireland.[25] Achieving this consensus was made possible by the decision in 1873 of the leadership of the Fenian, or Irish Republican Brotherhood, to give their conditional support to the constitutional movement for three years.[26] During those three years, however, the Fenian leadership seriously split into "opportunists," who thought the alliance with the constitutionalists should be continued, and the "ultras," who thought it should be discontinued. One of the chief supporters of the ultra-Fenian policy was John Daly of Limerick, and when the Odd Fellows Society of Limerick City invited their parliamentary members, one of whom was Butt, to visit in April 1876 during the Easter recess when they would be accorded the honor of a public entry into the city, Daly and two colleagues who represented themselves as "extreme nationalists," wrote Butt publicly informing him that though they esteemed him personally, they could not allow him to hold a Home Rule demonstration in Limerick. [27] While admitting that this might appear to be a refusal to extend "to each other the liberty we are seeking from England," they maintained that, because only they truly represented nationalist opinion in Limerick, they refused to have the opinion of a small minority forced on them and that if Butt and his friends persisted, they would break up their meeting by force.

Butt refused to be intimidated, and on his arrival in Limerick he was presented with an address from the Nationalists of Limerick, signed by five of their number, disassociating themselves from Daly and his ultra-Fenian friends.

We have no hesitation in declaring to you, sir, that we do not altogether agree in following up a Parliamentary agitation, as past experience has taught us to expect but very little concession from the English Government. Yet, we cannot as nationalists, de-bar our fellow citizens from seeking if they wish it, to obtain concessions in a constitutional manner. And why? Because while we are seeking for liberty in our own way, we would not be true or faithful to our country if we attempted by fraud or force to stifle the honest opinions of our fellow-citizens. [28]

"What we ask for ourselves," the Limerick nationalists then concluded, "we cannot deny to them, and we pledge our faith to you on this day that whoever interferes with the free expression of your sentiments will have our unanimous and determined opposition." In the meantime, Daly and some forty to fifty of his followers, armed with heavy bludgeons and blackthorns, had taken possession of the site for the meeting; in the general melee that resulted when Butt and his friends arrived, Daly and his small band were overwhelmed by the force of numbers and severely handled in the process.

Just as the centenary episode was a good example of the thwarting of any kind of effort to promote a Catholic ascendancy, so the Limerick affair was a reassuring illustration of the inability of a minority, claiming to represent the general will, to prevent the exercise of freedom of speech and assembly. This was not the first, nor was it to be the last, effort of a minority in Ireland to force the majority to accept its exclusive views with regard to what was appropriate in terms of the national ideal. In time, the Irish idea of freedom would have to face even more serious traumas on the national level, in the 1890s and the 1920s respectively, when Parnellite and republican minorities attempted to impose their views on the then constituted majorities in the name of the general will. These efforts all failed, and the Irish political system has continued to prove to be extraordinarily resilient in sustaining freedom in the face of all such threats to the unity of the community.

But why has the system remained so resilient in sustaining freedom? Because the system has remained over time both vital and stable. And why has it been able to retain its vitality and stability? Because it has continued to be essentially democratic and representative. The vitality of the system has been continually refreshed by the grass-roots populism that has continued to be one of its two chief features for over 160 years, and its stability has been the result of the evolution of a unique party system, which has been its other main feature. The grass-roots populism has produced that democratic ethos on which the real political egalitarianism of the system is founded, while the evolution of the unique party system has provided the mainstay for the representative nature of the system, which has allowed for that basic order that sustains real freedom. In a word, Irishmen are politically both equal and free because their system is functionally democratic and representative.

But how did all this come about? The development of the Irish political system took place in two main stages. The first began with the founding of the Catholic Association by O'Connell in 1823 and ended with the emergence of the Home Rule movement under Butt in the 1870s. The second stage may be dated from the New Departure under Parnell in the late 1870s to the present day. In the first period populism was the dominant feature in the system, and in the second, party has become more and more prominent. Still, from the beginning, it has been the tension between populism and party that has given the Irish political system its real dynamic as well as its basic uniqueness. Populism has not only provided the system with its vitality, but it has also shaped its radical nature. Through populism, the concepts of popular sovereignty, consent, and rights all have been made politically concrete, and because populism is essentially government from the bottom up, rather than the top down, as it is with the party, the Irish idea of freedom finds its chief safeguard in this vital element of its system. Indeed, from the day when it was first institutionalized in O'Connell's

Catholic Association to the recent emergence of Desmond O'Malley's Progressive Democratic party, the vitality of Irish populism has been remarkable. There has not been a decade in Irish life since the 1820s when the developing Irish political system has not been reinvigorated by the founding of a new association, league, or party, as well as given point at the grass roots by the inauguration of clubs and branches, or the holding of aggregate meetings and conventions. The populism of the Irish political system, in fact, has been and still remains a conspicuous phenomenon.

This can hardly be said about the second main feature of the Irish political system. Because the party's origins are more obscure, and because its emergence over time has been more tentative, something more will have to be said about its evolution. Like so much else in the Irish political system, the origins of party are to be found in the Catholic Association. In early August 1828, shortly after O'Connell's celebrated election in Clare and before the granting of emancipation, the association gave formal notice that to secure its endorsement, pledges would be required from those candidates seeking parliamentary honors on the popular interest.[29] Because the association was dissolved on the achievement of emancipation, this novel political experiment was delayed for a time, but the lesson was not lost on O'Connell. "In part," one distinguished historian has pointed out, "this was forced on him by circumstances; in part, it was the fruit of his extraordinary inventiveness."

O'Connell was the pioneer of the modern political party. By present-day standards, the discipline of his party in the House of Commons was loose, constituency organisation was weak and central control over the nomination of candidates unconstant and uncertain. But, by contemporary standards in a situation where MPs, unless they were office-holders or placemen, were independent and unpredictable agents, O'Connell's "tail" was a phalanx which the leadership could use at will and which, if the support of the clergy were available, possessed an impregnable power-base in at least one third of the Irish constituencies. Although O'Connell's development of constituency and national machinery and parliamentary management was necessarily rudimentary, it foreshadowed in almost every single feature the modern political organisation of the party.[30]

For some forty years after O'Connell all the various attempts to form an independent, disciplined Irish party in the House of Commons were frustrated because the Irish M.P.s were unwilling to pledge themselves to sit, vote, and act as the majority of them should direct. Most of the Irish M.P.s held to the sound radical view that they were responsible in the last analysis to their constituencies rather than to their parliamentary colleagues constituted as a party.[31] For these radical populists the proper mode of securing effective action on the part of the body of Irish M.P.s in the House of Commons was rather by holding annual national conventions, where the people's will would be made evident, than through the mechanism of a majority binding a minority. The populist mode of annual conventions, however, did not prove practicable in securing the discipline required of Irish M.P.s, and the national need to win self-government combined with the practical necessity to secure the political balance of power in the House of Commons, eventually resulted in the emergence of a pledge-bound Irish Parliamentary party under the leadership of Parnell in the 1880s. With the emergence of the party, the Irish political system finally crystallized, and the hallmark of that system is that it has been since its inception, and has remained almost down to the present day, a one-party system checked and balanced by its longer-standing populist tradition.

Over time the party has become the centerpiece in the Irish political system, but those other elements of the governing consensus in that system, the leader and the Catholic bishops as a body, have also had significant roles to play in checking and balancing the party and each other.[32] Indeed, it is in this functionally constitutional relationship of leader, party, and bishops that the tendencies inherent in any system of government to limit civil, political, and religious liberties in the interests of order have been checked or mitigated. But while this de facto arrangement has done much to help preserve the Irish idea of freedom, the populist tradition in the system has perhaps been even more important. It is necessary to understand how the populist tradition functions not only in terms of the governing consensus, but even more especially with regard to its survival in a one-party system.

A few words will have to be said first about that one-party system over the last one hundred years. Over that time three parties have succeeded each other and dominated their respective periods—the Irish Parliamentary party (1885-1918), Sinn Féin (1918-1932), and Fianna Fáil (1932-1986). The parliamentary party, which dominated Irish politics for a period of thirty-three years, never won less in a general election than 70 of the 103 Irish seats in the British House of Commons. That figure of 70 appears to have been the critical number necessary to both the party's moral authority in claiming to represent the Irish people and in its ability to secure the crucial balance of power in an English two-party system. The Irish Parliamentary party was literally destroyed in the general election of 1918 by Sinn Féin, which won 73 of the 103 parliamentary seats in Ireland, and thereby succeeded to the party's moral and political authority in the Irish political system. Three years later, in 1921, however Sinn Féin's own moral and political authority was seriously impaired when it split on the issue of accepting dominion status instead of a republic for Ireland. The majority of the Sinn Féin party, after accepting dominion status and establishing a free state in 1922, reconstituted themselves as the League of the Gael, or Cumann na nGaedheal, and proceeded to govern Ireland until 1932. In the meantime, the minority of the Sinn Féin party founded a new party, Fianna Fáil, in 1926, and in 1932 succeeded finally in bringing the ascendancy of the league to an abrupt end. Since 1932, Fianna Fáil has been the only political formation in Ireland able to secure a clear majority in the Dáil, or chamber of deputies, and it has governed Ireland for forty of the last fifty-four years.

How, it may well be asked, has the populist tradition fared in this remarkable succession of parties, each of which has not simply forced its predecessor to give way, but virtually to give up? The populist tradition has, in fact, not only fared well in the face of an essentially one-party system over the last one hundred years, but it bids fair in the very near future perhaps to effect yet another basic transformation in Irish politics. The populist tradition has, for example, been basic to the success of all three parties in achieving power in the Irish political system. Just as the Parliamentary party struck its grass roots in the Land League in the early 1880s, Sinn Féin was firmly rooted in the popular anticonscription movement in the spring of 1918. Like its predecessors, Fianna Fáil was also populist in its origins, being rural, reformist, republican, and radical, and drawing its initial electoral strength from the small farming and laboring classes in the west of Ireland. It very quickly expanded its base after coming to power in 1932 into urban areas, especially Dublin, and by 1938 it had gained considerable electoral ground among the urban working classes.[33]

The influence of the populist tradition, moreover, has been made manifest in the various constitutions that have been written for the Irish people over the last seventy years. From the proclamation establishing the Irish Republic in 1916, through the declaration of independence, democratic program, and provisional constitution of the first Dáil in 1919, to the more formal constitutions presented to the Irish people in 1922 and 1937, the themes of popular sovereignty, consent, and rights as well as the paramountcy of the interests of the community over its parts, have been fundamental in all of these documents. The proclamation in 1916, for example, declared "the right of the people of Ireland to the ownership of Ireland, and to the unfettered control of Irish destinies, to be sovereign and indefeasible," and that the republic guaranteed "religious and civil liberty, equal rights and equal opportunities to all its citizens and declares its resolve to pursue the happiness and prosperity of the whole nation and all of its parts, cherishing all the children of the nation equally, and oblivious of all the differences carefully fostered by an alien government, which have divided a minority from the majority in the past."[34]

These themes, which have been basic to the Irish populist tradition since the political heyday of Daniel O'Connell, were not only all reiterated in the various documents ratified by the first Dáil in 1919, but even more significantly, they were remarkably enlarged upon in the constitution of the Irish Free State in 1922. That constitution not only declared that all "powers of government, and all authority, legislative, executive, and judicial, are derived from the people," and guaranteed habeas corpus, domiciliary inviolability, and freedom of religion, speech, association, and assembly in its opening section of fundamental rights, but it also provided a number of safeguards for the ensuring of the sovereignty of the people—initiative, referendum, and proportional representation.[35] The constitution also included a very novel and interesting provision for external ministers, as distinguished from cabinet ministers, who were to be nominated by an impartial committee of the Dáil, and who were then to be appointed by that chamber and remain directly responsible to it.[36] This provision was obviously designed, like initiative, referendum, and proportional representation, not only to limit the power of the executive in favor of the legislative branch of government, but also to keep some real power within the reach of the people.

The genius, moreover, of the constitution drawn up by Eamon de Valera and ratified by the Irish people in 1937 was that it articulated better than any previous document the realities of the Irish political system. The keystone in the constitutional arch remained the doctrine of popular sovereignty, which power the people derived from God in the persons of the "Most Holy Trinity."[37] At the same time, the constitution, while exorcising the demon of the British Commonwealth in the person of its king, guaranteed all those civil and religious liberties that were the most significant part of its British inheritance. The most provocative and challenging feature of the new constitution, however, was that it not only finally and explicitly recognized the "special position of the Holy Catholic Apostolic and Roman Church as guardian of the Faith professed by the great majority of the citizens," but it endorsed Catholic moral teaching in regard to the family, education, marriage, and private property (regulated by the principles of social justice), and approved the establishment of a welfare state informed by Catholic social thought.[38] The constitution, in fact, explicitly established a Catholic confessional state, with an extraordinary degree of toleration for the miniscule religious minorities. This had been the basic political reality since Daniel O'Connell first focused the Irish political system in his quest for Catholic emancipation.

Besides being basic not only to understanding how parties achieve power in Ireland but also to explaining why the fundamental rights that guarantee the Irish idea of freedom are made explicit and formal in the written constitutions, the Irish populist tradition is crucial to appreciating why the transfer of power, that most delicate moment for all political systems, has been relatively successful in constitutional terms. In a two-party or a multiparty system, the processes of alternating or regrouping respectively in terms of a majority are fairly straightforward in effecting an orderly transfer of power compared to the complexities, not to mention the risks and dangers, of attempting to do so in an essentially one-party system. The key to this problem of effecting an orderly transfer of power in the Irish political system is that the system not only learned early how to tolerate dissent in principle, but also how to institutionalize it. Without a populist tradition to nourish and to vitalize dissent at the grass roots, however, that dissent could never have been eventually institutionalized. The beginnings of that institutionalization are to be found in the first real challenge to the consolidated system by Parnell and his supporters in the early 1890s. Because the governing consensus of leader, party, and bishops was only able to contain the Parnellites and not to destroy them politically, provision had to be made for the toleration of political dissent.[39] The eventual reincorporation of the Parnellites in a reunited party in 1900 under a Parnellite leader was not only a fundamental lesson in the long-term advantages of political toleration, but also a real act of political magnanimity on the part of a majority for a dissenting minority in the interests of national unity.[40]

In any case, as the besetting sin of all parties in one-party systems, longevity in power, began to take its inevitable toll, Sinn Féin, the All for Ireland League, and the Irish Labour party, all of which began as clouds no bigger than a man's hand, in the decade after the Parliamentary party's reunification in 1900, eventually and collectively brought the Irish Parliamentary party down in 1918 after an ascendency of some thirty-three years. The dilemma of an emergent and triumphant Sinn Féin sincerely claiming to represent a new and genuinely representative national consensus in Irish politics, while at the same time suffering from a real revulsion at the idea of becoming the very kind of political monster they had just overthrown, appears to be the ironic destiny of winners in one-party systems. Having spent some ten long years in the political wilderness, Sinn Féin, by 1918,

was fully committed to proportional representation as best suited to preserve the representation of minorities. As has been mentioned, proportional representation was incorporated in the Irish Free State constitution in
1922, and it has remained the electoral mode ever since, in spite of two
major efforts by Fianna Fáil in 1959 and 1968 to abolish it by constitutional
amendment.[41]

This formal institutionalization of dissent through proportional representation has allowed for its expression in the Irish political system. Indeed, it was the cumulative force of that dissent that finally brought the ten-
year political ascendancy of the Cumann na nGaedheal to an end in 1932 by
producing, in effect, the informal coalition between Fianna Fáil and the
Irish Labour party that secured the majority necessary to oust the government. Fianna Fáil then began its own first sixteen-year period of uninter-
rupted power, which was also brought to an end by the cumulative force of
dissent in a startling and unlikely coalition in 1948 of all the other five minor
parties and some half-dozen independents. That coalition broke up three
years later in 1951, but it was again resurrected in three years, proving that
the original formation was not a mere political freak. By the time this
second coalition broke up again in 1957, Fianna Fáil, which in its worst
political moments since 1932 had never received less than 42 percent of the
popular vote or held less than 44 percent of the seats of the Dáil, had
learned a profound political lesson in opposition, and so succeeded in the
next several years in refurbishing its populist and progressive image in the
country that it was able to secure for itself yet another sixteen successive
years in power. That second ascendancy was brought to an end in 1973 by
mobilizing the cumulative forces of dissent in the formation of a third
coalition. Though that coalition was routed in a general election four years
later in 1977, Fianna Fáil has not been able since then to refurbish its image
or to project its power as in the past. The reason why Fianna Fáil has not
been able to repeat its previous successes is that its thunder as the populist,
and particularly as the progressive party, has recently been stolen by the
transformation of the old Fine Gael party under Garrett FitzGerald into a
progressive party. In the first three general elections since 1981, Fine Gael
has finally been able to rival Fianna Fáil in both its popular vote and seats in
the Dáil, polling nearly 40 percent of the vote and securing about the same
percentage of seats. The last general election in May 1987 was indecisive,
with Fianna Fáil being returned as a minority government, and the next
general election, therefore, promises to be one of the most interesting in
recent Irish history as far as the political system is concerned.

The Irish populist tradition not only goes a long way toward explaining
the transformation of Fine Gael from a conservative to a progressive party,

but it also allows for a clearer appreciation of one of the more curious features of the Irish political system—the continued survival of the Irish Labour party. The critics and the would-be friends of the Irish Labour party have often complained that its basic weaknesses are that it is at one and the same time nonideological and rurally rooted, a fatal combination for a working-class party that aspired to winning power in the state.[42] The fact is, however, the Irish Labour party has survived because it is not a socialist, class-conscious, centralized, and urban-oriented party that has aspired to power at the center. The Labour party has always been, and still is, essentially a populist party—rural, radical, reformist, and above all an opportunist political formation. The reasons why the Labour party has survived and all the other Irish political formations have merely come and gone, are mainly three in number. First, the Irish Labour party has been able to build on a long-term political base.[43] The local Land and Labour leagues of the 1880s and 1890s, and especially the All for Ireland League just before the First World War, have provided the Labour party with a politically conscious constituency at the grass roots. It is no historical accident, for example, that labor's electoral strength has always been found south of a line drawn from Dublin to Galway cities, where the above leagues flourished between 1880 and 1914. Second, the Irish trade-union movement has provided the organizational frame, the funds, and the leadership for that constituency. Again, it is no accident that the Irish trade-union ethos is essentially populist in that it is reformist, radical, eminently opportunist, and above all nonideological.

Third, and finally, the Irish Labour party, for the greater part of its existence, has not really aspired to power at the center, but has viewed its role in basically populist terms—as a brake or check on that power at the center. In this scenario, the historic mission of the Labour party is to play the role of political midwife in bringing the populist or progressive party to power, realizing at the same time that because power at the center inevitably corrupts, the thankless task will always have to be repeated. Labor played just such a role, it will be recalled, in both 1918 and 1932 by helping to bring the long ascendancies of the Irish Parliamentary party and rump of the Sinn Féin party respectively to an end, and it repeated the performance in both 1948 and 1973 by checking what it perceived to be the political arrogance of Fianna Fáil by forming coalitions that ousted the latter from power. Indeed, the coalition policy has been the single most divisive issue in the Labour party since 1970, for it has resulted in a deep division of opinion between those who believe that the party should seize upon every opportunity to prevent Fianna Fáil from exercising power and those who are convinced that such a policy can only result in the loss of labor's identity and its absorption by Fine Gael in the long run.[44] The anticoalitionists argue that because labor since 1923 has not polled much more than 10 percent of the vote or held much more than the same percentage of seats in the Dáil, it cannot ever hope to win power in its own right, and it should, therefore, realistically face up to the fact that its role in the Irish political system is to check the abuse of power at the center in the interests of the people. Given the populist/party dynamic in the Irish political system, moreover, it should come as no surprise that the main opposition to participating in coalition has come consistently from the trade-union wing of the labor movement, while the aspiring professional politicians in the party have been more enthusiastic about the coalition policy. The moral to be drawn from this lesson, of course, is that the vitality and stability on which the survival of the Irish Labour party depends is but a microcosm of the macrocosm that is the Irish political system.

In conclusion it should be pointed out that the populist/party, or periphery/center, dichotomy is not only useful in explaining the survival of the Labour party in the Irish political system, but it is also helpful in elucidating a number of other apparent conundrums in that system; namely, the role of the leader as chief and/or chairman, the remarkable persistence of independent candidates in the electoral process, the Janus-like ambivalence of those elected in regard to their constituents and their parties, the parochial nature of machine politics in Ireland, and a good deal more. Any attempt, however, to come to terms with all of these problems here would only turn this effort at a conclusion into another paper.

The fundamental point to be made here is the same as it was in the beginning. The Irish political system is indigenous and therefore unique. To appreciate its uniqueness is to understand that its real dynamic is not supplied by parties, ideologies, or even personalities, but in the popularization of the center and the periphery. The dynamic is still what it was some 160 years ago when Daniel O'Connell mobilized Irish dissent against British power, and the Irish people were asked not only to face up to Dublin Castle, but to the British Parliament at Westminster. Irish nationalism and Catholicism have succeeded in again localizing the confrontation, and for more than a hundred years, the party in the de facto and de jure Irish state has been at the center of a stable Irish political system, while populism is what has given the periphery in the system its continued vitality. In a word, the party has become the institutional expression of the community, and defines its consensus. To guard against the long-term tendency of the party to express its particular interests, grass-roots populism and the minor parties or the other political institutions it produces (i.e., the Labour party) are necessary as a check on the party. This populism, therefore, has as much a claim as the party to be the legitimate expression of the community, and because it has, it does serve as an effective check on the party. When all is said and done, however, the fact is that, since the days of Daniel O'Connell, the center, whether it has been British or Irish, has never been allowed to take the periphery for granted, and this is what, in the last analysis, accounts for both the endurance and the strength of the Irish idea of freedom.

Thomas E. Hachey

IRISH NATIONALISM AND
THE BRITISH CONNECTION

IRISH NATIONALISM and the British connection during the seventeenth, eighteenth, and nineteenth centuries is a subject that has been especially well served by a number of excellent histories.[1] Similarly, Anglo-Irish relations during the earlier part of the twentieth century, up through the 1919-21 Irish War for Independence, is a field that already has yielded a score of important studies.[2] It is, therefore, the era from 1922 through 1949, from the founding of the Irish Free State through the establishment of the Irish republic, that has had to await the opening of the London government's archives, as well as the release of some Dublin government papers, before the continuing story of Irish nationalism and the British connection could be meaningfully attempted. But that task is now well underway thanks to the recent publication of important new monographs,[3] and to the almost unrestricted accessibility of British government archives relating to this eventful twenty-seven-year period in the Anglo-Irish relationship. This essay will highlight some of the books, as well as selected documents, that examine or portray the often confrontational character of Anglo-Irish relations during those three remarkable decades: the 1920s when the Irish Free State led the fight for greater dominion autonomy; the 1930s when Dublin effectively seceded from the Commonwealth; and the 1940s when the Irish remained neutral during World War II and ultimately declared the establishment of a republic shortly thereafter.

There is, however, scarcely an author of any of the works in this growing historiography who has not expressed regret over the fact that a large part of the Irish government archives either remain officially closed or are so badly organized as to render them of very limited value. Not only has this made definitive scholarship immeasurably more difficult, it inevitably has produced findings that are largely, if not exclusively, derivative of British evidence. And that is scarcely surprising. Except for Department of Taoiseach records that are thirty or more years old, there are comparatively few papers available for any worthwhile study of the various departments of the Irish government. Moreover, de Valera's personal disinclination to keep written accounts of political discussions, a practice often imitated by the Costello government after 1948, sometimes resulted in Irish Cabinet minutes which contain little more than a roll call of the members present and a sketchy outline of the topics presumably reviewed.[4] By contrast, the British have produced and preserved records with an almost Teutonic zeal. In addition to telegrams, dispatches, and memoranda, there are also internal minutes by officials of such ministries as the Dominions Office and Foreign Office that can help the reader to better appreciate those factors that dictated the formulation of a given policy or to see why the London government chose to respond in this or that instance as it did.

Britain, for obvious reasons of self-interest, could not and would not accept the 1919 Sinn Féin demand for a united and independent Republic of Ireland. Nor did the British leave it to the Irish themselves to resolve the northern question and the imperial issue. Thanks to John McColgan's 1983 book on Irish administration, we now have a better sense of how London in fact orchestrated the partition of Ireland rather than simply accepting it as an inevitability imposed by unionist perseverance. Ireland, after all, had been governed until 1920 as a single entity by a British administration centered in Dublin. But in September of that year, Sir Ernest Clark was appointed assistant secretary in Belfast as the first step in a program that would incrementally establish full civil authority in the Six Counties. By the time the Government of Ireland Act reached the statute book in December 1920, the administration of Ireland was already bureaucratically partitioned at its center, and the administrative machinery was in place to make both Home Rule and partition a reality. Sinn Féin did not appreciate the significance of this maneuver and, accordingly, failed to make a bargaining chip out of the full transfer of government services to the North, which followed in the wake of the treaty. London's political success was thereby achieved through the adroit exploitation of administrative apparatus and with the help and advice of the civil servants who managed that apparatus. To a very considerable extent, therefore, the British left Ireland on their own terms: specifically, the nonseparation of Ireland from the empire and the noncoercion of Ulster.[5]

It was not, however, an unqualified triumph. The confidential minutes of various British ministers reflect the fact that some of them recognized how Ireland's geographical proximity and distinctly different historical traditions made that country uniquely different from other dominions and that realization prompted London into making concessions even from the very outset of the 1921 treaty negotiations. British negotiators consented, for example, to the Irish demand that the oath of allegiance contained in the treaty not be addressed directly to the Crown, but to "the Constitution of the Irish Free State, and to the King only in his capacity as part of that constitution."[6] Lloyd George further agreed that the governor general of the Irish Free State would be an Irishman and a commoner, which all but assured that he would be chosen by the Irish themselves. Such a practice differed from that of the other dominions. And there were additional concessions. Article 2 of the proposed treaty stated that "all powers of government, and all authority, legislative, executive and judicial in Ireland are derived from the people of Ireland." Compare this with article 9 of the Canadian Constitution, the nation that ostensibly was to serve as the dominion model for the Irish Free State. The Canadian document reads: "The executive government and authority of and over Canada is hereby declared to continue to be vested in the queen."[7] Moreover, the governor-general in Canada, as in all other dominions, could dissolve Parliament on his own authority, a power not given to the Irish governor-general. Several other important concessions were made by the British in order to oblige Irish nationalist sensibilities, and some were remarkably indicative of the future direction of Irish policy. Article 49 of the Anglo-Irish Treaty is a case in point in that it sought to secure Ireland's right to remain free from involvement in wars in which Britain might participate. It reads: "Save in the case of actual invasion, the Irish Free State . . . shall not be committed to active participation in any war without the assent of the Oireachtas" (both houses of Parliament).[8]

None of this, of course, detracts from the fact that there were several matters of critical importance to Irish republicans on which the British refused to compromise. Six counties of Northern Ireland would remain a part of the United Kingdom; several Irish ports would remain under the control of the Royal Navy; and the Irish Free State's sovereignty would be clearly modified by a compulsory allegiance to the Crown and Common-wealth. Why London insisted that these terms were nonnegotiable is easy to understand. Many Britons were as passionately committed to the symbols of monarchy and empire as Sinn Féiners were to the goals of republi-canism, and they insisted upon Ireland remaining in association with Britain under the Crown. Moreover, government ministers were especially anxious about these two concerns: that the Irish Free State not compromise the security of the United Kingdom in the immediate aftermath of a hard-fought war, and that the colonial dependencies not be incited by an Irish example of independent sovereignty.

Eamon de Valera understood London's anxieties and thought that his

formula for "external association" would serve the national interests of both
Britain and Ireland. De Valera outlined the concept to his fellow Cabinet
members by drawing a large circle to represent the British Commonwealth, and placed within that circumference a number of smaller circles to
indicate dominion members. Outside of the large circle, but touching it,
was another smaller circle representing Ireland. The essential thought was
that Ireland would be *associated* with the Commonwealth, as opposed to
being an actual member. De Valera not only expected that the British might
perceive this as an acceptable compromise, he also imagined it would pave
the way for Ulster's inclusion in the new Irish state. That expectation, of
course, was entirely misplaced and serves to support John Bowman's
contention that de Valera never really understood the Ulster unionist
attitude toward interacting with *any* Dublin government.[9]

What does not require retelling here are the details of that now familiar
story of how the Irish negotiating team that de Valera sent to London
eventually accepted a twenty-six-county dominion, and how the Dail, after
an acrimonious debate over the resulting treaty, ratified it by the narrow
vote of 64 to 57.

Few people in 1922 could have foreseen the international role which
the Irish Free State was destined to assume over the next ten years. The
question of whether the Irish should be perceived as empire wreckers or as
dominion reformers was examined over a generation ago by William Keith
Hancock, Robert McGregor Dawson, and Nicholas Mansergh.[10] They
shared the view that the Irish Free State helped to expedite and expand
upon consitutional reforms which were already evolving within the Commonwealth. In recent years, however, the work of David Harkness, Paul
Canning, Robert Fisk, Deirdre MacMahon, John Bowman and Ronan
Fanning, to mention but a few, have further expanded our knowledge of the
Anglo-Irish relationship in the period from the 1920s through the 1940s,
through studies which have either fine-tuned or notably revised existing
interpretations for various parts of this history.

David Harkness produced the first modern reassessment of Anglo-
Irish affairs during the 1920s with his pioneer study, *The Restless Dominion*, published in 1969. In it, Harkness succeeds in disposing of Gordon
Walker's claim that Canada provided the lead for other dominions in the
transformation from empire to commonwealth. He explains, for example,
how Irish statesmen like Desmond FitzGerald, Patrick McGilligan and
Kevin O'Higgins, and not Mackenzie King of Canada or Herzog of South
Africa, provided the greatest impetus for change. Although the Harkness
book may contain a few assertions that are insufficiently supported by the
existing evidence, he is entirely persuasive when arguing that the 1926

Balfour Declaration was, in significant measure, the product of Irish lobbying. It was that declaration, later to be enshrined in the 1931 Statute of Westminster, that described the dominions as "autonomous communities within the British Empire, equal in status . . . though united by a common allegiance to the Crown."

Outside the Commonwealth, and in the forum of world affairs, the Irish Free State, under the leadership of President of the Executive Council William T. Cosgrave, acted on successive occasions to assert its separate sovereignty. The Irish, for example, went ahead in 1923 and registered the Anglo-Irish Treaty as an international treaty over the strenuous objections of the British who regarded dominion relations as an internal matter for the Commonwealth. Dublin further insisted on having separate diplomatic representation abroad, sending her own ministers, for instance, to Washington, D.C., and to the Vatican. In 1926 the Irish Free State became the first dominion to run for election to the Council of the League of Nations and, although defeated, her example helped persuade the Canadians to run and win with Free State support the following year. Moreover, the Free State won a term of its own in 1930.[11] As British Cabinet minutes and Dominions Office records make clear, the first ten years of the new Irish state, from 1922 to 1932, represented a decade of unrelenting challenges that often strained the forbearance and patience of His Majesty's ministers.[12] But whether under the premiership of Stanley Baldwin or Ramsay MacDonald, British policy toward Dublin was more frequently conciliatory than confrontational. That spirit of official tolerance was, of course, largely attributable to the fact that the dominions would not have supported any coercive measures taken against the Irish Free State.[13] It was also due in part to the shared view of many British officials, that the Irish could not reasonably be expected to share Australia's or New Zealand's receptivity toward dominion status. Ireland was different.

To men like Eamon de Valera, however, any form of dominion relationship was unacceptable and not surprisingly his electoral triumph in 1932 caused the British government no little concern. As early as June 1932, de Valera frankly informed London that his ultimate objective was an Irish republic in *association* with the Commonwealth.[14] It was, therefore, in response to what the British perceived as a constitutional challenge that Prime Minister Ramsay MacDonald created an Irish situation committee for the specific purpose of monitoring the activities of, and remediating any differences with, the de Valera government. The committee, which was chaired by the prime minister, included both Cabinet ministers and senior civil servants, and it met periodically for six years until the signing of the Anglo-Irish Agreements in 1938.[15]

It is also important to note that economic and political interests within the British Cabinet were, with great difficulty, eventually reconciled to changes that effectively abrogated the Treaty of 1921. Deirdre MacMahon's study, *Republicans and Imperialists: Anglo-Irish Relations in the 1930s*, offers the best assessment of Britain's response to a variety of Irish nationalist initiatives. de Valera, for example, began by terminating the oath of allegiance in 1933, and then proceeded to eliminate what he perceived as each of the remaining encumbrances to Irish sovereignty. The 1936 abdication of King Edward VIII took place as de Valera was hard at work on a new constitution that would delete all reference to the Crown. Since, however, Edward VIII had removed himself from the throne before De Valera had had the opportunity of removing him from the constitution, this unexpected development required prompt action. De Valera responded with the External Relations Act which took the Crown out of the internal government entirely, while retaining the king for limited external purposes only. Hence, the Irish Free State, which was renamed Eire in the new constitution of 1937, became a republic in everything but name. Britain could either accept de Valera's unilateral changes or expel Eire from the Commonwealth. If Britain chose the latter course, there was a good prospect that some dominions would not follow Britain's policy and the unity of the Commonwealth would be shattered, along with much of its influence in the world. A public acceptance of external association, however, could further encourage the already awakened national aspirations of India and other British colonies, creating a nightmare for the constitutional theory of the Commonwealth. The British answer was a masterpiece of political pragmatism: they chose to ignore, at least publicly, the implications of the new constitution and to maintain the fiction that Eire was still part of the Commonwealth.

De Valera chose not to challenge that pretense and the result was a modus vivendi whose value was manifested the following year when the Anglo-Irish Agreements of 1938 ended the six-year trade war that had resulted from de Valera's refusal to pay Britain the land annuities provided for in earlier treaties. What the recently opened British documents make clear is that this reconciliation would not have taken place had it not been for the rather fortuitous changes at this time in the London government. Indeed, it was not until Malcolm MacDonald and Neville Chamberlain, respectively, replaced J.H. Thomas and Stanley Baldwin as dominions secretary and prime minister, that British policy began to place a higher premium on the creation of goodwill than it did on the viability of treaty obligations. Malcolm MacDonald was a prime mover in this shift in priorities, as was Adolf Hitler whose increasing bellicosity persuaded even the

British military chiefs to concede the loss of the Irish ports rather than jeopardize Dublin's goodwill.

The transfer of the treaty ports from Britain to Ireland in the summer of 1938 was both a symbolic and a substantive component of de Valera's drive for total Irish independence. The symbolism was obvious, and the substance would become equally apparent a year later upon the outbreak of the Second World War when control of the ports made possible Eire's policy of neutrality. But Anglo-Irish relations plummeted to their lowest point since the creation of the Free State when de Valera, in 1940, refused to trade neutrality for the vague promise of Irish unity that was made by the new prime minister, Winston Churchill. Robert Fisk's study, *In Time of War*, explains how Churchill's hostility to both de Valera and neutrality was due in part to the fact that Churchill had helped to negotiate the Treaty of 1921 and took very personally the Irish prime minister's role in unilaterally dismantling it.[16] Moreover, the evidence clearly indicates that both protagonists were, in part, unwilling and, in part, unable to barter neutrality for Irish unity. Churchill, for instance, could sacrifice neither Northern Ireland's value to the war effort nor his own concept of empire. De Valera, on the other hand, could risk neither the alienation of advanced Irish nationalists nor the prospect of German air strikes against his defenseless country. Hence, the often repeated references to the lost opportunity for Irish unification in 1940 is fallacious. There was no such window of opportunity either then or later.

Eire's policy of neutrality during World War II was supported by virtually every constituency within the twenty-six counties, and it succeeded spectacularly in demonstrating the legitimacy of the 1937 Constitution, just as it also affirmed unequivocally the sovereignty of the Irish state. But it was not without cost. John Bowman believes that Irish neutrality in fact thickened the partitionist wall between northern and southern Ireland and sacrificed much of the goodwill that had characterized Anglo-Irish affairs during the MacDonald-Chamberlain era.[17] Indeed, the strain on the relationship between Dublin and London was palpable by the end of the first year of the war.

The extent to which Irish nationalism, in general, and Eire's policy of neutrality in particular, placed still further strain upon the British connection during the war years is graphically apparent from the documentary correspondence among the London government archives that have been opened in recent years. We see, for example, how Eamon de Valera summoned Britain's representative to Eire, Sir John Maffey, on 20 November 1940 to protest the publication of an article entitled "Irish Harbours" which had appeared in *The Economist*. The article quoted Prime Minister

Churchill as having declared that the loss of the Irish ports had handicapped the English at sea. De Valera disputed that claim by insisting that the ports were not so vital as the Admiralty chose to contend, and he remarked to Maffey that the press could not print such defamatory articles in wartime without at least the tacit consent of the London government. The British diplomat replied that the Irish premier erred in assuming that press censorship was as rigid in Britain as it was in Eire and in believing that such newspaper accounts were a product of government inspiration. Maffey agreed, nonetheless, to communicate de Valera's strong misgivings on the matter to Dominions Secretary Lord Cranborne.[18]

Churchill's antipathy toward de Valera was so intense that he might have seized the desired ports by invading Eire had it not been for the fear that such a step would jeopardize sensitive Anglo-American relations.[19] But the British prime minister did nonetheless contemplate an equally sinister plan of coercion. On 23 November 1940, he sent a confidential message to Minister of Food Lord Woolton which read: "Let me know exactly the effect that would be produced on your department by the cutting off of Irish supplies of food for say six months."[20] Woolton reported that he would support such action if it were accompanied by a complete prohibition of British food exports, both for human or for animal consumption, to Eire. And he concluded by remarking that such a step would so profoundly disturb Irish agriculture over a three-month period "as to render negotiations possible with them subsequently on our terms."[21]

Churchill next made secret inquiries to Chancellor of the Exchequer Sir K. Wood and President of the Board of Trade Sir O. Lyttelton. Wood advised the prime minister that the Irish would be unable to take any effective retaliatory measures against Britain in the face of a food boycott.[22] On 4 December Lyttelton wrote Churchill: "There is nothing in the terms of the Trade Agreements of 1938 to prevent us from cutting off our exports to Eire . . . [but] it will make us rather than Mr. de Valera unpopular with the Irish people."[23] Although there is no evidence in the government papers to explain why the prime minister's scheme was never implemented, it seems safe to assume that the anticipated response of Irish opinion in the United States was a restraining influence.[24]

Precisely how much the denial of the treaty ports was to cost Britain in terms of vessels sunk by German U-boats is difficult, if not impossible, to estimate. But it should be remembered that the Germans had cracked the Royal Navy's secret code in 1936, a security breach which was not entirely remedied until 1943. Indeed, by the year 1943 the British were to become far less aggressive in their representations to the Eire government on the subject of the ports for two reasons. One is that experience in the early and critical years of the war had shown that the Irish ports simply were not as vital as was previously assumed; the other, which underscored the wisdom of de Valera's policy, was that Britain did not have the capability of effectively defending Eire if that country were also to become involved in the war. That assessment was candidly conceded in a memorandum of 5 March 1943 from Dominions Secretary Clement Attlee to Foreign Secretary Anthony Eden. Attlee, in responding to a recommendation by a junior minister urging that the Dublin government be asked once more to allow British military facilities at the treaty ports, reminded Eden of the stark realities should de Valera suddenly agree. Attlee concluded: "It would be tantamount to bringing Eire into the war, and we should have to supply her not only protection (anti-aircraft equipment, etc.), [but] also with civilian supplies. I thought it doubtful that we could spare enough of this at the present time and that the strategic facilities would probably be dearly bought at such a price."[25]

Aside from the treaty ports and the partition issues, another aspect of Eire's policy of neutrality which further aggravated her relations with Britain was the involvement or participation of Irishmen in the war effort. Eamon de Valera not only insisted upon keeping Eire neutral but also warned London not to impose conscription upon Ulster. Other opponents of compulsory military service included the Catholic hierarchy and the Labour party of Northern Ireland, in addition to the substantial nationalist minority in that province, who promised to resist conscription by the most effective means at their disposal. There is, moreover, reason to assume that the representations made in London by United States Ambassador Joseph P. Kennedy and by the prime minister of Australia helped to influence the British government in its determination to seek only volunteer enlistments in Northern Ireland.[26]

The decision of the government of the United Kingdom not to extend compulsory military service to Ulster rankled many Ulster loyalists. Northern Ireland Prime Minister Lord Craigavon used all of the influence at his disposal to urge the inclusion of Ulster in the military training bill. But the British Cabinet, mindful of the sorry attempt to impose conscription on Ireland during the First World War, was disinclined to provoke needlessly the Eire government in the early and critical months of hostilities. Accordingly, Northern Ireland was totally excluded from the Military Training Act. Neville Chamberlain publicly commended Lord Craigavon for displaying "the purest kind of patriotism" because, as John Blake tells us in his study, *Northern Ireland in the Second World War*, Craigavon gracefully accepted London's decision and placed the resources of Northern Ireland unreservedly at the disposal of Britain in the event of war.[27]

In point of fact, the determination not to extend conscription to Northern Ireland was keenly resented by hard-liners at both Westminster and Stormont. Among these irreconcilables were Winston Churchill and the man who was soon to become the prime minister of Northern Ireland, J.M. Andrews. Efforts to extend conscription to the province of Ulster were attempted on two further occasions, one in the spring of 1941 and the other in the spring of 1943. Although both Churchill and Andrews were then in power, the British Cabinet overwhelmingly opposed altering the conscription policy because of the formidable and widespread opposition which such a move was likely to engender both in Ireland and in Irish nationalist communities abroad.[28]

It is now very clear that the Stormont government had been embarrassed by the comparatively low rate of voluntary enlistment from Ulster, where only 38,000 volunteered out of an eligible male population of 212,000, and it was obviously hopeful that conscription would cover up this apparent lack of enthusiasm among loyalists to fight for the imperiled empire. By contrast, some 60,000 Irishmen from Eire volunteered for the British armed forces, 40,000 of whom crossed the border to enlist in Belfast, while the remainder joined up in Britain.[29] These were the unsung warriors whose contribution was never effectively recognized by either London or Dublin. As a neutral, the Eire government could scarcely acknowledge the participation of its citizens in the military forces of a belligerent power, but neither did it seek to prevent them from enlisting, insisting only that these volunteers wear civilian attire whenever they returned to Eire on furlough.

The British government did take appropriate notice of the individual efforts of Irish volunteers, awarding no fewer than seven Victoria Crosses, as well as a host of other military distinctions, to citizens of Eire. But when the Irish-born General Sir Hubert Gough initiated a campaign to revive the historic Irish regiments from Munster and Leinster in which all the southern Irishmen in the British Army might serve, he provoked an immediate reaction in Belfast. The fact that General Gough was the Ulster hero who, in 1914, had declined to use the army against the Ulster unionists who were revolting against Home Rule did not deter Stormont officials from informing the Dominions Office on 28 November 1941 that they "did not wish any publicity given to the services of recruits from Eire, [and] that they were sorry to see encouragement given to the idea put forward by General Gough and his associates."[30]

London ultimately decided against authorizing the formation of a southern Irish brigade, but not because of the objections raised by the Ulster government, which, incidentally, at least one high British official had deemed to be "absurd and shortsighted."[31] Rather, the Dominions and War offices considered the merits and/or shortcomings of the Gough plan from a purely pragmatic perspective. The consensus view of these two ministries was that whatever goodwill might be fostered in Eire by the creation of military units exclusively comprised of southern Irish would be more than offset by the potential complications of such a scheme. It was feared, for example, that the special recognition accorded citizens of neutral Eire fighting with the British forces might compromise the Dublin government and compel it to prevent the departure of further volunteers. Moreover, there was apprehension that instead of serving as a symbol of the close connection between Britain and Ireland, an Irish brigade might become a fertile breeding ground for subversive agitation by members of the IRA. After providing this analysis to Prime Minister Churchill in a joint memorandum of 25 October 1941, the Dominions and War offices concluded with this not uncharacteristic recommendation: "In the meantime, a suitable measure of publicity could be given . . . [to] the deeds of individual Irishmen, particularly in the air [force], which has apparently a special appeal to the Irish people."[32]

Another dimension to the manpower contribution that the citizens of Eire made to the British war effort was the 100,000 or more Irish men and women who worked in Britain's munitions factories. Again, there is an interesting contrast between these Irish and those in Ulster. In May 1941 Prime Minister Churchill asked Home Secretary Herbert Morrison if laborers from Northern Ireland, one-eighth of whose insured population was then out of work, might not be encouraged to take employment in Britain as semiskilled workers in munitions production. Churchill wrote on 4 May that "Northern Ireland does not appear to be making its utmost contribution to the war effort."[33] In his reply on 8 May to the prime minister, the home secretary recalled that the Stormont government had been pressing for a larger share of armaments contracts since the beginning of the war and that an estimated one thousand men per month had moved from Northern Ireland to Britain for employment as of that date. He did add, however, that "not all of these men are willing to remain permanently in this country and there was a marked tendency, until Belfast became a target for bombing, for such men to return to Northern Ireland if bombs fell in their vicinity while over here."[34]

One month later, on 23 June 1941, Minister of Labour and National Service Ernest Bevin sent Churchill a confidential memorandum urging that the admission of Eire citizens into Britain be regularized in the interest of security. Bevin noted how the recruitment of southern Irish laborers was being done by employers' agents, and he requested that his department, in collaboration with Irish authorities, assume responsibility for that task. He further suggested that Eire citizens be kept under close supervision while in the United Kingdom and that arrangements be made for the immediate return of any unsatisfactory worker. Across the bottom of Bevin's recommendation Churchill scrawled the following directive: "Approved. But keep a tight hand over them. They are really enemy aliens in many cases."[35]

The anomalous character of neutral Eire's relations toward the belligerent powers inevitably produced some rather bizarre developments. There never was any secret about the enlistment of Irish citizens in the British forces, but the Dublin government's censors would not allow any reference whatever to it in the Irish press. Obituary notices of men who died in battle could not be published. Moreover, when a young journalist from one of the Dublin dailies who had joined the British Navy went down with the HMS *Prince of Wales* and was rescued, the only means his editor had of informing readers of his safety was through the subterfuge of a notice in the social and personal column that the young man in question had completely recovered from the effect of his recent boating accident.[36]

If Prime Minister de Valera had wished to prevent Eire citizens from joining the British armed forces, he might easily have followed the example of other neutral countries by passing a foreign enlistment act making it an offense, punishable by the loss of all civil rights, to join the fighting services of any of the belligerent powers. He did nothing of the kind, and all through the war Irishmen were at liberty to join the British forces. The fact that they did so in comparatively large numbers caused de Valera no notable concern, although he doubtless would have preferred that the enlistments not include men on active duty in the Irish Army who deserted in order to fight for Britain. At the end of 1945 it was admitted in the Dáil Éireann that some four thousand of the Irish Army, about 10 percent of its total force, had deserted during the war to join the British Army. When one of them was arrested and tried on a charge of desertion on his return to Dublin after V-E Day, it was argued by his lawyer that the man could not be guilty of desertion in the military sense of the word since desertion meant running away from danger to a place of safety, whereas in the case of the Irish soldiers who went to the British forces, precisely the opposite procedure had been adopted. There were a few test cases to satisfy military regulations, and suspensory sentences were pronounced, but denials of government employment or participation in government relief schemes were the most severe penalties suffered by these Irish "deserters."[37]

The pro-British tilt of Eire's neutrality did not, however, in the view of Winston Churchill, compensate for her unpardonable determination to remain neutral. And the prime minister was actively encouraged by the American minister to Dublin, David Gray, to engage in economic warfare against southern Ireland and to "bring home to a people who have been persistently misled by their Government as to the true basis of their economy."[38] Churchill was deterred from acting on that advice, which would have had dire consequences for Eire, primarily because he suspected that the Roosevelt administration did not share David Gray's views on this issue. But on 4 November 1943, the prime minister told Foreign Secretary Eden that a forthcoming food conference sponsored by the United Nations provided a splendid opportunity to make Irishmen feel the "ignominy of their conduct." In observing that neutrals had not been invited to the conference, Churchill told Eden: "Southern Ireland is a neutral and this is the moment to make her feel her isolation and the shameful position she will occupy at the peace."[39]

By the following year, 1944, as the war was approaching its desperate climax, both Washington and London became increasingly concerned with the question of Allied security. American Minister David Gray recommended that the Eire government be asked to close the Axis legations in Dublin lest they somehow compromise the D-Day preparations then underway. This time both Churchill and Roosevelt agreed with Gray. It was decided that the United States would take the initiative, while Britain would send de Valera a separate communication in support of the American note. Privately, Churchill told Dominions Secretary Viscount Cranborne that it might be necessary to sever all communication between Ireland and the Continent for a period of several months if the Axis missions were not expelled from Eire.[40]

On 21 February 1944, David Gray personally delivered a message from President Roosevelt to Prime Minister de Valera which requested the Irish government to take appropriate steps for the recall of German and Japanese representatives in Ireland because of the opportunity that they afforded for highly organized espionage at a critical juncture in the war.[41] De Valera replied that his government had done all it could to prevent espionage against the Allies, and it could not and would not do more. He was courteous but firm, both to Gray and to the British representative to Eire, Sir John Maffey, who brought a similar appeal from Churchill the very next day. Maffey reported that de Valera denounced the proceedings as an ill-disguised attempt to push him into war and to deprive Eire of the symbols of neutrality and independence. It was obvious, observed Maffey, that the Irish prime minister attached immense importance to the symbolic factor.[42] Washington and London accepted this rebuff with something less than equanimity, but for several reasons, which included a reluctance to alienate the Irish-American vote or the Eire citizens then serving in the British armed forces, the Allies took no retaliatory action against southern Ireland.

What de Valera found particularly objectionable about the American note was Roosevelt's contention that the Irish government, in spite of its declaration of friendly neutrality, had in fact pursued a policy which operated in favor of the Axis. It seems reasonable to conclude that the German government would not have shared that view. German airmen who bailed out or were shot down over Eire were interned for the duration of the war, while nearly all British servicemen were returned to their units. Furthermore, the Irish government compelled the German minister, Dr. Edward Hempel, to surrender his wireless transmitter during the war and denied Berlin's 1940 request to add two additional members to its five-man legation in Dublin. For its part, the German government refused to accept Eire's newly appointed minister to Berlin without the usual letters of credence, which in the existing circumstances still needed to be signed by the British king. His Majesty could hardly be expected to accredit a minister to a power with which he was at war, with the consequence that Eire's Berlin legation was left to the supervision of a chargé d'affaires. And when the legation premises in the Drakestrasse were demolished by an RAF bomb in 1943, the chargé was offered no other facilities, whereupon he transferred the legation's business to a stud farm outside Berlin owned by an Irishman. [43] There was little cordiality, and still less cooperation, between the governments of Dublin and Berlin. Although there undoubtedly was a certain amount of German espionage, particularly in the early years of the war, when spies parachuted into Eire, it never got very far, thanks to an efficient Irish secret service and a vigilant home defense force. By any fair standard of judgment, Roosevelt's claim that Irish neutrality operated in favor of the Axis was simply misinformed.

Eamon de Valera provoked another storm of protest in Britain and in the United States when, on 2 May 1945, he called on the German minister to express condolence upon the death of Adolf Hitler. Eire's Secretary of the Department of External Affairs Joseph Walshe, who accompanied de Valera for the ceremonial visit, was apprehensive about the wisdom of that gesture because he anticipated what world reaction would be. But the Irish prime minister had paid a similar visit to the American minister upon the death of President Roosevelt a few weeks earlier, and he felt it only correct diplomatic procedure to be consistent in matters such as these. [44]

De Valera's visit to Hempel took place just when the full horror of Buchenwald and other Nazi extermination camps was being revealed, and even those who had otherwise been sympathetic to Eire's neutrality joined in denouncing the Irish prime minister for his diplomatic courtesy on the occasion of Hitler's death. Ironically enough, it was Prime Minister Churchill who helped restore de Valera's popularity, at least among his countrymen in Eire. In his May 13 victory speech, Churchill bitterly attacked his nemesis in an immoderate diatribe that succeeded in offending southern Irishmen: "Had it not been for the loyalty and friendship of Northern Ireland we should have been forced to come to close quarters with Mr. de Valera . . . [and] though at times it would have been quite easy and quite natural, we left the Dublin Government to frolic with the Germans . . . and the Japanese . . . to their hearts content."[45] De Valera waited four days before making a reply, and the moderate, statesmanlike tone of his address gave the Irish prime minister a psychological and moral advantage. Churchill had admitted that he would have justified violating Ireland's neutrality if Britain's necessity had so required. This was an unfortunate remark with the Nazi example so close at hand, and de Valera took full advantage of it by asking if the prime minister intended to say that if Britain's necessity became sufficiently great, other peoples' rights were not to count. But then de Valera went on to say, "Mr. Churchill is proud of Britain's stand alone, after France had fallen and before America entered the war. Could he not find in his heart the generosity to acknowledge that there is a small nation that stood alone, not for one year or two, but for several hundred years against aggression . . . a small nation that could never be got to accept defeat and has never surrendered her soul?"[46]

Sir John Maffey advised London of the spontaneous change in the national mood of Eire. "After de Valera's call on Hempel," Maffey wrote, "the public mind had been too stunned to react quickly, but overnight there came the collapse of the Reich and with the sudden end of censorship there came the atrocity stories and pictures of the concentration camps."[47] To many Irishmen, de Valera's condolences seemed morally reprehensible, and a sense of disgust emerged with the growing belief that ideals had been sacrificed for symbols. But Churchill's inflammatory remarks had allowed the Irish prime minister to regain his lost prestige and had also undermined several months of plotting by Dominions Secretary Cranborne to marshal international opinion against admitting Eire to the United Nations. No one recognized this better than Maffey, who in his report from Dublin in July 1945 wrote: "I sympathize very deeply with the Dominions Office. . . . But how are you to control ministerial incursions into your china shop? Phrases make history here."[48]

Indeed, the truth of Maffey's observation was eloquently demonstrated by R. M. Smyllie a short time later in an article for *Foreign Affairs*. Smyllie was the editor of the *Irish Times*, which was associated with both

the diminishing Anglo-Irish acendancy and ex-servicemen with pro-union-
ist sympathies who regarded de Valera's ideal of a Gaelic and Catholic
Ireland as rather repugnant. But Smyllie spoke for many Irishmen of
different creeds and politics when he wrote, "Neutrality, almost by definition, is something negative; but Mr. de Valera raised it to the dignity of a
national principle, largely because he wanted to be able to prove to the
world at large that, after more than seven hundred years of subjection to
England, the 26 counties of Southern Ireland at last were really free."[49]
Professor John Murphy would later put it more simply but no less eloquently: "Neutrality in a world conflict is the ultimate exercise in national
sovereignty."[50] Perhaps, therefore, Eire's much-maligned abstention from
World War II may yet be recognized by her wartime critics as one of this
century's most impressive feats of statecraft.

As Donald Akenson, Patrick Keatinge, and others have shown, the
London government nurtured a spiteful attitude toward Dublin even after
Churchill left office following his party's electoral defeat in the general
election of 1945.[51] The Irish, for example, were thought to have forfeited
their right to membership in the United Nations organization that had been
established by the victorious Allies, and some British officials even opposed the granting of American reconstruction aid to Eire because of that
country's wartime neutrality. But despite such efforts to punish de Valera
and to prevent Dublin's rehabilitation within the international community,
the Labour government which was elected to office in 1945 soon discovered
that there still existed compelling reasons for sustaining a close relationship
with Eire.

Clement Attlee's government was no less keen than its predecessor
had been about preserving the essential links of Commonwealth, but
Labour ministers were perhaps more pragmatic and less sentimental when
pursuing that objective. Attempts by London to draw Eire back into a
closer Commonwealth relationship were unavailing precisely because the
trend in Irish politics was clearly in the other direction. Nevertheless,
postwar shortages and rationing in Britain prompted the Labour government to appreciate the value of Eire as a source of food and labor, and as a
market for British goods. It was becoming painfully apparent that the
continuation of Commonwealth trade preferences to Eire were very likely
to be at least as beneficial to Britain as they were to Eire.

British Cabinet minutes and other documents relating to London's
policy toward Eire between 1945 and 1949 further reveal sharp differences
of opinion within the Labour leadership. Herbert Morrison, Ernest Bevin,
and Harold Wilson, among others, deeply resented Dublin's repeal of the
External Relations Act and believed that the end of Eire's membership in

the Commonwealth must also end reciprocal citizenship rights and imperial preferences. Unlike Churchill, their objections did not relate to any
romantic concerns about the sanctity of empire, but rather to the more
materialistic issue of Britain's trade relations with other nations. Even those
ministers who sought accommodation with the Irish, like Lord Addison and
Philip Noel-Baker, did so without any apparent affection for the Irish, or for
the merits of the Irish viewpoint. They simply held to the view that any
other solution than the one that was eventually adopted would pose un-
manageable difficulties for His Majesty's government.[52]

London's response to the 1948 Republic of Ireland Act deliberations in
Dublin was initially hostile. Realizing that it was no longer possible to
perpetuate the fiction that Eire had not left the Commonwealth in 1937,
the British suggested to Dublin that there would be serious implications
involving nationality questions and trade preferences if Ireland became a
foreign country in relation to the Commonwealth. The dominions, however, already worried about the negative impact that punitive measures of
any kind might have upon their own constituents of Irish descent, demanded that London find some way of protecting the Irish from the
consequences of their own action. Even members of Prime Minister Attlee's own Labour party who represented urban constituencies with a large
Irish vote spoke openly of the need for Britain to do something. London's
response was characteristically innovative. Under the terms of the Ireland
Act of 1949, the Westminster Parliament accorded the Republic of Ireland a
"nonforeign" status which insulated the Irish in the two areas where they
were most vulnerable—citizenship and trade.

The retention of Commonwealth trade preferences for Ireland was
important, but so too was the question of Irish citizenship which de Valera
had attempted to resolve sometime earlier with the Irish Nationality Act of
1935. But London and Dublin had never shared a common interpretation
of that particular law—and it was not until the British Nationality Act of
1948, which was mutually agreed upon by both countries, before the
question was put to rest. The effect of the 1948 law was that citizens of Eire,
although no longer British subjects, would, when in Britain, be treated as if
they were British subjects—a concession of enormous importance for the
many Irish men and women living and working in Britain. Reciprocity was
accorded to British subjects who, when in Ireland, would be accorded the
same treatment as Irish citizens. What is sometimes overlooked, however,
is the fact that there existed a very real distinction between the way in
which each country perceived this nonalien status. British subjects in Eire
could not vote, hold public office, or work in the government service of
Eire, whereas Eire citizens in Britain could do all of these. Therefore, the

British Parliament's 1948 Nationality Act, and its subsequent Ireland Act of 1949, had a profound and enduring impact upon the focus of nationalist expression in Ireland. National elections since 1951, for example, have been devoid of the "green card" which set the tone during so many previous campaigns. Elections in the republic have tended to be fought since that time on economic and social issues rather than on relations with Great Britain. Even the rhetoric about coercing an end to partition became decidedly muted, and there has developed a tendency among Irish citizens to view partition as a fact of life "far removed from their daily concerns."[53]

In conclusion, then, the period between 1922 and 1949 witnessed a remarkable evolution in Anglo-Irish relations. Although Britain may have succeeded in dictating the terms of partition and dominion status in 1921, the course of events that began almost immediately thereafter would eventually reverse, except for partition, every imposed provision of the treaty. Irish lobbying and dominion opinion in the 1920s, and international tensions in the 1930s, were the principal occasions for British concessions to the demands of Irish nationalism. Remaining neutral in World War II, of course, gave credence to Irish sovereignty, but that policy also had the effect of diminishing the cordial Anglo-Irish spirit that typified the 1938 agreements. Indeed, after 1945 the tenor of domestic politics in Ireland made it increasingly difficult for any government to allow the country's constitutional status to remain ambiguous. All the same, when Eire's remaining links with the Commonwealth were finally severed, the change that ensued was more symbolic than substantive. Neither Britain nor Ireland could afford to ignore the stern realities of the postwar world. Both recognized how their respective economies were interdependent, and likely to remain so, irrespective of the political relationship of the moment. And that is essentially what the two governments acknowledged in accommodating Erie's symbolic need for a separate citizenship without changing its practical effects on individuals. Irish national opinion required an end to the British connection, but the basic interests of both peoples made inevitable that special and exceptional relationship that endures to this day.

NOTES

Components of Irish Nationalism

1. D. George Boyce, *Nationalism in Ireland* (Baltimore, 1982), and Robert Kee, *The Green Flag* (New York, 1972) are excellent discussions of the manys strands of Irish nationalism. Shorter but perceptive examinations are Maurice Goldring, *Faith of Our Fathers* (Dublin, 1982) and Owen Dudley Edwards, "Ireland," *Celtic Nationalism* (New York, 1968). Boyce's first three chapters discuss the growth of local self-consciousness in Ireland's first English colony and its implications for nationalism.

2. Maureen Wall, *The Penal Laws, 1691-1760*, Irish History Series, no. 1 (Dundalk, 1961) is the best study of its subject.

3. Mary Edith Johnson, *Ireland in the Eighteenth-Century* (Dublin, 1974) is a good survey. Boyce, *Nationalism in Ireland* chaps. 3 and 4, and Kee, *The Green Flag*, pt. 1, chaps. 5 and 6, provide valuable insights into Protestant patriotism.

4. Tom Dunne, *Theobald Wolfe Tone, Colonial Outsider* (Cork, 1982) is a brief, perceptive, revisionist portrait of the first hero of Irish revolutionary republicanism.

5. Marianne Elliott, *Partners in Revolution:United Irishmen and France* (New Haven, 1982) is an excellent and exhaustive analysis of the United Irishmen. Other valuable examinations are Thomas Pakenham, *The Year of Liberty: The Great Rebellion of 1798* (London, 1967); Edwards, "Ireland"; Kee, *The Green Flag*, pt. 2; and Boyce, *Nationalism in Ireland*, chap. 4. One of the best ways to understand 1798 is by reading Thomas Flanagan's National Book Critics Circle Award novel, *The Year of the French* (New York, 1979). He sets his story in Mayo, but it reveals the essence of the entire 1798 situation. The Ulster Protestant mind that birthed the Orange Order is best described in David Miller, *The Queen's Rebels* (New York, 1978), and A.T.Q. Stewart, *The Narrow Ground* (London, 1977).

6. G.C. Bolton, *The Passing of the Act of Union* (London, 1966). Oliver MacDonagh, *The Hereditary Bondsmen: Daniel O'Connell, 1775-1829* (New York, 1988) is an excellent scholarly study of O'Connell's life through the Catholic emancipation crisis. Volume II will follow. Of the many O'Connell biographies, Sean O'Faolain, *The King of the Beggars* (Dublin, 1980), originally published in 1938, remains the most readable and insightful total profile of the creator of modern Irish nationalism. Maurice O'Connell, *The Correspondence of Daniel O'Connell*, (Dublin and New York, 1972-80) has made possible significant scholarly investigation into the life of Catholic Ireland's Liberator.

8. For interesting examinations of the priest's role in Irish life and politics, see Emmet Larkin, *The Historical Dimensions of Irish Catholicism* (Washington, 1984); Patrick Corish,

The Irish Catholic Experience (Wilmington, 1985); Theodore Hoppen, *Elections, Politics, and Society in Ireland, 1832-1885* (Oxford, 1984); S. J. Connolly, *Priests and People in Pre-Famine Ireland, 1780-1845* (New York, 1982); James O'Shea, *Priest, Politics and Society in Post-Famine Ireland: A Study of County Tipperary, 1850-1891* (Atlantic Highlands, N.J., 1983); Donal A. Kerr, *Peel, Priest and Politics* (Oxford, 1982).

9. Fergus O'Ferrall, *Catholic Emancipation: Daniel O'Connell and the Birth of Irish Democracy, 1820-30* (Dublin, 1985) has superseded James A. Reynold's valuable, *The Catholic Emancipation Crisis in Ireland* (New Haven, 1954) as the best study of the Irish Catholic struggle for civil rights.

10. Kevin Nowlan, *The Politics of Repeal* (Toronto, 1965).

11. John Whyte, *The Independent Irish-Party, 1850-1859* (London, 1958).

12. "We aim at founding a republic based on universal suffrage, which shall secure to all the intrinsic value of their labor. The soil of Ireland at present in the possession of an oligarchy belongs to us, the Irish people, and to us it must be restored. We declare also in favour of absolute liberty of conscience, and the separation of church and state" ("Fenian *Proclamation of an Irish Republic*," London *Times*, 8 March 1867).

13. Lawrence J. McCaffrey, *Irish Federalism in the 1870s: A Study in Conservative Nationalism* (Philadelphia, 1962), and David Thornley, *Isaac Butt and Home Rule* (London, 1964).

14. F.S.L. Lyons, *Charles Stewart Parnell* (New York, 1977); Conor Cruise O'Brien, *Parnell and His Party, 1880-1890* (Oxford, 1960); Kee, *The Green Flag*, 403.

15. F.S.L. Lyons, *John Dillon* (Chicago, 1968); Denis Gwynn, *The Life of John Redmond* (London, 1932); David Miller, *Church, State, and Nation in Ireland, 1898-1921* (Pittsburgh, 1973).

16. "The Irish Republic is entitled to, and hereby claims, the allegiance of every Irishman and Irishwoman. The Republic guarantees religious and civil liberty, equal rights and equal opportunities to all its citizens, and declares its resolve to pursue the happiness and prosperity of the whole nation and all its parts, cherishing all the children of the nation equally, and oblivious of the differences fostered by an alien government, which have divided a minority from a majority in the past" (POBLACHT NA H EIREANN, THE PROVISIONAL GOVERNMENT OF THE IRISH REPUBLIC TO THE PEOPLE OF IRELAND, Easter Monday, 1916).

17. George Dangerfield's *The Strange Death of Liberal England* (New York, 1961) gives a vivid account of the impact of the Irish question on pre-World War I Britain.

18. Kerby A. Miller, *Emigrants and Exiles: Ireland and the Irish Exodus to North America* (New York, 1985) is the best analysis of Irish-American nationalism as alienation.

19. Thomas N. Brown, *Irish-American Nationalism* (Philadelphia, 1966), and "The Origins and Character of Irish-American Nationalism," *The Review of Politics* 18, no. 3 (July 1956): 327-58, emphasize the respectability motive in Irish-American nationalism.

20. Brian Jenkins, *Fenians and Anglo-American Relations During Reconstruction* (Ithaca, N.Y., 1969); Joseph Patrick O'Grady, *Irish-Americans and Anglo-American Relations, 1880-88* (New York, 1976); Alan J. Ward, *Ireland and Anglo-American Relations, 1899-1921* (London, 1969); Jack Holland, *The American Connection: U.S. Guns, Money, and Influence in Northern Ireland* (New York, 1987); Sean Cronin, *Washington's Irish Policy, 1916-1986* (Dublin, 1986).

21. Brown, *Irish-American Nationalism*, details the Clan's role in authoring the New Departure.

22. Thomas E. Hachey, *Britain and Irish Separatism: From the Fenians to the Free State, 1867-1922* (Washington, 1985).

23. R.V. Comerford, *The Fenians in Context: Irish Politics and Society, 1848-82* (Atlantic Highland, N.J., 1985); Brian Griffin, "Social Aspects of Fenianism in Connacht and Leinster, 1858-70," *Eire-Ireland* 22, no. 1 (Spring 1986): 16-39; and Tom Garvin, *The Evolution of Irish Nationalist Politics* (Dublin, 1984) discuss the relationships between Americanization as expressed in Fenianism and egalitarian values and diminished deference among Irish Catholics.

24. E.R. Norman, *The Catholic Church and Ireland in the Age of Rebellion, 1859-73* (Ithaca, 1965); Philip Magnus, *Gladstone* (New York, 1964); and J.L. Hammond, *Gladstone and the Irish Nation*, 2d ed. (Hamden, Conn., 1964).

25. The land struggle is discussed in Samuel Clark and James S. Donnelly, Jr., ed., *Irish Peasants Violence and Political Unrest 1780-1914* (Madison, Wis., 1983); E.D. Steele, *Irish Land and British Politics: Tenant Right and Nationality, 1865-1870* (Cambridge, 1974); Paul Bew, *Land and the National Question in Ireland, 1858-82* (Dublin, 1978); Charles Townshend, *Political Violence in Ireland: Government and Resistance Since 1848* (New York, 1983); W.E. Vaughan, *Landlords and Tenants in Ireland, 1848-1904* (Dublin, 1984); and Laurence M. Geary, *The Plan of Campaign, 1886-1891* (Cork, 1987).

26. The unionist Irish policy and its logic are discussed in L.P. Curtis, Jr., *Coercion and Conciliation in Ireland, 1880-92* (Princeton, N.J., 1963), and Catherine Shannon, *Arthur J. Balfour and Ireland 1874-1922* (Washington, 1987). Paul Bew, *Conflict and Conciliation in Ireland, 1890-1910* (Oxford, 1987) analyzes the unionist policy in regard to land and its dissension effects within the Irish party. Andrew Gailey, *Ireland and the Death of Kindness: The Experience of Constructive Unionism* (Cork, 1987) argues that there was more pragmatism than policy in the unionist approach to Ireland.

27. Samuel Clark, *Social Origins of the Irish Land War* (Princeton, N.J., 1979) explores the emergence of the shopkeeper leadership class in the Land League.

28. The role of literature in defining Irish cultural identity is the main theme in Thomas Flanagan, *The Irish Novelists, 1800-1850* (New York, 1959); Malcolm Brown, *The Politics of Irish Literature from Thomas Davis to W.B. Yeats* (Seattle, 1972); Herbert Howarth, *The Irish Writers: Literature and Nationalism, 1880-1940* (New York, 1959); R.V. Comerford, *Charles Kickham (1828-82): A Study in Irish Nationalism and Literature* (Dublin, 1979).

29. Anti-Irish Catholic Anglo-Saxon racism is the topic in L.P. Curtis, Jr., *Anglo-Saxons and Celts: A Study in Anti-Irish Prejudice in Victorian Britain* (Bridgeport, Conn., 1968).

30. Sean Ó Tuama, ed., *The Gaelic League Idea* (Cork, 1972).

31. Splits and controversies within Irish cultural nationalism in the late nineteenth and early twentieth centuries are described in F.S.L. Lyons, *Culture and Anarchy in Ireland, 1890-1939* (Oxford, 1979) and in Boyce's *Nationalism in Ireland*.

32. "The symbol system of the new nationalism was parallel to that of Irish Catholicism and was a translation of the latter into political terms. Neo-Gaelic nationalism retained the values of self-sacrifice for the group, religious communalism, purity, respect for women, fear of external evils and idealism which were taught by the Irish Catholicism of the period. The use of cultural-linguistic rather than religious terminology obscured in the nationalists' own mind the practical near identity between their 'Irish' or 'Gaelic' nation-to-be and the mainly English-speaking Catholic community in Ireland" (Garvin, *Irish Nationalist Politics*, 104).

33. Ruth Dudley Edwards, *Patrick Pearse: The Triumph of Failure* (London, 1977); Richard Loftus, *Nationalism in Modern Anglo-Irish Poetry* (Madison, Wis., 1964); Alan J. Ward, *The Easter Rising: Revolution and Irish Nationalism* (Arlington Heights, Ill., 1980); William Irwin Thompson, *The Imagination of an Insurrection Dublin, Easter 1916* (New York, 1972); Francis Shaw, S.J., "The Canon of Irish History—A Challenge," *Studies* 61 (Summer 1972): 113-53.

34. The essential moderation of Irish nationalism is an important theme in Kee, *The Green Flag.*

35. Joseph M. Curran, *The Birth of the Irish Free State* (University, Ala., 1980). David Fitzpatrick, *Politics and Irish Life, 1913-21* (Dublin, 1977) discusses the allegiance shift in nationalism from Home Rule to Sinn Féin.

36. For informative studies of posttreaty Ireland, see Ronan Fanning, *Independent Ireland: the First Fifty Years* (Dublin, 1981); Garvin, *Irish Nationalist Politics*, 135 ff.; F.S.L. Lyons, *Ireland Since the Famine* (New York, 1971), 465 ff.; John A. Murphy, *Ireland in the Twentieth-Century* (Dublin, 1975).

37. See the Larkin essay in this volume.

38. Lawrence J. McCaffrey, "Irish Nationalism and Irish Catholicism: A Study in Cultural Identity," *Church History* 42, no. 4 (Dec. 1973): 524-34.

39. See the Comerford essay in this volume.

40. Daniel Corkery, *The Hidden Ireland* (Dublin, 1967) and *Synge and Anglo-Irish Literature* (Cork, 1955). For analyses of literature and nationalism in Ireland after 1921, see Lawrence J. McCaffrey, "Trends in Post-Revolutionary Irish Literature," *College English* 8, no. 1 (Oct. 1956): 26-30; Lawrence J. McCaffrey, "Daniel Corkery and Irish Cultural Nationalism," and Emmet Larkin, "A Reconsideration: Daniel Corkery and His Ideas on Cultural Nationalism," *Eire-Ireland* 8, no. 1 (Spring 1973): 35-51; and Terence Brown, *Ireland: A Social and Cultural History, 1922-1979* (Ithaca, N.Y., 1985).

41. Maurice Harmon, "By Memory Inspired: Themes and Forces in Recent Irish Writing," *Eire-Ireland* 8, no. 2 (Summer, 1973) discusses the post-O'Faolain and O'Connor content and themes in Irish writing.

42. Seamus Deane, Seamus Heaney, Richard Kearney, Declan Kiberd, Tom Paulin, Marianne Elliott, and Terence Brown are some of the poets and scholars associated with *Ireland's Field Day* pamphlets and their search for an Irish identity beyond religion and language. E. Rumpf and A.C. Hepburn, *Nationalism and Socialism in Twentieth-Century Ireland* (New York, 1977) demonstrates the difficulty of such a search. It argues that nationalism associated with sectarianism has frustrated efforts in Ireland to achieve class solidarity on social and economic issues.

Nation, Nationalism, and the Irish Language

1. John A. Murphy, "O'Connell and the Gaelic World," in *Daniel O'Connell: Portrait of a Radical*, eds. K.B. Nowlan and M.R. O'Connell (Belfast, 1984), 32-52.

2. Ibid., 28.

3. See Maureen Wall, "The Decline of the Irish Language", in *A View of the Irish Language*, ed. Brian Ó Cuív (Dublin, 1969), 81-90.

4. Garrett FitzGerald, "Estimates for Baronies of Minimum Levels of Irish Speaking Amongst Successive Decennial Cohorts, 1771-81 to 1861-71," *Royal Irish Academy Proceedings*, ser. C, 84 (1984): 127.

5. My translation from Tomás de Bhaldraithe, ed., *Cín Lae Amhlaoibh* (Dublin, 1970), 9.

6. Demond Bowen, *Souperism: Myth or Reality?* (Cork, 1970), 79, 110-11; V.E. Durkacz, *The Decline of the Celtic Languages* (Edinburg, 1983), ch. 3; and see Pádraig de Brún, "The Irish Society's Bible Teachers, 1818-27," in *Éigse*, 19, no. 2 (1983), and subsequent issues.

7. Finlay Holmes, *Henry Cooke* (Belfast, 1981), 134-37.

8. Breandán Ó Buachalla, *I mBéal Feirste cois cuain* (Dublin, 1968), 74-77.

9. *Nation*, April 1, 1843.

10. R.V. Comerford, *The Fenians in Context: Irish Politics and Society, 1848-1882* (Dublin, 1985); John Devoy, *Recollections of an Irish Rebel*, (1929; reprint, Shannon, 1969), 264.

11. *Irishman* (Dublin), June 1, 1861.

12. John O'Mahony, *The History of Ireland from the Earliest Period to the English Invasion by the Reverend Geoffrey Keating, D.D., Translated from the Original Gaelic and Copiously Annotated* (New York, 1857).

13. Devoy, *Recollections*, 261-65.

14. Nollaig Ó Muraile, "Staid na Gaeilge i gConnachta in aimsir Sheáin Mhic Héil" in *Leon an Iarthair*, ed. Áine ní Cheannain (Dublin, 1983).

15. Fr. Ulick Bourke, *Easy Lessons in Irish* (1863); Proinnsias Ó Maolmhuaidh, *Uilleog de Búrca: athair na hathbheochana* (Dublin, 1981), 66.

16. Máirtín Ó Cadhain, "Conradh na Gaeilge agus an litríocht" in *The Gaelic League Idea*, ed. Seán Ó Tuama (Cork, 1972), 53.

17. Intermediate Education (Ireland) Act, 1878 *(41 & 42 Vict.*, c.66).

18. Vivian Mercier, "Victorian Evangelicalism and the Anglo-Irish Literary Revival," in *Literature and the Changing Ireland*, ed. P. Connolly (Gerrard's Cross, 1982), 59-101.

19. Matthew Arnold, *On the Study of Celtic Literature and Translating Homer* (1867; reprint, New York, 1883).

20. J.L. McAdams, *Ellen, Countess of Desart, and Captain the Hon. Otway Cuffe* (n.p., n.d.); Diarmuid Breathnach agus Máire Ní Mhurchú, *1882-1982: Bethaisnéis a hAon* (Dublin, 1986).

21. *Kilkenny Journal*, Aug. 27, 1902.

22. Pádraig Ó Snodaigh, *Hidden Ulster*, rev. ed. (Dublin, 1977), 28-31.

23. R.B.D. French, "J.D. Hannay and the Gaelic League," in *Hermathena* 102 (1966), 26-52.

24. Ibid., 49.

25. Ruth Dudley Edwards, *Patrick Pearse: The Triumph of Failure* (London, 1977), 33.

26. A.E. Clery, "The Gaelic League, 1893-1919," in *Studies* 8, no. 31 (Sept. 1919), 401.

27. Donal McCartney, "MacNeill and Irish-Ireland," in *The Scholar Revolutionary: Eoin MacNeill (1867-1945) and the Making of the New Ireland*, eds., F.X. Martin and F.J. Byrne (Shannon, 1973), 81.

28. Edwards, *Patrick Pearse*, 99.

29. Earnán de Blaghd, "Hyde in Conflict," in *The Gaelic League Idea*, ed. Ó Tuama, 36.

30. David Greene, "The Irish Language Movement," in *Irish Anglicanism, 1869-1969*, ed. Michael Hurley (Dublin, 1970), 116-17.

31. Thomas O' Fiaich, "The Great Controversy," in *The Gaelic League Idea*, ed. O' Tuama, 67-69.

32. 8 Edw. VII, c. 38.

33. T.J. Morrissey, *Towards a National University: William Delany, S.J., 1835-1924* (Dublin, 1983),323-24.

34. Ibid., 336.

35. Ibid., 340-41.

36. 3 Edw. VII, c. 1.

37. B.S. Mac Aodha, "Was This a Social Revolution?" in *The Gaelic League Idea*, ed. Ó Tuama, 22. See also M.J. Waters, "Peasants and Emigrants: Considerations of the Gaelic League as a Social Movement," in *Views of the Irish Peasantry, 1800-1916*, eds. D.J. Casey and R.E. Rhodes (Hamden, Conn., 1977), 160-77.

38. Morrissey, *Delany*, 330.

39. F.S.L. *Lyons Culture and Anarchy in Ireland, 1890-1939* (Oxford: Clarendon Press, 1979), and see Margaret O'Callaghan, "Language, Nationality and Cultural Identity in the Irish Free State, 1922-27," in *Irish Historical Studies* 24, no. 94 (Nov. 1984), 226-45.

40. David Miller, *Church, State and Nation in Ireland 1898-1921* (Dublin, 1973), 36-37.

41. Seamus O' Buachalla, "Educational Policy and the Role of the Irish Language from 1831 to 1981," in *European Journal of Education* 19, no. 1 (1984), 75-92.

42. See D.H. Akenson, *A Mirror to Kathleen's Face: Education in Independent Ireland, 1922-60* (Montreal, 1975), 35-45, 59-61.

43. R.V. Comerford, *Charles J. Kickham (1828-82): A Study in Irish Nationalism and Literature* (Dublin, 1979), 209.

44. Gearóid S. Mac Eoin, "Twentieth-century Irish Literature," in *View of the Irish Language*, Ó Cuív, 57-69.

45. P.C. Power, trans., *The Poor Mouth* (London, 1972).

46. Máirtín Ó Murchú, *The Irish Language* (Dublin, 1985), 29.

47. Mac Aodha, "Was This a Social Revolution?" 28.

48. John MacNamara, *Bilingualism and Primary Education: A Study of Irish Experience* (Edinburgh, 1966).

49. Pádraig Ó Riagáin, *Public and Teacher Attitudes Towards Irish in the Schools: A Review of Recent Surveys* (Dublin, 1986).

50. There is a valuable listing of secondary literature in John Edwards, *The Irish Language: An Annotated Bibliography of Sociolinguistic Publications, 1772-1982* (New York, 1983).

The Folklore of Irish Nationalism

1. Augusta Gregory, "The Canavans," *The Collected Plays*, vol. 2 (Gerrards Cross, 1971), 207.

2. Thomas Davis, *Literary and Historical Essays* (Dublin, 1865), 240.

3. *Paddy's Resource: Being a Select Collection of Original and Modern Patriotic Songs, Toasts and Sentiments Compiled for the Use of the People of Ireland*, 3 vols. (Belfast and Dublin, 1795-98), 1: 10-12.

4. *Paddy's Resource*, 3: 119-20.

5. Charles Gavan Duffy, *The Ballad Poetry of Ireland* (Dublin, 1869), 70-72.

6. Donal O'Sullivan, *Songs of the Irish* (Cork, 1960), 146.

7. Seán Ó Tuama, "Introduction," *An Dunaire: An Irish Anthology 1600-1900: Poems of the Dispossessed*, ed. Seán Ó Tuama and Thomas Kinsella (Philadelphia, 1981), xxii.

8. O'Sulivan, *Songs*, 149.

9. Ibid., 150.

10. Ibid., 153.

11. Duffy, *Ballad Poetry*, 112-13.

12. Georges-Denis Zimmermann, *Songs of Irish Rebellion: Political Street Ballads and Rebel Songs 1780-1900* (Dublin, 1967), 158-59.

13. Colm O Lochlainn, *The Complete Irish Street Ballads*, 2 vols. (London, 1984), 2:198-200.

14. Alan Bruford, *Gaelic Folk-Tales and Medieval Romances: A Study of Early Modern Irish 'Romantic Tales' and Their Oral Derivatives* (Dublin, 1969), 8, 16.

15. James MacKillop, *Fionn mac Cumhaill: Celtic Myth in English Literature* (Syracuse, 1986), 23-27.

16. O'Sullivan, *Songs*, 102, 106.

17. Roger McHugh, "The Famine in Irish Oral Tradition," *The Great Famine: Studies in Irish History 1845-52*, ed. R.D. Edwards and T.D. Williams (New York, 1976), 391-436.

18. O'Sullivan, *Songs*, 137.

19. F.S.L. Lyons, *Ireland Since the Famine* (1971; reprint, London, 1985), 104.

20. *The Book of Irish Verse*, ed. John Montague (New York, 1976), 180-81.

21. Thomas Crofton Croker, *Researchers in the South of Ireland* (1824; reprint, Shannon, 1969), 361.

22. George Cornewall Lewis, *On Local Disturbances in Ireland and on the Irish Church Question* (London, 1836), 39.

23. Fergus O'Ferrall, *Catholic Emancipation: Daniel O'Connell and the Birth of Irish Democracy* (Dublin, 1985), 263-65.

24. Donal MacCartney, "The Writing of History in Ireland," *Irish Historical Studies* 10 (1957): 347-62.

25. Charles Gavan Duffy, *Young Ireland: A Fragment of Irish History* (New York, 1881), 181.

26. Duffy, *Ballad Poetry*, 103.

27. Samuel Ferguson, "Hardiman's Irish Minstrelsy—No. II," *Dublin University Magazine* 4 (1834): 154-67.

28. Terence Brown, *Northern Voices: Poets from Ulster* (Totowa, N.J., 1975), 31.

29. Davis, *Essays*, 98.

30. Ibid., 98.

31. Ibid., 372-74.

32. Duffy, *Ballad Poetry*, 25-26.

33. O'Sullivan, *Songs*, 131.

34. Zimmermann, *Songs*, 134.

35. *The Spirit of the Nation: Ballads and Songs by the Writers of 'The Nation'* (1845; reprint, Wilmington, 1981), 133-34.

36. *Songs, Ballads and Poems by James Clarence Mangan* (Dublin, n.d.), 6.

37. Ó Tuama, *An Dunaire*, 309.

38. O'Sullivan, *Songs*, 133.

39. Douglas Hyde, *The Songs of Connacht I-III*, ed. Breandan Ó Conaire (Dublin, 1985), 31-33.

40. *Spirit of the Nation*, 5-6.

41. Davis, *Essays*, 161.

42. Turlough Faolain, *Blood on the Harp: Irish Rebel History in Ballad* (Troy, 1983), 186-87.

43. Arthur Griffith, "Preface," John Mitchel, *Jail Journal* (1913; reprint, Dublin, 1982), 372.

44. Zimmerman, *Songs*, 250-52.

45. Ibid., 262-63.

46. Frank O'Connor, *Kings, Lords, and Commons: An Anthology from the Irish* (Freeport, N.Y., 1969), 122.

47. D. George Boyce, *Nationalism in Ireland* (Baltimore, 1982), 146.

48. Mary Helen Thuente, "Violence in Pre-Famine Ireland: the Testimony of Irish Folklore and Fiction," *Irish University Review* 15 (1985): 145-47.

49. Gearóid Ó Tuathaigh, "The Folk-Hero and Tradition," *The World of Daniel O'Connell*, ed. Donal McCartney (Cork, 1980), 30-42; "Gaelic Ireland, Popular Politics and Daniel O'Connell," *Galway Archeological and Historical Society Journal* 35 (1975): 21-34.

50. Zimmerman, *Songs*, 206-7.

51. Daithi Ó hÓgain, *The Hero in Irish Folk History* (Dublin, 1985), 99-119.

52. William Carleton, *Traits and Stories of the Irish Peasantry*, 4th ser. (London, n.d.), 219.

53. Zimmermann, *Songs*, 144-60.

54. Louis Cullen "The Cultural Basis of Modern Irish Nationalism," *The Roots of Nationalism: Studies in Northern Europe*, ed. Rosalind Mitchison (Edinburgh, 1980), 101.

55. John O'Leary, *How Irishmen Should Feel* (Dublin, 1886), 12.

56. Lyons, *Ireland*, 112.

57. O'Ferrall, *Catholic Emancipation*, 289.

Nationalism: The Literary Tradition

1. John Mitchel, *The History of Ireland. From the Treaty of Limerick to the Present Time: Being a Continuation of the History of the Abbe MacGeoghegan* (New York, 1868).

2. M. l'Abbe (James) ma-Geoghegan, *Histoire de l'Irlande, Ancienne et Moderne, Tiree des Monumens les plus authentiques*, 3 vols. (Paris and Amsterdam, 1758-63).

3. For the MacGeoghegans, James, but more especially Alexander, see mentions throughout John D'Alton, *King James' Army List*, 2 vols. (Dublin, 1860); John Cornelius O'Callaghan, *History of the Irish Brigades in the Service of France* (Dublin, 1869); and *Dictionary of National Biography*.

4. Mrs. Morgan John O'Connell, *The Last Colonel of the Irish Brigade, Count O'Connell, and Old Irish Home Life at Home and Abroad*, 2 vols. (London, 1892) 1: 207. But Lieutenant Rick O'Connell, the colonel's dashing young relative, saw matters differently: "Would to God, my dear Maurice, that we were at this moment two hundred thousand strong in Ireland, and that I had the command of our single company of Oak Park! I would kick the Members and their Volunteers and their unions and their Societies to the Devil! I would make the rascally spawn of Damned Cromwell curse the hour of his Birth!" O'Connell, 1: 223. Mrs. Morgan John O'Connell remarks primly that "there is a bitter anti-English tone in this, wanting in all the other Irish Brigade letters I have seen." Daniel Corkery, on the other hand, was rather fond of Rick and his sentiments.

5. Charles O'Conor, especially *Dissertations on the Ancient History of Ireland . . .* (Dublin, 1753); John Curry, *An Historical and Critical Review of the Civil War in Ireland*, 2 vols. (Dublin, 1775).

6. Sylvester O'Halloran, *A General History of Ireland From the Earliest Accounts to the Close of the Twelfth Century, Collected From the Most Authentic Sources . . .* 2 vols. (London and Dublin, 1778). See also his *Introduction to the Study of the History and Antiquities of Ireland* (Dublin, 1772).

7. Terence Brown, "The Whole Protestant Community: The History of a Historical Myth," *Field Day Pamphlet*, no. 7 (Derry, 1985); Oliver MacDonagh, "Time's Revenges and Revenge's Time: A View of Anglo-Irish Relations," *Anglo-Irish Studies* 4 (1979): 1-19.

8. O'Halloran, *History of Ireland*, 1: 130.

9. Richard Lovell and Maria Edgeworth, *Essays on Irish Bulls*, 3rd ed. (London, 1808), 262-63.

10. Charlotte Brooke, *Reliques of Irish Poetry* (Dublin, 1789); Joseph Cooper Walker, *Historical Memoirs of the Irish Bards*, 2 vols. (Dublin, 1786).

11. Owen Dudley Edwards, "Ireland," in *Celtic Nationalism*, eds. Edwards and others (London, 1968), 61.

12. Lady Ferguson, *Sir Samuel Ferguson in the Ireland of His Day*, 2 vols. (Edinburgh and London, 1896), 1: 40. She is quoting from Ferguson's essay.

13. "Hardiman's *Irish Minstrelsy*," *Dublin University Magazine* (April 1834).

14. Malcolm Brown, *Sir Samuel Ferguson* (Lewisburg, Pa., 1973).

15. Robert O'Driscoll, *An Ascendancy of the Heart: Ferguson and the Beginnings of Modern Irish Literature in English* (Dublin, 1976).

16. Thomas Davis, *Selections from His Poetry and Prose* (London and Dublin, n.d.), 103-4.

17. William Butler Yeats, *Autobiography* (New York, 1953), 123, as are the two quotations immediately following.

18. He is quoting from his translation of a famous Gaelic poem.

19. Thomas Flanagan, "Yeats, Joyce, and the Matter of Ireland," *Critical Inquiry* 2, no. 1 (Autumn 1975): 45.

20. William Butler Yeats, "Red Hanrahan's Song About Ireland," in *In the Seven Woods* (London, 1903).

21. *Dublin University Review* (November 1886). Reprinted in *Uncollected Prose by W.B. Yeats*, vol. 1, ed. John Frayne (London, 1970), 87-104. For the references to the essays by Dr. Mahaffy and Miss Stokes, I am indebted to Mr. Frayne's scholarship.

22. Frayne, *Uncollected Prose*, 100.

23. Yeats, *Autobiography*, 286.

24. Ibid., 137, 133-34, 127.

25. Malcolm Brown, *The Politics of Irish Literature: From Thomas Davis to W.B. Yeats* (Seattle, 1972), 297. He is quoting from O'Grady's 1886 pamphlet, *Toryism and the Tory Democracy.*

26. Lady Ferguson, *Sir Samuel Ferguson*, 1: 256-66.

27. Ibid., 254.

28. Conor C. O'Brien and Maire O'Brien, *A Concise History of Ireland* (London, 1972), 85-86.

29. Seamus Deane, in "Heroic Styles: the Tradition of an Idea," Ireland's *Field Day* (Notre Dame, 1986, 47-48.

The Land Question in Nationalist Politics

1. James S. Donnelly, Jr., "Propagating the Cause of the United Irishmen," *Studies* 69 (Spring 1980): 5-23; idem, "Pastorini and Captain Rock: Millenarianism and Sectarianism in the Rockite Movement of 1821-4," in Samuel Clark and James S. Donnelly, Jr., eds., *Irish Peasants: Violence and Political Unrest, 1780-1914* (Madison, 1983), 102-39.

2. *Dublin Evening Post*, 27 Dec. 1821.

3. R.B. McDowell, *Irish Public Opinion, 1750-1800* (London, 1944), 198-202; idem, *Ireland in the Age of Imperialism and Revolution, 1760-1801* (Oxford, 1979), 374-77.

4. Donnelly, "Propagating the Cause," 20-21, 23 n. 18.

5. Marianne Elliott, *Partners in Revolution: The United Irishmen and France* (New Haven, 1982), 369, 371-72.

6. James S. Donnelly, Jr., "Republicanism and Reaction in the 1790s," *Irish Economic and Social History*, 11 (1984): 99-100.

7. Daniel O'Connell to Lord Duncannon, 14 Jan. 1833, in Maurice R. O'Connell, ed., *The Correspondence of Daniel O'Connell*, 8 vols. (Dublin, 1972-80), 5: 3-4 (hereafter cited as *O'Connell Corr.*).

8. See, e.g., Thomas Steele to Daniel O'Connell, 6 Jan. 1841; Steele to O'Connell, 8 Jan. 1841, in *O'Connell Corr.* 7: 3-4.

9. Donnelly, "Pastorini and Captain Rock," 136-37.

10. Gearóid Ó Tuathaigh, "The Folk Hero and Tradition," in Donal McCartney, ed., *The*

World of Daniel O'Connell (Dublin, 1980), 30-42; Diarmuid Ó Muirithe, "O'Connell in Irish Folk Tradition," in Kevin B. Nowlan and Maurice R. O'Connell, eds., *Daniel O'Connell: Portrait of a Radical* (Belfast, 1984), 53-69.

11. Fergus O'Ferrall, *Catholic Emancpation: Daniel O'Connell and the Birth of Irish Democracy, 1820-30* (Dublin, 1985), 48-55, 71-74, 78-79, 262-65.

12. Daniel O'Connell to Pierce Mahony, 26 Apr. 1845, in *O'Connell Corr.* 7: 315-16.

13. Kevin B. Nowlan, *The Politics of Repeal: A Study in the Relations between Great Britain and Ireland, 1841-50* (London, 1965), 5-6.

14. Daniel O'Connell to Pierce Mahony, 12 Oct. 1844, in *O'Connell Corr.* 7: 277-78.

15. Angus Macintyre, *The Liberator: Daniel O'Connell and the Irish Party, 1830-1847* (London, 1965), 279-80.

16. See note 14.

17. Joseph Lee, "The Social and Economic Ideas of O'Connell," in Nowlan and O'Connell, *Daniel O'Connell,* 71.

18. Daniel O'Connell to Pierce Mahony, 25 Apr. 1845, in *O'Connell Corr.* 7: 277-78.

19. *Nation,* 4, 11 July 1846.

20. *Hansard,* 3rd ser., 87: 377; Lee, "Social and Economic Ideas," 71.

21. See note 18.

22. Thomas Davis, *Literary and Historical Essays* (Dublin, 1865 ed.), 88-89.

23. *Nation,* 15 Oct. 1842.

24. Malcolm Brown, *The Politics of Irish Literature: From Thomas Davis to Y.B. Yeats* (Seattle, 1972), 52-54.

25. Nowland, *Politics of Repeal.*

26. Ibid., 148-51.

27. Sir Charles Gavan Duffy, *Young Ireland: Part 2, or Four Years of Irish History, 1845-1849* (Dublin, 1887), 476-77.

28. *Nation,* 1 Sept. 1849.

29. Ibid., 8 Sept. 1849.

30. J.H. Whyte, *The Independent Irish Party, 1850-9* (London, 1958).

31. R.V. Comerford, *The Fenians in Context: Irish Politics and Society, 1848-82* (Dublin, 1985), 115.

32. Ibid.

33. Ibid., 115-16.

34. *Irish People,* 16, 23 Jan. 1864.

35. Ibid., 19 Dec. 1863, 1 Apr. 1865; Comerford, *Fenians,* 112-14.

36. Comerford, *Fenians,* 182-83, 213-15, 222.

37. Donald E. Jordan, Jr., "Land and Politics in the West of Ireland: County Mayo, 1846-82" (Ph.D. diss. Univ. of California, Davis, 1982), 179-88, 203-10.

38. Samuel Clark, "The Social Composition of the Land League," *Irish Historical Studies* 17 (Sept. 1971): 447-69; idem, *Social Origins of the Irish Land War* (Princeton, 1979), 272-75. See also Jordan, "Land and Politics," 193-200, 232-35.

39. Jordan, "Land and Politics," 249-302; Paul Bew, *Land and the National Question in Ireland, 1858-82* (Dublin, 1978), 98-114.

40. Bew, *Land,* 115-44.

41. Jordan "Land and Politics," 302-10.

42. Ibid., 311-52.

43. Conor Cruise O'Brien, *Parnell and His Party, 1880-90* (corrected impression, Oxford, 1964), 65-79; Bew, *Land,* 185-213.

44. C.S. Parnell to Capt. W.H. O'Shea, 28 Apr. 1882, quoted in David B. King, *The*

Irish Question (New York, 1882), 189-90. See also Bew, *Land*, 213-16; F.S.L. Lyons, *Charles Stewart Parnell* (New York, 1977), 180-207.

45. Paul Bew, *C.S. Parnell* (Dublin, 1980), 57.

46. Thomas N. Brown, *Irish-American Nationalism, 1870-1890* (Philadelphia, 1966), 120-24.

47. Ibid., 124-30; T.W. Moody, *Davitt and Irish Revolution, 1846-82* (Oxford, 1981), 516-27; King, *Land Question*, 341-50.

48. Moody, *Davitt*, 537-46; Bew, *Parnell*, 60-64.

49. Quoted in Bew, *Parnell*, 84. See also Bew, *Parnell*, 81-84. For the land purchase bill of 1886, see James Loughlin, *Gladstone, Home Rule, and the Ulster Question, 1882-93* (Atlantic Highlands, N.J., 1987) 80-94.

50. Bew, *Parnell*, 97-104; Michael Barker, *Gladstone and Radicalism: The Reconstruction of Liberal Policy in Britain, 1885-94* (Hassocks, 1975), 75-87.

51. Liam Kennedy, "Farmers, Traders, and Agricultural Politics in Pre-Independence Ireland," in Clark and Donnelly, *Irish Peasants*, 339-73; David S. Jones, "The Cleavage between Graziers and Peasants in the Land Struggle, 1890-1910," Clark and Donnelly, *Irish Peasants*, 374-417.

52. F.S.L. Lyons, *John Dillon: A Biography* (London, 1968), 178-215, 222-29.

53. Ibid., 236.

54. *Cork Constitution*, 18 Nov. 1887.

55. Davis, *Essays*, 89.

56. *Freeman's Journal*, 26 Sept. 1888.

57. W.S. Blunt, *My Diaries* (London, 1932), 468.

58. Lyons, *Dillon*, 230-41.

59. William O'Brien, *Evening Memories* (Dublin, 1920), 480-87.

60. *Irish People*, 2 Jan. 1864.

61. Bew, *Land*, 49-54.

62. Quoted in F.S.L. Lyons, "The Economic Ideas of Parnell," in Michael Roberts, ed., *Historical Studies* (London, 1959), 2: 69.

The Irish Political Tradition

1. Michael Gallagher, *Political Parties in the Republic of Ireland* (Dublin, 1985), 1-2.

2. Tom Garvin, *The Evolution of Irish Nationalist Politics* (New York, 1981), 4-5, 209.

3. Leonard Krieger, *The German Idea of Freedom* (Chicago, 1972), 4-5.

4. *Scritture Riferite nei Congressi, Irlanda*, 34, fol. 1281, Archives of the Sacred Congregation for the Evangelization of Peoples, Rome.

5. Ibid., fols. 165-72.

6. Emmet Larkin, *The Consolidation of the Roman Catholic Church in Ireland, 1860-1870* (Chapel Hill, 1987), 344-47.

7. Proinsias MacCana, "Notes on the Early Irish Concept of Unity," in M.P. Hederman and R. Kearney, eds., *The Crane Bag Book of Irish Studies, 1977-1981* (Dublin, 1982), 215.

8. Daniel Corkery, *The Hidden Ireland: A Study of Gaelic Munster in the Eighteenth Century* (Dublin, 1975), 28.

9. Ibid.; see also Henry Glassie, *Passing the Time at Ballymenone* (Philadelphia, 1982).

10. M. McGrath, ed., *Diary of Humphrey O'Sullivan* (London, 1936), Irish Texts Society, 33: 10.

11. Emmet Larkin "The Devotional Revolution in Ireland, 1850-75," *American Histor-*

ical Review 75 (1972), reprinted in Emmet Larkin, *The Historical Dimensions of Irish Catholicism* (Washington, D.C., 1984), 82-83.

12. John MacHale, *The Letters of the Most Rev. John MacHale, D.D.* (Dublin, 1888), 9. The letter is dated 12 February 1820.

13. Maurice O'Connell, ed., *The Correspondence of Daniel O'Connell* (Dublin, 1974), 3: 141-42.

14. Arthur Houston, *Daniel O'Connell: His Early Life and Journal, 1795-1802* (London, 1906).

15. Ibid., 106-7 (1/5/96), 119-20 (1/30/96).

16. Ibid., 110 (1/13/96), 116 (1/19/96).

17. Ibid., 215.

18. John O'Connell, ed., *The Select Speeches of Daniel O'Connell, M.P.* (Dublin, 1865), 1: 9.

19. Ibid., 215.

20. Patrick F. Moran, ed., *The Pastoral Letters and Other Writings of Cardinal Cullen* (Dublin, 1882), 3: 647-55.

21. David Thornley, *Issac Butt and Home Rule* (London, 1964), 266.

22. Cullen Papers, Dublin Diocesan Archives.

23. *Freeman's Journal*, 16 September 1875.

24. Ibid., 21 September 1875.

25. Ibid., 19-22 November 1873.

26. Emmet Larkin, *The Roman Catholic Church and the Emergence of the Modern Irish Political System, Part One, 1870-1874* (forthcoming).

27. *Freeman's Journal*, 19 April 1876.

28. Ibid.

29. Fergus O'Ferrall, *Catholic Emanicpation, Daniel O'Connell and the Birth of Irish Democracy, 1820-30* (Dublin, 1985), 215.

30. Oliver MacDonagh, "The Contribution of O'Connell," in Brian Farrell, ed., *The Irish Parliamentary Tradition* (Dublin, 1873), 163-64.

31. Larkin, *Roman Catholic Church, 1870-1874.*

32. Emmet Larkin, *The Roman Catholic Church and the Creation of the Modern Irish State 1878-1886* (Philadelphia, 1975), 36. See also Emmet Larkin, *The Roman Catholic Church and the Plan of the Campaign in Ireland, 1886-1888* (Cork, 1978), 314-22.

33. Gallagher, *Political Parties*, 15.

34. Basil Chubb, ed., *A Source Book of Irish Government* (Dublin, 1964), 3-4.

35. Darrel Figgis, *The Irish Constitution*, (Dublin, n.d.). See articles 26, 46, 47 of the Free State Constitution for proportional representation, referendum, and initiative, respectively.

36. Ibid., Articles 50, 52, 53, 55.

37. F.S.L. Lyons, *Ireland Since the Famine* (London, 1982), 538.

38. Ibid., 545-49.

39. Emmett Larkin, *The Roman Catholic Church in Ireland and the Fall of Parnell, 1888-1891* (Chapel Hill, 1979), 297.

40. The reunification of the Irish Parliamentary party in 1900 under the leadership of John Redmond is yet another illustration of the fundamental importance of populism in the Irish political tradition. The reunification was the result of the launching of a new grass-roots organization, the United Irish League, in the country by William O'Brien in 1898, and by 1900 the pressure of the demand by the league for unity in party proved to be irresistible.

41. Cornelius O'Leary, *Irish Elections, 1918-1977; Parties, Voters, and Proportional Representation* (Dublin, 1979), 46-58, 66-70.

42. Gallagher, *Political Parties*, 91.

43. Arthur Mitchell, *Labour in Irish Politics*, 1890-1930 (Dublin, 1974), 16.

44. Gallagher, *Political Parties*, 86-87.

Irish Nationalism and the British Connection

1. Representative examples include J.C. Beckett, *The Anglo-Irish Tradition* (Ithaca, N.Y., 1976); Karl Bottigheimer, *Ireland and the Irish* (New York, 1982); F.S.L. Lyons, *Ireland Since the Famine* (New York, 1971); Lawrence J. McCaffrey, *The Irish Question, 1800-1922* (Lexington, Ky., 1968); Patrick O'Farrell, *Ireland's English Question* (New York, 1972); and Eric Strauss, *Irish Nationalism and British Democracy* (New York, 1961).

2. Representative examples include D. George Boyce, *Englishmen and Irish Troubles: British Public Opinion and the Making of Irish Policy 1918-1922* (Cambridge, Mass., 1972); David Miller, *Church, State and Nation in Ireland, 1898-1921* (Pittsburgh, 1973); and Alan Ward, *Ireland and Anglo-American Relations, 1899-1921* (London, 1969).

3. In addition to those titles that appear later in this essay, such works include Joseph Curran, *The Birth of the Irish Free State, 1921-1923* (Alabama, 1980), and Paul Canning, *British Policy Towards Ireland, 1921-1941* (Oxford, 1985).

4. See, for instance, various minutes in State Paper Office, Dublin, Republic of Ireland, CAB 2/10, 11.

5. John McColgan, *British Policy and the Irish Administration, 1920-22*, London, 1983.

6. David Harkness, *The Restless Dominion* (New York, 1970), p. 21.

7. Ibid., 22-23.

8. *Constitution of the Free State of Ireland* (Dublin, 1922), 16.

9. See John Bowman, *De Valera and the Ulster Question, 1917-1922* (Oxford, 1983), 323-38.

10. See Sir W. Keith Hancock, *Survey of British Commonwealth Affairs, vol. 1 of Problems of Nationality, 1918-1936* (London, 1937); Robert McGregor Dawson, ed., *The Development of Dominion Status*, 1900-36 (Oxford, 1937); and Nicholas Mansergh, *Survey of British Commonwealth Affairs: Problems of Imperial Policy, 1931-39*. (Oxford, 1952).

11. See Harkness, 74-79, 137-38, and 174-76.

12. See British Public Record Office, Kew Gardens, Cabinet Papers: CAB 23, 24, 27; see also DO 35, 114, 117, 121; FO 371, 800.

13. See Deirdre MacMahon, *Republicans and Imperialists: Anglo-Irish Relations in the 1930s* (London, 1984).

14. Hancock, *Problems of Nationality*, 1: 369.

15. David Harkness, "Mr. de Valera's Dominion: Irish Relations with Britain and the Commonwealth, 1932-1938," *Journal of Commonwealth Political Studies* 8, no. 3 (Nov. 1970): 207.

16. See Robert Fisk, *In Time of War: Ireland, Ulster and the Price of Neutrality, 1934-45* (Philadelphia, 1983), 103.

17. See Bowman, *De Valera*, 255-61.

18. Telegram No. 319, United Kingdom Representative to Eire John Maffey to Dominions Secretary Lord Cranborne, 20 Nov. 1940. Premier 3/127/1.

19. Joseph T. Carroll, *Ireland in the War Years, 1939-1945* (New York, 1975), 46.

20. Premier, 3/128.

21. Ibid.

22. Ibid.

23. Ibid.

24. Even the British military chiefs of staff were sensitive to the need for not permitting Eire to imperil Anglo-American relations, and they further believed that the United States government itself might yet agree to approach Dublin over the ports issue. Memorandum from the Joint Chiefs to the War Cabinet, 8 March 1941. Premier 3/127/2.

25. F.O. 371/36602.

26. David Kennedy, "Ulster During the War and After," in Kevin B. Nowlan and T. Desmond Williams, eds., *Ireland in the War Years and After, 1939-1951* (Dublin, 1969), 53-54.

27. John Blake, *Ireland in the War Years and After, 1939-1951*, (Belfast, 1956), 194.

28. It is evident from the Cabinet memoranda that the opposition of the Northern Ireland Labour party and the Catholic hierarchy were also important considerations. See Memorandum from Home Secretary Herbert Morrison to the War Cabinet, 23 May 1941. CAB 66/16, w.p. (41) 110. One minister argued in favor of conscription for Ulster on the grounds that it would help eliminate the high unemployment rate in that region. Memorandum from Minister of Labour and National Service Ernest Bevin to the War Cabinet, 21 May 1941. CAB 66/16, w.p. (4) 107.

29. Carroll, *Ireland in the War Years*, 108-9.

30. D.O. 35/1109.

31. Ibid.

32. Ibid.

33. Premier 4/53/3.

34. Ibid.

35. Ibid.

36. R.M. Smyllie, "Unneutral Neutral Eire," *Foreign Affairs* 24 (1946): 323.

37. Ibid., 320-21.

38. Minutes, F. Evans at the Foreign Office, 8 March 1943. F.O. 371/366.

39. F.O. 371/35368.

40. Winston S. Churchill, *Closing the Ring* (Boston, 1951, 1948-54), 693.

41. U.S. Department of State *Bulletin* 10, no. 246 (Washington, D.C., 1944): 236.

42. F.O. 371/42679.

43. Carroll, *The War Years*, 31. See also Smyllie, "Unneutral Neutral Eire," 319.

44. The Earl of Longford and Thomas P. O'Neill, *Eamon de Valera* (Boston, 1971), 411.

45. The London *Times*, 14 May 1945.

46. *New York Times*, 17 May 1945.

47. Carroll, *The War Years*, 166.

48. D.O. 35/1229.

49. Smyllie, "Unneutral Neutral Eire," 317.

50. John A. Murphy, *Ireland in the Twentieth Century* (Dublin, 1975), 99.

51. See Donald H. Akenson, *The United States and Ireland* (Cambridge, 1973), and Patrick Keatinge, *A Place Among Nations* (Dublin, 1978).

52. See British PRO: CAB 21, 128-134; Dominions Office 35, 37, 99; Foreign Office 369, 371.

53. Ronan Fanning, *Independent Ireland* (Dublin, 1983); 212. For a more comprehensive account of the 1947-49 period, see Thomas Schunk, "A Special Relationship: Britain, Eire and the Commonwealth, 1947-1949," (Ph.D. diss., Marquette University, 1986).

CONTRIBUTORS

R.V. COMERFORD is senior lecturer of modern history at St. Patrick's College (Maynooth), the National University of Ireland. He is the author of *Charles J. Kickham (1828-82): A Study in Irish Nationalism and Literature* (1979), *The Fenians in Context: Irish Politics and Society, 1848-1882* (1985), and many articles. He is general editor of the Wolfhound Press's Topics in Modern Irish History series. Comerford also is the author of the section on 1850-70 for a forthcoming volume of the *New History of Ireland*.

JAMES S. DONNELLY, JR. is professor of modern British and Irish history at the University of Wisconsin, Madison. Among his many publications on Irish agrarian history are *Landlord and Tenant in Nineteenth-Century Ireland* (1973); *The Land and the People of Nineteenth-Century Cork: The Rural Economy and the Land Question* (1975), which the American Historical Association awarded the Herbert Baxter Adams prize; *Irish Peasants: Violence and Political Unrest* (1983), coeditor; and *Agrarian Violence and Secret Societies in Ireland, 1760-1845* (1988).

THOMAS FLANAGAN is professor of Anglo-Irish literature at the State University of New York at Stony Brook. His *The Irish Novelists, 1800-1850* heads a list of seminal essays interpreting Anglo-Irish literature and Irish intellectual history. Flanagan's fictional analysis of the 1798 rebellion in Mayo, *The Year of the French* (1979) won the National Book Award. *The Tenants of Time* (1988) is his latest historical novel.

THOMAS E. HACHEY is professor of Irish, Irish-American, and British history and chair of the department at Marquette University. He wrote *Britain and Irish Separatism: From the Fenians to the Free State, 1867-1922* (1977); coauthored and edited *The Problem of Partition, Peril to World Peace* (1972); coedited *Voices of Revolution: Rebels and Rhetoric* (1972); and edited *Anglo-Vatican Relations, 1914-1939: Confidential Annual Reports of the British Ministers to the Holy See* (1972) and *Confidential Dispatches: Analyses of America by the British Ambassador, 1939-45* (1974). Hachey also has published numerous essays.

EMMET LARKIN is professor of modern British and Irish history at the University of Chicago. In addition to *James Larkin, Irish Labor Leader, 1876-1947* (1965) and *The Historical Dimensions of Irish Catholicism*, (1985), he has published five volumes of his monumental history of the Catholic church in nineteenth-century Ireland. Along with McCaffrey, Larkin was one of the cofounders of the American Conference for Irish Studies.

LAWRENCE J. MCCAFFREY is professor of Irish and Irish-American history at Loyola University of Chicago. He has published a number of articles and books, including *Daniel O'Connell and the Repeal Year* (1966), *The Irish Question, 1800-1922* (1968), and *The Irish Diaspora in America* (1976). He coauthored *The Irish in Chicago* (1987).

MARY HELEN THUENTE is associate professor in the Department of English and Linguistics at Indiana University–Purdue University at Fort Wayne. Her *W.B. Yeats and Irish Folklore* (1980) and a wide ranging number of articles emphasize Thuente's historical, literary, and anthropological interdisciplinary approach to Irish studies. She is at present secretary of the American Conference for Irish Studies.

INDEX